Diagnostics for a Globalized World

World Scientific–Now Publishers Series in Business

ISSN: 2251-3442

Vol. 1 Games and Dynamic Games
by Alain Haurie, Jacek B. Krawczyk and Georges Zaccour

Vol. 2 Dodd–Frank Wall Street Reform and Consumer Protection Act: Purpose, Critique, Implementation Status and Policy Issues
edited by Douglas D. Evanoff and William F. Moeller

Vol. 3 The History of Marketing Science
edited by Russell S. Winer and Scott A. Neslin

Vol. 4 The Analysis of Competition Policy and Sectoral Regulation
edited by Martin Peitz and Yossi Spiegel

Vol. 5 Contingent Convertibles [CoCos]: A Potent Instrument for Financial Reform
by George M. von Furstenberg

Vol. 6 Superpower, China? Historicizing Beijing's New Narratives of Leadership and East Asia's Response Thereto
by Niv Horesh, Hyun Jin Kim and Peter Mauch

Vol. 7 Diagnostics for a Globalized World
by Sten Thore and Ruzanna Tarverdyan

World Scientific – Now Publishers Series in Business: **Vol.7**

Diagnostics for a Globalized World

Sten Thore
The University of Texas at Austin, USA

Ruzanna Tarverdyan
The Geneva Consensus Foundation, Switzerland

now
World Scientific

Published by

World Scientific Publishing Co. Pte. Ltd.
5 Toh Tuck Link, Singapore 596224
USA office: 27 Warren Street, Suite 401-402, Hackensack, NJ 07601
UK office: 57 Shelton Street, Covent Garden, London WC2H 9HE

and

now publishers Inc.
PO Box 1024
Hanover, MA 02339
USA

Library of Congress Cataloging-in-Publication Data
Thore, Sten A. O.
Diagnostics for a globalized world / Sten Thore, The University of Texas at Austin, USA, Ruzanna Tarverdyan, The Geneva Consensus Foundation, Switzerland.
pages cm. -- (World scientific-now publishers series in business ; 7)
Includes bibliographical references and index.
ISBN 978-9814641432 (hardcover) -- ISBN 981464143X (hardcover)
1. Economic policy. 2. Social policy. 3. Sustainable development. 4. Globalization--Economic aspects. I. Tarverdyan, Ruzanna. II. Title.
HD87.T556 2015
330--dc23
2014038403

British Library Cataloguing-in-Publication Data
A catalogue record for this book is available from the British Library.

In-house Editor: Philly Lim

Typeset by Stallion Press
Email: enquiries@stallionpress.com

Printed in Singapore by B & Jo Enterprise Pte Ltd

Dedicated to the memory of W. W. Cooper,
friend and mentor

who participated in this research effort from an early stage,
who co-authored one of our previous reports,
who passed away as the last pages of this book were being completed.

Foreword

by Dr. David V. Gibson, Associate Director
IC^2 Institute, The University of Texas at Austin

Inspired by the vision of George Kozmetsky, the IC^2 (Innovation Creativity and Capital) Institute was founded in 1977 at The University of Texas at Austin as a "Think and Do Tank" focusing on entrepreneurship and science and technology commercialization initiatives, locally, nationally and internationally. In 1987, The University of Texas at Austin held the first International Technopolis Conference at the IC^2 Institute and in 1989, with regional support, established the Austin Technology Incubator (ATI) to serve as an "experiential learning laboratory" for students and faculty in the creation and growth of technology companies. As the high tech environment in Austin grew into a true technopolis, the Institute's international efforts matured in similar directions, with regional economic development collaborations in such countries as Mexico, Russia, China, Taiwan, Poland, Brazil, Portugal, Japan, South Korea, India and Norway. In 1996, scholars tied to the IC^2 Institute launched a UT Austin MS degree focused on the commercialization of science and technology that, over the years, has included training and online instruction in Russia, Poland, Mexico, Portugal, and Australia. Today, the Institute's roster of about 200 Fellows from academia, business, and government has a strong international representation and organizes conferences, programs, and education activities worldwide.

It is with pleasure that we welcome the book's focus on some of the achievements and some of the great failures of international economic and social policy — and explaining, at some length, novel metrics designed to gauge and rank the performance (or lack of performance) of nations. This enabling technique, *data envelopment analysis* (DEA), was developed by University of Texas scholars who were also Fellows at the IC^2 Institute which was, from the beginning, involved in the promotion of this methodology, including the organization of a 1989 conference on uses of DEA in management and public policy. The towering figures in these efforts were Professors Abe Charnes and W. W. Cooper who explored — together, and with their UT Austin colleagues and numerous PhD students — the mathematical ramifications and the ever-widening possibilities of this numerical technique. Sten Thore, who George Kozmetsky brought to the Institute in 1978, was an especially important colleague in these research and writing activities. Thanks to the efforts of Sten Thore and Ruzanna Tarverdyan, the present volume extends this work by ranking nations and providing a series of diagnostics to assist the conduct of economic and social policy.

Preface

The technological advance of our age is breathtaking and so is the extent of human needs and suffering. The United Nations Millennium Development Goals of economic and social progress are still distant dreams for the citizens of many nations, and UN agencies are scrambling to measure those shortcomings: to find diagnostics that would gauge the accomplishments of policy and the failures of policy.

This book examines the promise in this regard that is offered by *data envelopment analysis* (DEA), a quantitative technique invented by A. Charnes and W. W. (Bill) Cooper and their PhD students. This promise is documented in publications spanning a twenty-year period and in the chapters to follow — but the large-scale practical application is still awaiting. To prepare for this practical phase, my coauthor Ruzanna Tarverdyan has established the foundation The Geneva Consensus which operates out of Geneva, Switzerland.

This book is dedicated to the memory of Bill Cooper and will appear in print close to his centenary. It is being sponsored by the IC^2 Institute (my former academic home) as kindly arranged by Dr. Robert A. Peterson as Director. I would like to thank him, along with Associate Director, Dr. David V. Gibson. Margaret Cotrofeld, Technical Writer & Editor, did a wonderful job in compiling the index and preparing the book for print.

The Algarve, Portugal, February 2014, S. Th.

Introduction

One of the failings of today's economic science is the growing disconnect between the problems and tasks of the real world and the subject matters dealt with in economic textbooks. The calculation of national income and its determination in a system of competitive markets somehow does not seem to have the same priority as half a century ago. Instead, the current economic debate deals with concepts and entities that were not even mentioned those days: the competitiveness of nations, sustainable development, globalization, the environment, the liberation of gender and race, a decent income for all, and nutrition and health.

The explosion of new information technology and the opening-up of global markets for high tech products seemed to promise unlimited bounties of a new technological age but attendant economic and social problems quickly manifested themselves: workers being laid off in non-competitive industries, social turmoil in developing countries, and increasing poverty in areas relying on traditional means of livelihood. The International Labour Organization (ILO), an arm of the United Nations based in Geneva, puts it this way:

> On the one hand, the process of economic cooperation and integration has helped a number of countries to benefit from high rates of economic growth and employment creation, to absorb many of the rural poor into the modern urban economy, to advance their developmental goals, and to foster innovation . . . . On the other hand, global economic integration has caused many countries and sectors to face major challenges of income inequality, continuing high levels of unemployment and poverty, vulnerability of economies to external shocks . . . [ILO, 2008].

These are the realities that a modern theory of economic and social policy would have to wrestle with.

As a first and modest step toward developing economic theory more in tune with the requirements of our own age, the present book examines means of *measuring* multidimensional concepts like "Decent Work" (the preferred term used by ILO), or "A Fair Globalization." Considering the list of recent accomplishments and failures of nations cited just now, the economic and social performance of a nation is always multidimensional. Once we have agreed on a single numerical measure of such performance, it becomes possible to document numerically how policymakers succeed (or fail) in achieving their goals.

Rather ironically, the roots of the present work can be traced back to a piece by Paul Krugman that appeared in *Foreign Affairs* in 1994 titled, "Competitiveness: A dangerous obsession," which argued that such multidimensional concepts were meaningless. In a riposte, Golany and Thore [1997a], using data collected by the US Council of Competitiveness, calculated a single numerical measure of the competitiveness of each of the G-7 countries (Canada, France, Germany, Italy, Japan, the United Kingdom, and the United States) for each of the years 1972–1992. To effect the calculations they employed the (then) novel technique of *data envelopment analysis* (DEA), explicitly designed to rank multidimensional observations.

Subsequent work along similar lines involved comparisons of the productive efficiency of market-oriented economies in the West and state capitalism in the Soviet Union and Eastern Europe, and work by Golany and Thore ranking the performance of social and economic policy in 72 nations, including poor and developing nations drawn from all continents. DEA splits all observations into two classes: observations that are "efficient" (Pareto-optimal) and "subefficient" observations that are in disequilibrium. The possibility of poorly coordinated or even chaotic policy is explicitly recognized.

The original work by Golany and Thore appeared in a *Festschrift* to the late George Kozmetsky, founder of the IC^2 Institute (Innovation, Creativity and Capital) at The University of Texas at Austin. The IC^2 Institute is a powerhouse of new ideas, promoting generously the stupendous academic success of the technique of DEA, invented by A. Charnes and W. W. Cooper, two grand old men of management science, and their numerous colleagues and students. As the work assessing the international achievements of social and economic policy was resurrected by Thore and Tarverdyan (at the time working for the ILO in Geneva), Cooper followed these developments with great interest and in 2010 joined forces with Thore and Tarverdyan to publish a remarkable extension of his original pioneering work on DEA [Charnes, Cooper & Rhodes, 1978]. In this Cooper's last published work, a novel and surprising interpretation of the efficiency measure of DEA emerged when applied to policy data: as the maximal ratio between the social utility of the policy goals and the social cost of the policy instruments applied.

The Millennium Declaration by the United Nations was a major achievement in spelling out the priorities and goals of international economic and social policy. The concept of Decent Work as earlier promoted by the International Labour Organization quickly became reinterpreted in terms of the millennium goals. Similarly, the idea of "A Fair Globalization" was full-heartedly embraced by the international community. In the text to follow, assembling and processing data for 102 nations from all continents, we demonstrate how envelopment methods can be employed to assess the achievements of nations in terms of Decent Work and A Fair Globalization. Also, returning to the subject of the international competitiveness of nations, we have rerun the World Economic Forum competitiveness data, thus not only establishing a world ranking order but identifying the competitiveness *frontier* — the frontier of optimal performance of policy.

The frontier in all these cases is defined by the "best" performers, those nations that are able to convert their policy instruments into maximal returns of goals. In a sense, these are the countries that conventional economic equilibrium theory, and planning economists of former generations, would recognize and feel comfortable with. But, as it turns out, most of the countries fall short of these ideals. For them there is a "deficit" as in the "Decent Work Deficit" identified by the International Labour Office in Geneva. The actual goal achievements then fall short of the frontier achievements. The metrics to be developed deliver a numerical estimate of each such deficit. In other words, the frontier calculations not only identify the ideal performance but also the steps that need to be taken in order to improve actual performance.

For instance, our study of the competitiveness of nations in 2012 (reported in Chapter 7) reveals that 42 countries were located at the envelope that year, among them countries as diverse as France, Italy, Malawi, and Tanzania. The procedure of envelopment selects no single winner but a number of countries that are ranked as "equally good." They all served as "role models" to one or more of the 49 sub-frontier countries (located behind the envelope). In particular, Malawi was found to serve as a role model for Senegal and several other African countries.

For each sub-frontier country its performance deficit is calculated. The target performance is obtained as a linear amalgam of the performance of its role models. The envelopment provides not only a ranking of all the sub-frontier countries but is also a *diagnostic*: it calculates the improvement in goal performance that should have been possible, considering the achievements of its peers. The ranking methods proposed in the present volume identify policy goals that are realistic and achievable for all nations.

The recognition of the possibility of sub-frontier (suboptimal) behavior involves more than just a willingness to tolerate some short-term deviations from the equilibrium world. As we see it, it indicates the need to rewrite the entire neoclassical economic system, just as developments in physics has led to a reformulation of the Newtonian system. The Nobel laureate Ilya Prigogine has proposed such a reformulation, based on the idea that most physical systems are located far from equilibrium and stay in disequilibrium most of the time (see Part III in this book). Similarly, our numerical work has led us to believe that the achievements of economic and social planning in most countries in the world are located far from equilibrium and fall short of optimum most of the time.

And yet — we believe that our present inquiry into economic and social policy rests solidly on the works of those who went before us. The great Jan Tinbergen wrote in the 1950s two standard works on economic policy, much admired, that for a long time codified the subject of economic policy. They have now gradually faded from memory as Tinbergen's high hopes for economic verification never materialized. Our present work should be seen as a revival of Tinbergen's ambition, complementing it with the recognition of suboptimal behavior and thereby opening the door to large-scale statistical estimation.

To sum up, we believe that the envelopment procedures described in this book will have a great future on the international scene for evaluating national economic and social policy and for monitoring progress toward sustainable development goals. For some time, the international community has actually actively been looking for such a tool, recognizing the limits of simple constant-weights indices and searching for ways of evaluating the entire spectrum of the millennium goals. The effectiveness ratings (the scores) proposed in this book:

- transcend the standard measures of economic, social, and environmental performance;
- can serve as the basis for comprehensive packages of policy advice for regional, industry, and global agendas;
- can serve as a surveillance instrument for tracking development progress, increasing the benefits, and reducing the social costs of globalization.

The proposed metric will hopefully assist the harmonic convergence of national and international efforts toward economic development, social progress, and environmental protection.

Contents

Part I

The Economic and Social Policy of Nations: Achievements and Failures

Part I

Overview

The present work is directed to readers who would like to assess and compare the effectiveness of economic and social policy on the international scene, identifying opportunities and mechanisms for possibly improved performance. A new type of metrics will be proposed — rating current or past policy achievements — identifying laggards and winners.

The existing theory of economic policy was put in place by the Dutch economist Jan Tinbergen who wrote the classical tome on the subject, *Economic Policy: Principles and Design* (Amsterdam 1956). This work still stands as a major theoretical achievement, yet it is not well suited for empirical application, and in many ways it came to represent a dead end, providing little help to today's economist. A new departure is needed.

Appointed after the war as director of the newly established Central Planning Bureau for the Netherlands, Tinbergen constructed mathematical models of the Dutch economy where many variables could be considered as "instruments" of policy, like financial aggregates, interest rates, and data on the government budget. Could such variables be manipulated by economic policy to meet desired ends?

Tinbergen postulated the presence of a "social welfare" function expressed as a function of an array of suitable economic goals. These would include aims such as international peace, maximum real expenditure per capita, and the distribution of income over social groups and countries. Tinbergen suggested maximizing social welfare subject to constraints imposed by technology, resources, and (to some extent) political feasibility.

In the pages to follow, we shall present a set of numerical calculations that attempt to breathe empirical life into the programming problem of economic policy suggested by Tinbergen. In so doing, we shall select a set of realistic and implementable goals for economic and social policy relating to labor markets, globalization, and social conditions in both developed and less developed countries. These goals will not be made up in some kind of Tinbergenesque introspective exercise but will be brought from the working programs of international organizations, like the millennium development goals. In what follows, we intend to assemble a social preference function featuring dimensions that reflect the working program of the ILO (the International Labour Organization, an arm of the UN based in Geneva). As causal variables ("instruments" in Tinbergen's parlance) we employ a range of economic and social policy variables actually being used in contemporary economic policy.

The present work draws on some remarkable developments in data analysis that, 60 years after Tinbergen's pioneering account of the theory of economic policy, finally opens the door to meaningful empirical work that was so close to his heart. Following up on Tinbergen's original intentions, we shall indeed maximize a generalized welfare function subject to constraints, drawing on the techniques of *data envelopment analysis* (DEA). The calculations will be made for a large number of countries brought from all continents. Breaking with the received doctrines of economic equilibrium, however, DEA permits for some decision makers (here: countries) to fall short of the maximization of social preference. It is key to realize that real-world attempts at optimization are not necessarily successful, so that there may exist a *gap* between the idealized solution policy and actual performance. Optimization and the attainment of the optimal equilibrium point is thus not assumed but rather considered as a matter for empirical investigation.

Those countries that most effectively realize the goals formulated for economic policy together define an economic and social *frontier* — an effectiveness frontier of the selected social goal function. For those countries that fall short of the frontier, and thus are characterized by disequilibrium rather than equilibrium, the shortcomings (shortfall of goals or excessive use of instruments) will be calculated numerically. We shall assess the success of nations in reaching the three goals:

- decent work for men and women in the workforce,
- a fair globalization,
- international competitiveness.

These are all worthy strivings; they are continually discussed at international conferences and embodied in various ways in national legislation. They are all multi-dimensional and thus fall outside the confines of conventional economic theory and yet are of fundamental importance for understanding events on the international economic and social scene. All three of them also involve *compromise*: decent work is paid work but requires also acceptable work conditions, fair globalization means open borders but requires also protection for vulnerable industries, while competitiveness means productivity advantage but not at unlimited social cost.

For each such multi-dimensional goal complex we shall identify the frontier countries defining the "best" performance. For those countries that fall behind the frontier a numerical index of sub-effectiveness (an "effectiveness score") will be calculated and the scope for possible improved performance will be evaluated.

Our investigation of *Decent Work*, as defined by the International Labor Office in Geneva, identifies sixteen out of 102 nations that define the envelope, headed by Denmark, the United States, Burkina Faso, and Jamaica. (Poor countries also need "peers" to define their best practice!) Rather attractively, the kingdom of Bhutan joins the group of peers, preaching the message of gross national happiness to the world!

Using the same data set, we identify eighteen nations that define the envelope for *A Fair Globalization*, as defined by the World Commission on the Social Dimension of Globalization [WCSDG, 2004a]. One of the goals entering our list of success criteria is the equality of the vertical income distribution (measured by one minus the Gini coefficient). Denmark still is on the list but several of the former winners now slip badly, among them the United States. More generally, our results prompt us to investigate the blessings and costs of free trade. In an expanded causal tree depicting the cause-effect relationships covering both Decent Work and A

Fair Globalization at the same time, we continue the numerical analysis through a hybrid or two-stage procedure.

The World Economic Forum (WEF) kindly made available to us their extensive data base from which they calculate their regularly published, *Global Competitiveness Index*. However, the WEF more or less sidesteps the issue of the goals of national competitiveness policy, spending its efforts on enumerating and assessing all possible policy instruments (their twelve "pillars" of policy). Accordingly, our ranking of nations is at great variance with that of the Forum: The winners in their annual ranking list are those countries that have excellent *reason* to be competitive; our rankings reward those countries that actually *perform* more competitively than others.

Many countries reveal long-standing effectiveness deficits, some of them no doubt connected to internal strife, war, pestilence, or other national misfortunes — and others tied to turbulent growth. Also, as some countries go through rapid technological and social upheaval, they sacrifice short-term equilibrium. In such cases, effectiveness is a distant ideal and economic equilibrium theory is of little help. To conclude our investigation, trying to understand the prevalent presence of ineffectiveness, we survey some relevant elements of modern chaos theory and the mathematics of non-equilibrium orbits.

* * *

The core of Part I as presented in the three chapters 4, 5, and 6 consists of material brought from three papers [Thore & Tarverdyan, 2008; 2009; Cooper, Thore & Tarverdyan, 2010]. Our numerical calculations were this time, however, carried out with a much larger data set (111 nations rather than the earlier 52 nations). Chapter 7 presents a study of the international competitiveness of 101 nations, drawing on statistical data collected by the World Economic Forum. This material is published here for the first time. Throughout our joint work, Thore has been responsible for the written text; Tarverdyan contributed her extensive knowledge of the work of international organizations and was responsible for the acquisition, assembly, and processing of all data.

Chapter 1

The Theory of Economic and Social Policy Reconsidered

1.1 International Initiatives

A series of international accords has recently brought attention to the wide variety of social and economic problems facing nations in a world of globalization, economic development (or lack of development), and scarce resources. The need for policy coherence, coordination, and cooperation has intensified during past years. A notable event occurred with the formulation of the United Nations Millennium Declaration (New York) [2000]. It laid down a series of "millennium development goals" (MDGs), giving a sharper focus and impetus to the international quest for social and economic development.

The Millennium Declaration resolved "to ensure greater policy coherence and better cooperation between the United Nations (UN), its agencies, the Bretton Woods Institutions and the World Trade Organization, as well as other multilateral bodies, with a view to achieving a fully coordinated approach to the problems of peace and development." The development community reached a consensus around the shared objectives of achieving the MDGs and the partnership between developed and developing countries:

- the developing countries are expected to focus on good governance, sound economic and social policies, and robust institutions that will help mobilize resources from all sources — public, private, foreign, and domestic;
- the developed countries are expected to reduce barriers to trade and promote an international economy more conducive to growth and development, to provide adequate aid resources in the form of private

capital flows, to provide additional development assistance to support those efforts, and (under the Heavily Indebted Poor Country Initiative) help the developing world to ease the debt burdens and support them in effective management of their external debts (see also UN Department of Economic and Social Affairs [2004]).

The MDGs include poverty reduction, full and productive employment and Decent Work for all, educational goals, health goals, and other measures. The Monterrey Consensus of the UN [2004] International Conference on Financing for Development emphasized the need for coherent action of all stakeholders in the international community, including the need to enhance the efficacy of macroeconomic policies. The Millennium Declaration was followed by a report by Secretary-General Kofi Annan titled, *Road Map towards the Implementation of the United Nations Millennium Declaration* [UN, 2001], which brought together the goals listed in the declaration under eight separate chapters:

- MDG 1: Eradicate extreme poverty and hunger;
- MDG 2: Achieve universal primary education;
- MDG 3: Promote gender equality and empower women;
- MDG 4: Reduce child mortality;
- MDG 5: Improve maternal health;
- MDG 6: Combat HIV/AIDS, malaria, and other diseases;
- MDG 7: Ensure environmental sustainability;
- MDG 8: Develop a global partnership for development.

MDG 1 and MDG 8 are overarching goals toward poverty reduction. They, along with MDG 7 on sustainable development, rely on Decent Work (a term to be explained in a moment) for their attainment. Achieving MDG 3 on gender equality is a condition for meeting all the other goals. Decent Work for parents and the elimination of child labor are essential to attain MDG 2. Social protection contributes directly to the health-related goals (MDG 4, 5, and 6).

Founded in Geneva in 1919, the International Labour Organization (ILO) is a specialized agency of the UN to promote opportunities for women and men to obtain decent and productive work in conditions of freedom, equity, security, and human dignity. Working through dialogue with governments, employers, and workers, the ILO has set international labor standards that form part of international human rights law and national legal systems. From its inception, through the means of research, advocacy, and technical cooperation, the ILO seeks the promotion of social justice and internationally recognized human and labor rights. The ILO constitution, *Declaration of Philadelphia* [2004], states:

> ... the attainment of the conditions in which ... [social justice] shall be possible must constitute the central aim of national and international policy ... it is the responsibility of the International Labour Organization to examine and consider all international economic and financial policies and measures in the light of this ... fundamental objective.

In his 1999 annual report, the director-general of the ILO, Juan Somavia, set out the *Decent Work Agenda* [ILO, 1999] with four elements:

(1) *employment*: the principal route out of poverty is through work and income;
(2) *rights*: without them, people will not be empowered to escape from poverty;
(3) *social protection*: it safeguards income and underpins health;
(4) *dialogue:* the participation of employers' and workers' organizations.

Since then, the concept of "Decent Work" has provided a strategic framework for organizing ILO's activities as the simultaneous pursuit of these four objectives. The concept of Decent Work draws on the long experience that the ILO has gained, working with constituents in a variety of programs and in interaction with employment, labor markets, and social protection policies in many countries and under many different circumstances [ILO, 2001a].

The logical relationship between the millennium development goals and various instruments of economic and social policy may be illustrated by a cognitive map as in Figure 1.1. The cognitive map is a common tool in multi-criteria analysis (see *e.g.*, Bana e Costa and Thore [2002]). Figure 1.1 highlights the logical structure of the causal relationships, tying causes to effects. More detailed cognitive maps will be presented in this book as we proceed.

For the purposes of empirical analysis, it is necessary that the goals and policy inputs referred to in Figure 1.1 can be *measured*, requiring

Figure 1.1 Casual relationship between inputs and goals.

that suitable *metrics* are available to measure them. In the empirical work reported in this book, data will be analyzed from readily available international data sources, compiled by international bodies like the World Bank and the Organisation for Economic Co-operation and Development (OECD).

The purpose of the millennium development goals and subsequent work carried out by the UN is to recognize the strivings of nations toward social and economic betterment. Admittedly, the goals are ambitious — some would even say unrealistic. But the shortcomings of performance from the goals are spelled out without compunction.

A framework for monitoring has been designed by the World Bank and the International Monetary Fund (IMF) in close collaboration with the UN, the World Trade Organization (WTO) and regional multilateral development banks. Together with the European Commission, they have initiated a series of annual global monitoring reports reviewing international efforts to support the Millennium Declaration and assess the implementation of policies and actions for achieving the MDGs and related development outcomes. They provide systematic reviews and analysis of national performances including a discussion of a wide range of issues, and thus enable developing and developed countries to benchmark their policies, actions, and outcomes *vis-à-vis* others.

The monitoring reports emphasize the need to improve policy coherence, the management of inputs into the production process, and result management. They call for instituting a results management agenda with an effort to develop a "common performance management system" and for integrating management of development results into the practices of the development banks. Consider, for instance, the annual "progress charts" published by the UN statistics division. The *Progress Chart for 2011* delivers verdicts as cited (in part) below.

- MDG 1: *very high hunger* in Sub-Saharan Africa and *high hunger* in Southern Asia;
- MDG 2: *moderate enrollment in universal primary education* in Sub-Saharan Africa and Western Asia;
- MDG 3: *very low representation of women in national parliaments* in Western Asia;
- MDG 4: *high child mortality* in Sub-Saharan Africa;
- MDG 5: *mothers suffering very high mortality at childbirth* in Sub-Saharan Africa;
- MDG 6: *high mortality from tuberculosis* in Sub-Saharan Africa and Southeastern Asia;
- MDG 7: *very high proportion of slum dwellers* in Sub-Saharan Africa.

Reading this list, an obvious challenge cries out — the challenge to construct a new kind of economic theory that can deal with deviations between optimal policy and actual policy. Optimality is fine, but how large are the real-world shortcomings from optimum and how can policymakers correct them? A true believer in equilibrium economics may think that such deviations will somehow "go away." The profound lesson of a considerable body of disequilibrium theory later to be reviewed in this book is that they will not. Many economic activities may be stuck in disequilibrium permanently. For generations to come, there will be hunger, poverty, high mortality, and slum dwellers in many regions of the world. The Utopia dreamed up by Thomas More five hundred years ago is still just that: a beautiful dream. Economists and social scientists must do better.

Since the days of Adam Smith and Alfred Marshall, economics has been the science of the behavior of "economic man," some fictitious rational individual who, weighing all possible courses of action, chooses the one that maximizes "utility." A widely used definition of economics states that it is the science of allocating given means to obtain a set of desirable ends. But suboptimal individuals and suboptimal companies are not very good at solving that optimizing problem. And yet, they are very much part of the reality that economists need to come to grips with. Some companies are not very good at maximizing profit. Engineers may not see or understand technological opportunities. Managers may simply be poor at managing. In order to understand the real world, the science of economics needs a theory to describe management that falls behind, as well as management that operates at the cutting edge of technology.

Similarly, political bodies in many countries may act irrationally. Politicians may pay lip service to the true needs of the common citizen, but actually promote their own pet projects. The tools of national economic and social policy may be poorly coordinated. A realistic analysis requires that we allow for the existence of "non-economic man" executing economic and social policy. And so, there is an urgent need for the more mundane task of measuring the true performance of the nations of the world, the ineffectiveness of policy rather than its effectiveness, identifying the laggards rather than the victors and suggesting steps — even small steps — toward improvement.

1.2 Goals of Economic and Social Policy

In order to measure the relative success (or failure) of economic and social policy in a given country, one may identify a set of goal variables

$$r = 1, 2, \dots, s \tag{1.1}$$

and the goal achievements

$$Y = (Y_1, Y_2, \dots, Y_s) \tag{1.2}$$

To characterize the achievement of a goal, a long array of numerical information may need to be recorded. Some of the data may be cardinal, but much information will typically be qualitative rather than quantitative; to provide an account of this information a long list of categorical variables may be specified. To facilitate the numerical analysis, it is assumed that all this information has been compressed into a set of $r = 1, 2, \dots, s$ single-attribute cardinal numbers.

Next, a set of weights μ_r, $r = 1, 2, \dots, s$ are defined to be used calculating the total index of the policy achievements of this country

$$\sum_r \mu_r Y_r \tag{1.3}$$

The index (1.3) is a weighted amalgam of the observed goal achievements. Other names are the "scorecard" for the country examined, or the number of "points" scored. (These are common terms of multi-criteria analysis.)

A well-publicized and ambitious example of the calculation of an index like (1.3) is the World Economic Forum *Index of Global Competitiveness* [2014]. It aims at measuring the economic, social, and environmental competitiveness of 144 countries. The index is a weighted average of many components, each measuring a different aspect of competitiveness, culminating in a final competitiveness score for each country.

More generally, and in the time-honored language of economic theory, we may see (1.3) as a particular (linear) form of social preference or *social utility* obtained in each country, say

$$V = V(Y) \tag{1.4}$$

While the linear expression (1.3) is attractive and easy to work with, there is something to be said for a slightly weaker assumption, only assuming that (1.4) is concave. In practical terms, the curvature of the function would measure how a country could compensate for some lack of attainment of one goal by providing more of some other goal. In educational policy for instance, it may be considered to be socially acceptable to compensate for a shortfall of university entrance openings by offering more vocational schools. Differentiating (1.4), it would then be possible to determine the exact amount of marginal improvement of one goal that is required to offset a given shortfall of another.

For an illustration, turn to the *map of indifference* or *iso-utility curves* as commonly used in economic textbooks; along each such curve $V =$ *constant*. In Figure 1.2, two goods are exhibited: Good 1 is measured along the horizontal axis and Good 2 along the vertical axis. In our present application the two "goods" are identified as goals: Goal 1 and Goal 2. The *marginal rate of substitution* between the two goals can be read from the diagram as the slope of an indifference curve. For most goals the marginal rate of substitution is not constant, so their indifference curves are convex to the origin, describing a negative substitution effect: as the coverage of one goal gets less and less, the policymaker needs to be compensated by a greater achievement in terms of the other goal.

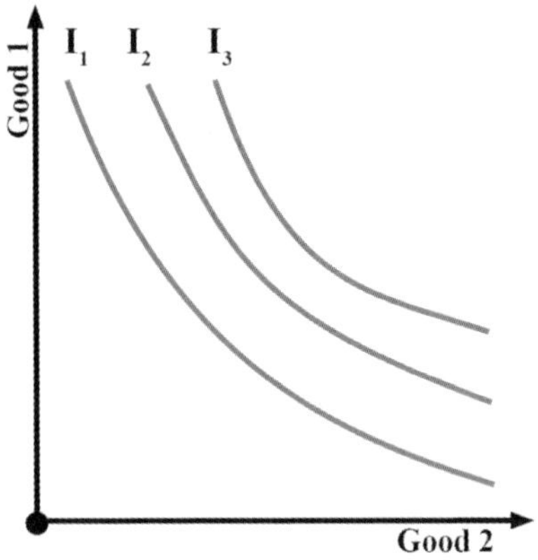

Figure 1.2 Map of indifference or iso-utility curves for the two goals Goal 1 and Goal 2.

An example of a utility function that generates indifference curves that are convex toward the origin is the Cobb-Douglas function. For the calculations to follow, we assume that the function $V(Y)$ as spelled out in (1.4) is generalized Cobb-Douglas, so that the relationship between social preference and the goals is linear in the logarithms of the variables:

$$log V(Y) = \sum_r \mu_r log Y_r \tag{1.5}$$

where the μ_r, $r = 1, 2, \ldots, s$ are weights to be determined empirically (a possible constant term is suppressed).

1.3 The Policy Parameters

The task of economic and social policy is not only to formulate goals, but more importantly to find ways of realizing those goals within the constraints set by existing conditions. Those constraints are not just budget constraints but all sorts of political constraints as well. There is a "cost" involved in every mix of policy action, not just in economic terms but more generally a *political opportunity cost.*

The opportunity foregone referred to in this expression is the opportunity of an idealized optimal or *equilibrium* array of policy actions (rather than the possible shortcomings of actual policy). The "opportunity" is the opportunity of optimal planning rather than the reality of actual planning.

In other words, the political opportunity cost brings in a *comparison* between idealized actions and actual policy actions. Denoting the list of $i = 1, 2, \ldots, m$ policy inputs by the column vector $X = (X_1, X_2, \ldots, X_m)$, we identify the political opportunity cost as

$$U(X) \tag{1.6}$$

We have already introduced a map of indifference curves for total economic and social welfare $V(Y)$ — see Figure 1.2. Now let us use the same diagram to illustrate the indifference curves of social policy costs. The two "goods" in the figure are then identified as Policy instrument 1 and Policy instrument 2. Again there will exist a map of indifference curves of the policy parameters X. Along each such indifference curve, the political opportunity cost $U = constant$. The slope of such an indifference curve at a given point indicates the rate of substitution between the policy actions X. These curves will also be taken to be convex toward the origin, indicating that along a given indifference curve a decreasing use of one policy parameter must be compensated by ever increasing amounts of one or more other policy parameters. For a practical example brought from the field of crime prevention, consider the use of alternative sentences by the courts such as community service and incarceration. In this case, the policy cost to society is not only the cost of administration and cost of operating prisons but also the risk of renewed crimes in the future. Presumably, it should be possible to compensate for some shorter prison sentences by extending the practice of compulsory community services, but there are obvious limits to such practices.

Just as we have assumed actual economic and social welfare to be Cobb-Douglas, we shall also assume that the political cost of that welfare is Cobb-Douglas, writing

$$logU(X) = \sum_i v_i logX_i \tag{1.7}$$

where the v_i, $i = 1, 2, \ldots, m$ are weights to be determined empirically (again, a possible constant term is suppressed).

The cognitive map illustrated in Figure 1.1 can now be spelled out in more detail as in Figure 1.3, featuring explicitly the instruments of economic social policy X_i, $i = 1, 2, \ldots, m$ and the goals Y_r, $r = 1, 2, \ldots, s$.

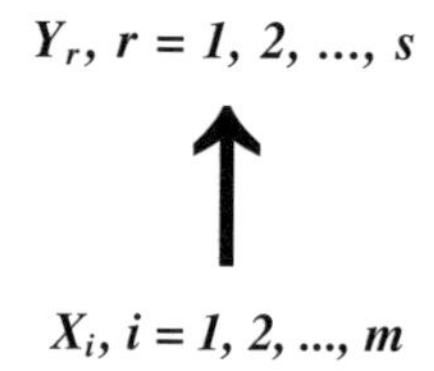

Figure 1.3 Cognitive map illustrating casual relations between policy parameters and goals.

The virtual social cost $U(X)$ should be compared with *actually attained* total societal welfare $V(Y)$. For the purpose of such comparison, form the ratio

$$V(Y)/U(X) \tag{1.8}$$

which one may identify as the *effectiveness rating* of the chosen policy. Obviously, the aim of economic and social policy in a country is to make this ratio as large as possible — to maximize the economic and social preference function for any given political opportunity cost.

The idea of forming a ratio like (1.8) goes back to standard concepts in engineering where the effectiveness of a machine would be calculated as the ratio between actual energy delivered and total energy spent. It would be less than one; only under idealized conditions would it equal one. In neoclassical economic theory based upon axioms of rational behavior, the effectiveness rating (1.8) would similarly equal one: actual value created is exhausted by costs. But in the real world that we shall be concerned with in our numerical calculations, economic plans sometimes fall short of the possibilities. Opportunities are missed and errors are made. There is a discrepancy between actual policy and the optimal ideal. The effectiveness ratio (1.8) may fall below unity. The numerical value of the ratio then serves as a metric to indicate the relative success of actual economic and social policy in a country.

With a slight modification of (1.8) and rather employing the logarithmic specifications of U and V, we shall subsequently choose to define the effectiveness rating of the chosen policy by the ratio

$$log V(Y)/log U(X) \tag{1.9}$$

which then reduces to

$$\left(\sum_r \mu_r logY_r\right) \Big/ \left(\sum_i v_i logX_i\right) \tag{1.10}$$

Again, the effectiveness ratio (1.10) may fall below unit, signaling a discrepancy between actual policy and the optimal ideal. But if the ratio (1.10) equals unity, the vector of economic and social policy is optimal, generating goals providing the maximal potential social welfare.

The numerical calculation of the effectiveness rating (1.10) requires information about the goal weights μ_r and the policy weights v_i. Rather than assuming these weights to be fixed and known numbers (as in the calculation of a conventional index, see Section 1.2 above) we shall now treat these weights as unknowns. *More precisely, we shall determine a unique set of goal weights and policy weights for each nation, drawing on a process of mathematical programming termed fractional programming.* (The numerical calculation will be demonstrated in Chapter 2.)

At the moment we can make one simple observation. The solution of the unknown weights ($\mu_r, r = 1, 2, \ldots, s; v_i, i = 1, 2, \ldots, m$) is not uniquely determined by the ratio (1.10) since that ratio will remain unchanged if we multiply all the weights by a fixed constant. Doubling all the weights, for instance, will leave the ratio unchanged. In what follows, we shall take advantage of this property by normalizing the weights, imposing either the condition

$$\sum_i v_i logX_i = 1 \tag{1.11a}$$

which will be said to generate an "instruments-oriented" or "input-oriented" calculation of the effectiveness rating, or

$$\sum_r \mu_r logY_r = 1 \tag{1.11b}$$

which generates a "goal-oriented" or "output-oriented" calculation of the effectiveness rating. Note that the goal-oriented version of the rating equals the inverted value of the social cost of the bundle of policy instruments. The instruments-oriented rating, on the other hand, simply equals the social welfare or utility of the chosen set of goals. In any case, if the effectiveness rating equals 1, it follows that the social welfare of the set of goals and the social cost of the policy instruments are both equal to 1. The following two propositions then follow:

- If a collection of goals and policy instruments is effective (the rating being equal to 1), then no goal can be increased without lowering the fulfilment of at least one other goal.
- Similarly, the use of no policy instrument can be lowered without increasing at least one other instrument.

These are statements that will ring familiar to any student of neoclassical equilibrium theory, evoking the well-known properties of Pareto efficiency. In order not to mix the concepts, however, we are deliberately using the term "effective" (rather than "efficient") to indicate that these are properties of variables that transcend the inputs and outputs of narrow production theory.

1.4 Tinbergen on Economic Policy

For the reader to put in perspective our presentation of goals and policy instruments, we need to say a few words about the inherited classical theory of economic and social policy, formulated in the 1950s by one of the giants of economic theory — the Dutch economist Jan Tinbergen.

In the early 1930s, the League of Nations engaged Tinbergen to evaluate empirically and test the proliferating flora of business cycle theory of the times. It is easy to understand how this work gradually led him to develop a theory of economic planning. Behind the work on business cycles was the constantly nagging question of how it might be possible by the central bank or the government to counteract the onset of apparently ever-deepening business downturns. His models were large systems with as many as 50 relations and 70 variables; these included many variables that could be considered as "instruments" of policy, like financial aggregates, interest rates, and data on the government budget. Could such variables be manipulated by economic policy in order to dampen business fluctuations?

Appointed after the war as director of the newly established Central Planning Bureau for the Netherlands, Tinbergen was expected to forecast the effects of economic policy and to advise the government on related matters. It led to the writing of two key tracts on the theory of economic policy [Tinbergen, 1952; 1956]. The 1952 book is the slimmer of the two, only 78 pages. He begins by explaining the nature of the model to be used. It contains four types of quantified entities: targets (goals), instruments, other variables of the economic system, and data. He goes on to argue that consistent economic policy requires that the number of targets equal the number of instruments. If the number of targets exceeds the number of instruments, the targets are "incompatible." If the number of targets is smaller than the number of instruments, the instruments are "alternative;" that is, one instrument may be used instead of another or a combination of others. (We should point out that these assertions do not hold up in the non-optimal framework that we will describe in subsequent chapters.) The book used simple examples illustrated with the aid of two models, one of which was used by the Central Planning Bureau.

The 1956 work introduces welfare functions for policymakers or entire nations. For the simplest case, when the number of targets equals the number of instruments, the mathematics goes like this (using Tinbergen's own notation):

Let

x_i, $i = 1, 2, \ldots, I$ be the economic variables that are not targets
y_j, $j = 1, 2, \ldots, J$ be the targets where $I = J$
z_k, $k = 1, 2, \ldots, K$ be the instruments controlled by a policymaker
u_l, $l = 1, 2, \ldots, L$ be the data
and write the equations of the model

$$\phi_n(x, y, z, u) = 0, \quad n = 1, 2, \ldots, N \tag{1.12}$$

where x, y, z, u are vectors as defined a moment ago. If the model is "consistent," the number of equations equals the number of unknowns, $I + K = N$. Under standard regularity conditions, the model will then possess a well-defined and unique solution. The general format is illustrated by a great number of examples, ranging from monetary and currency policy to tax policy. In all cases, the problem is considered not only theoretically but also numerically, using plausible values of the coefficients derived from econometric work.

When the number of targets exceeds the number of instruments, however, solution requires the presence of a social welfare function, say

$$\theta(y, z) \tag{1.13}$$

The problem at hand, then, is one of maximizing $\theta(y, z)$ subject to the side conditions (1.12). In almost all applications, however, he assumes fixed targets so that there is little practical maximization in the book.

Tinbergen's work was an immediate sensation. The prestigious *Journal of the American Statistical Association* asked one of the young and coming economists at Stanford by the name of Ken Arrow to write a detailed report on the book [Arrow, 1958]. One future Nobelist reviewing another future Nobelist! In many ways, the present reader may find the referee report as thought-provoking as the original work. Arrow starts out by examining Tinbergen's discussion of the aims or goals of economic policy, listing the following goals:

- international peace;
- maximum real expenditure *per capita* with full employment and monetary equilibrium;
- distribution of income over social groups and countries;
- emancipation of underprivileged groups;
- "as much personal freedom as compatible with the other aims."

Agreeing that peace should be treated as an overarching aim, Arrow nevertheless finds it difficult to see how the economics profession can contribute to it. (With 50 years of hindsight, we can only admire the cleverness of the authors of the MDGs who were able to articulate a series of economic and social goals that all directly and without question contribute to peace.)

Discussing the very last point in the list — about personal freedom — Arrow makes a very poignant observation: the freedom of one person may be seen as compulsion by another:

> I think the matter is more complex than is sometimes supposed. Man is a social animal and the freedom in question must extend to organizations of various kinds, not excluding labor unions [*ibid.*, p. 91].

In other words, some policy goals may be inherently contradictory. We shall later return to this issue in some detail, discussing the goal of free trade. (We shall also point at possibilities of resolving such conflicts of aims, breaking up the causal link from policy instruments to policy aims into two or several sub-links.)

Arrow reviews in some detail Tinbergen's discussion of "qualitative economic policy," where the institutions and methods of economic control are altered. This includes built-in stabilizers and changes in the types of taxation, monopoly policy, administrative centralization or decentralization, and appraisal of investment projects. Widening the scope of his investigation even further, Tinbergen also considered social security schemes, guarantees of minimum income or minimum employment, equalization of opportunities, monetary reforms, centralization of production decisions, industrial democracy, and nationalization. To the modern reader, the issue of qualitative economic variables boils down to the problem of identifying bundles of suitable quantitative target variables characterizing the situation at hand. Admittedly, this may involve a very large number of variables interacting with each other through complex interdependent causal networks. The cognitive map in Figure 1.3 is then far too simplistic and needs to be replaced by a detailed mapping of the causal structure.

1.5 Quasi-welfare

What happened to Tinbergen's vision of an overarching social welfare function of all economic and social goals? When the great man died, the book closed on his theory of global optimization and few if any seemed to be ready to pick up his mantle.

Work by P. A. Samuelson [1952] and T. Takayama and J. J. Judge [1971] opened up the possibility of estimating consumer welfare, called "quasi-welfare." More precisely, quasi-welfare is an economic potential function of all consumer demand. It is obtained by integrating the demand price functions of consumers (a demand price function is the inverse of an ordinary demand function, writing the demand price as a function of all quantities consumed). If the demand price functions are indeed integrable and if they are linear, quasi-welfare becomes a quadratic function of consumer demand. The income of consumers is supposed to be given, so that the works based on Takayama-Judge models are all *partial* economic models, developed for a sector of the economy only (typically an agricultural sector).

As an example one might refer to the regional activity analysis model of the US apple industry featuring a quadratic quasi-welfare function due to Fuchs, Farrish, and Bohall [1974].[1] These models can include an account of the production sector with explicit modelling of final goods, intermediary goods and resources, all controlled by the overriding principle of maximizing quasi-welfare.

Perhaps the most ambitious work along these lines was a study on multi-level regional planning in Mexico sponsored by the World Bank [Goreux and Manne, 1973]; see also the subsequent study of the Ivory Coast [Goreux, 1981]. In models like these, it becomes possible to demonstrate and evaluate how the total demand for various farm products is causally related to inputs into the production chain and their costs (including agricultural subsidies, say, which indeed are an example of public policy instruments).

But this is still a far cry from what Tinbergen had in mind. One can think of at least three reasons why the concept of quasi-welfare will never serve as an entry point to a general theory of economic and social policy. First, the goals of policy extend further than just to consumer demand. It is clearly not possible to write the goals of international policy (like the MDGs) as some kind of "demand functions" of possible policy parameters. Second, the goals laid down by international organizations like reducing poverty or establishing A Fair Globalization are all multidimensional involving complex (and sometimes self-contradictory) causal relationships. (How far should considerations of "fairness" be allowed to intervene, delaying further globalization?) Politicians set policy as they see fit and their choices cannot be captured by some overriding neoclassical quasi-welfare function. Third, while some countries presumably act more rationally than others, any theory of economic policy worth its name must also recognize the presence non-optimality: of setbacks, of failed efforts, of hunger, disaster, and war. To deal with them we need to look "outside the box" and be willing to accept an economic world that exists outside the orderliness of neoclassical equilibrium.

[1] For the general mathematical format, see the textbook *Economics Logistics* [Thore, 1991], Chapter 4.

Chapter 2

Rating Country Performance by Frontier Analysis

Frontier analysis is a recent development in economics that explicitly recognizes that some decision makers use sub-optimal solutions. When applied to the field of national economic and social policy, the purpose of frontier analysis is to identify those nations that effectively convert policy parameters into maximal goal achievements. These countries are said to be located at the frontier. Ineffective or sub-effective countries are located away from (or below) the frontier.

Since there may be several countries (or a given country measured at different time intervals) located at the frontier, the multiple answers provided by frontier analysis indicate that planning effectiveness may exist in several forms corresponding to different ways of organization and management of policy. However, countries that are not on the frontier do not make as effective use of their policy inputs as some linear combination of other countries, indicating that their performance might be improved by changing some of their planning procedures.

For most readers of these pages, the disequilibrium technique of data envelopment analysis (DEA) will be unknown. DEA has been used extensively during the last 30 years in the estimation of production functions and production frontiers for manufacturing corporations, hospitals, commercial banks, and electric utilities. Some of these units can be represented as profit maximizers, but others cannot. DEA works just as well for a study of farming in a developing country in which most of the farm produce is consumed on the farm, as it does for US farms in the wheat belt. It works just as well for a study of hospitals in Great Britain (which has a socialized health care system) as it does for profit-maximizing hospitals in the United States. For some such units there may be decreasing returns to scale, as required by standard equilibrium theory. For others there may be rapidly increasing returns to scale, even hypergrowth (in the semiconductor or computer industries). In all of these applications, the task of DEA is to identify a production frontier and to determine the location of each observation (hospital, bank, electric utility) relative to the frontier. On-frontier observations are ascribed an efficiency rating of 100%, off-frontier observations efficiency ratings less than 100%. For each off-frontier observation, the "distance" (shortcomings) to the frontier is calculated and thus the scope for possible improvement is determined. DEA is a diagnostic technique that delivers advice for enhanced performance.

Using DEA to rate the economic and social policy of a group of entire countries, the performance or effectiveness of each country will be assessed on the basis of its ability to realize the list of policy goals that has been laid down. Again, frontier observations will be ascribed an effectiveness rating of 100%. Geometrically, the frontier is constructed as the envelope of the 100% effective countries ("envelope" as in the term "data envelopment analysis"). In modern hi tech lingo, the word envelope is used in expressions such as "pushing the envelope," meaning going beyond what is technically possible today. More strictly, envelope is a geometrical term, referring to the piece-wise linear locus of tightest closure around a given collection of points. Off-frontier countries are ascribed an effectiveness rating of less than 100%. These countries fall behind (or below) the envelope. Projecting an off-frontier country onto the envelope, one finds its ideal performance. The difference measures the potential for possible improvement of economic and social policy.

2.1 Constructing the Frontier

A simplified illustration of an economic and social policy frontier is provided in Figure 2.1. The achievements of six countries A, B, C, D, E, and F are compared, plotting for each country the use of a single policy instrument X (an "input") and the resulting performance in terms of the single goal Y (the "output"). Each observed instrument-goal pair is marked as a separate point. To carry out the envelopment calculations, the observations of each country have to be divided into two classes: outputs or

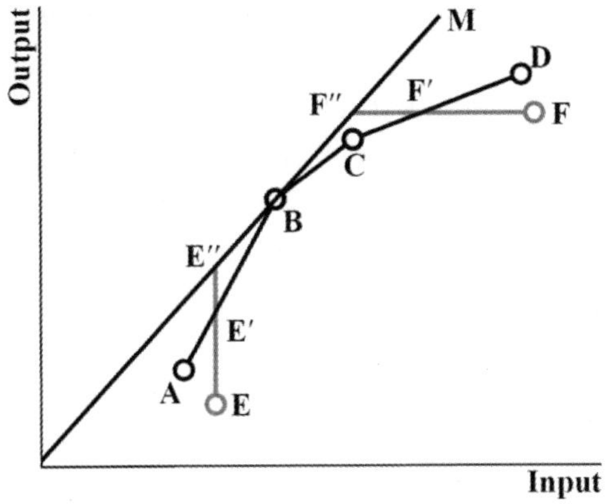

Figure 2.1 Illustration of instrument — goal effectiveness frontier.

goals, and inputs or policy parameters. DEA ranks the countries in terms of their ability to convert inputs into outputs. That is, the effectiveness rating is a measure of the relative performance of a country — relative to its use of policy parameters, not of its absolute goal performance. It is this relative measure that we call "effectiveness."

Quite generally, in a multidimensional space with many inputs and outputs, the effectiveness frontier can be drawn as a multifaceted multidimensional surface, a so-called linear polyhedron (the "envelope"). The polyhedron can be obtained by constructing the upper convex hull to the observed points. In Figure 2.1, the resulting effectiveness frontier A-B-C-D is piece-wise linear. It consists of three linear facets: AB, BC and CD. The frontier is said to be "spanned" by the four countries A, B, C, and D. These four countries are located on the instrument — goal effectiveness frontier. They are effective. The two remaining countries E and F are located behind the frontier. They are ineffective.

The geometric construction that underlies the techniques described in this book proceeds by drawing a slightly different kind of envelope: the *conical hull* or convex cone to the given points. The conical hull is the multidimensional plane passing through the origin O satisfying the "ray property" — if (X, Y) is a feasible observation, then (kX, kY) is also a feasible observation, where k is a non-negative scalar. In Figure 2.1 the conical frontier is then simply the ray OB. On this measure, country B is effective but the countries A, C, D, E, and F are all ineffective.

Historically, it was this latter envelope OB with constant returns throughout that was applied in the pioneering paper of Charnes, Cooper and Rhodes [1978]. For the first few years, the CCR-model (named after the initials of the authors) was the only enveloping procedure around. But with the publication of the Banker, Charnes, and Cooper [1984] — later referred to as the BCC-model — the alternative with flexible returns to scale (A-B-C-D) became also investigated.

The envelopment provides a ranking of all ineffective countries. (There is no ranking of the effective units because they all receive the rating of 100%. They are "the best.") An effectiveness score less than 100% signals non-optimal and nonequilibrium behavior. The performance of such a country is non-Paretoan in the sense that, given the policy instruments, it should be possible to increase the attainment of one or more goals. Fitting a polyhedral envelope in Figure 2.1, the effectiveness ratings of the countries A, B, C, and D are all 100%; all countries below A, B, C and D will be assigned a rating of less than 100%. Fitting a conical hull instead, the effectiveness rating of point B is 100% and the rating of each point below OB is less than 100%.

There are two ways of characterizing the ineffectiveness of points. One way of examining an ineffective point is *goal-oriented*, noting that the outputs obtained fall short of what should be possible. Given the instruments actually used, it should be possible to increase the goal achievements. Projecting point E vertically upwards toward the polyhedron frontier A-B-C-D, one finds point E$'$. The projection is carried out as an *equiproportional* increase of the goal outputs Y, keeping the policy inputs X unchanged. Projecting it even further upwards toward the conical hull, one finds point E$''$. Note that E$'$ and E$''$ are not observed points; rather, they are hypothetical points using the same inputs as E but generating more output. The goal-oriented version of envelopment will be used throughout the present book. It represents the natural way of looking at things in most applications involving social and economic policy, searching for the maximal possible achievements of goals, given the actual use of policy instruments.

A second way of examining an ineffective point would be *instruments-oriented*, searching for the lowest combination of inputs (policy instruments) that would be possible, given the goals obtained. For instance, projecting point F horizontally to the left onto the polyhedral frontier, one finds point F′. In this case the projection is carried out reducing all the policy inputs equiproportionally while keeping the goal outputs unchanged. Projecting the observation F further horizontally onto the conical hull, one finds point F″. F′ and F″ are both hypothetical points generating the same output but using fewer inputs.

Input-oriented envelopment is the standard mode of analysis in applications involving studies of the productive operations of firms, hospitals, banks, and other productive units, searching for the lowest use of inputs that will deliver a given bundle of outputs. In social and economic policy, something could perhaps be said for looking at the input-oriented envelopment as well. Such a choice could be motivated by the widespread feeling that the quest toward global harmonization during the new century has occurred too swiftly, at the cost of deteriorating economic and social conditions. The overwhelming agenda today seems to be to safeguard the results that have been won. During the present global debt crisis, treasuries all over the world are facing the challenge of implementing a program of fiscal austerity while maintaining the social protection networks that have already been put in place. The policy-oriented version of envelopment then asks how countries can minimize their use of their policy instruments while keeping their current achievements of social and economic goals intact.

The projection on the frontier is referred to as "best practice." As we shall see, best practice is obtained as a weighted average of the practices of two or more effective countries (located on the frontier), called the "peers." It is an "amalgam" of the performance of those peers. Thus, DEA is not only diagnostic in that it identifies those practices that perform optimally, but it is also normative or prescriptive in that it delivers information how the actual performance of a sub-optimal practice might be improved. Assessing the performance of a collection of countries, we shall be able to

- identify and separate the frontier and sub-frontier countries;
- identify the peers of the sub-frontier countries;
- pinpoint the shortcomings of lagging countries and provide advice for corrective policy action.

Data envelopment analysis ascribes a 100% performance ranking to all frontier countries. They are all "equally good." But when it comes to the sub-frontier countries, we shall be able to calculate an effectiveness rating (less than 100%), thus obtaining a measure of the *relative* performance of each country, and to calculate the weights of all peers of the country currently rated. The effectiveness rating is obtained by computing the total societal welfare/policy cost ratio of the country currently rated (see equation 1.8 above).

2.2 Logarithmic Considerations

It is not a new idea to construct an envelope for a set of logarithmic data, and several such models have been discussed in the literature, including the early textbook by Charnes, Cooper, Lewin, and Seiford [1994]. The recent paper by Cooper, Thore, and Tarverdyan [2011], preceding the efforts in the present volume, took a further step postulating a logarithmic utility or preference function of all goals and a logarithmic cost function of all the policy parameters. This leads to a novel and appealing interpretation of the DEA efficiency rating.

We now propose to fit a CCR envelope to the logarithmic data

$$(logX_j, logY_j), \quad j = 1, 2, \ldots, n \tag{2.1}$$

where, as before, X_j is the vector of policy instruments employed by the policymaking unit (PMU) identified by the index j and Y_j is the vector of goals formulated by the same PMU. Form the weighted average

$$\Sigma_j[(logX_j)\lambda_j, \Sigma_j(logY_j)\lambda_j], \tag{2.2}$$

where λ_j is a vector of non-negative weights (one weight for each country $j = 1, 2, \ldots, n$). If the weights sum to one $\Sigma_j \lambda_j = 1$, the expression (2.2) quite generally defines the convex hull or convex envelope for the set of observations (2.1) as plotted in logarithmic space. It is piece-wise linear, and consists of corner points and facets.

Given data for an observed country, expression (2.2) may be interpreted as a vector of policy instruments and goals of a "composite country" located on the frontier. It projects the observed country onto the envelope. The envelopment procedure determines the weights λ_j so that the composite country represents "best practice" in the logarithmic space. In the spirit of the CCR-model, however, no assumption is made that the weights λ_j, $j = 1, 2, \ldots, n$ necessarily add up to unity. This means that the composite country (2.2) is not necessarily a point *on* the convex hull to the observations (2.1) but could also be a point *inside* the convex hull (the sum of weights is less than one) or a point *outside* the hull (the sum of weights is greater than one).

A best practice point *inside* the convex hull means that best practice involves a convex combination of the observations but also an equiproportional contraction of the goals. In other words, the scale of operation of best practice is smaller than the convex combination at which there would be constant returns to scale. To achieve constant returns in the space of logarithmic input and output variables, the inputs and outputs of the given observation would have to expand. A best practice point *outside* the convex hull, on the other hand, means that best practice not only involves a convex combination of the observations but also an equiproportional expansion of the goals. The scale of best practice is larger than the convex combination at which there would be constant returns to scale. To achieve constant returns in the space of logarithmic inputs and outputs, the inputs and outputs of the given observations would have to shrink.

Once the envelope has been determined, it is easy to convert back to the original non-logarithmic data. Write the fitted ray frontier in logarithmic data

$$logY = c\, logX \tag{2.3}$$

where c is a positive constant. Converting back to a diagram drawn in the original variables X and Y one finally finds

$$Y = X^c, \tag{2.4}$$

that is, an exponential surface passing through the origin. It exhibits decreasing returns to scale throughout (if c is less than one), constant returns to scale (if $c = 1$) or increasing returns to scale throughout (if c is larger than one). For numerical illustrations see Chapters 4 and 5.

2.3 The Ratio Model of DEA

In the pioneering paper by Charnes, Cooper and Rhodes [1978] the authors reminded their readers how the concept of "relative efficiency" is routinely used in the engineering literature. It is defined as the ratio of output obtained per use of inputs. This concept is straightforward enough when the project has only a single output and a single input. But in the multidimensional case one needs first to form some kind of aggregate of the outputs, and another aggregate of the inputs. Only then can the ratio between the two be calculated. To form those aggregates, it is necessary to attach individual weights — virtual weights — to each output and each input. If only the numerical values of those weights were known, the values of the aggregates could be calculated, and the ratio between aggregate output and aggregate input would serve as the desired efficiency measure. Furthermore, if the ratio were equal to 1, one would say that the project was efficient. Sub-efficient values would be associated with ratios less than 1.

Charnes, Cooper and Rhodes found an ingenious programming approach that enables one to determine the weights endogenously, rather than assuming that they be known and given. Their idea was to determine them so as to maximize the obtained efficiency measure, while seeing to it that the efficiency measures of all other projects (including the project currently being rated) remain meaningful, *i.e.*, that they all be less than or equal to 1. This was the famous ratio model of DEA.

In the recent work by Cooper, Thore, and Tarverdyan [2010] dealing with situations of economic and social planning, the same approach was used to determine the relative effectiveness of the policy achievements. Again, an aggregate of outputs is formed — the social welfare $V(Y)$ of the goals. Similarly, an aggregate of inputs is formed — the function $U(X)$ of the policy parameters. We have already defined (see equation 1.5) the effect-tiveness rating of a given policymaking unit (PMU), such as a country, as the ratio between the social welfare obtained $V(Y)$ and the utility cost of the policies employed $U(X)$. The set of calculations now indicated aim at maximizing the effectiveness ratio $V(Y)/U(X)$ while seeing to it that the effectiveness measures of all other PMUs remain meaningful, *i.e.*, that they all be less than or equal to 1. For the PMU currently to be rated (say $j = 0$), the maximization problem would then read

$$\max\ V(Y_0)/U(X_0) \tag{2.5}$$

subject to

$$V(Y_j)/U(X_j) \leq 1, \quad j = 1, 2, \ldots, n.$$

Using the logarithmic specifications U and V (see equation 1.6) one rather gets

$$\begin{aligned}&\max\ \mu logY_0/\nu logX_0\\&\text{subject to}\\&\mu logY_j/\nu logX_j \leq 1, \quad j = 1, 2, \ldots, n\\&\mu, \nu \geq 0.\end{aligned} \tag{2.6}$$

Program (2.6) is an instance of fractional programming (there are fractions in both the maximand and in the constraints). As it stands, it is indeterminate. If $\mu*$, $\nu*$ solves the program, so does $k\mu^*$, $k\nu^*$ where k is an arbitrary positive number. To deal with a similar situation, Charnes, Cooper and Rhodes suggested *normalizing* the virtual weights. Preferring the goal-oriented version of envelopment, we normalize the virtual goal weights μ by adjoining to program (2.6) the condition $\mu logY_0 = 1$. In simple words, the index of goals is normalized to equal unity. The entire programming problem then reads

$$\begin{aligned}&\max\ \mu logY_0/\nu logX_0\\&\text{subject to}\\&\mu logY_j/\nu logX_j \leq 1, \quad j = 1, 2, \ldots, n\\&\mu logY_0 = 1, \quad \mu, \nu \geq 0.\end{aligned} \tag{2.7}$$

A linear programming equivalent is immediately obtained as

$$\begin{aligned}&\min\ \nu logX_0\\&\text{subject to}\\&-\mu logY_j + \nu logX_j \geq 0, \quad j = 1, 2, \ldots, n\\&\mu logY_0 = 1, \quad \mu, \nu \geq 0.\end{aligned} \tag{2.8}$$

Consider also the corresponding dual program

$$\begin{aligned}&\max\ \Phi\\&\text{subject to}\\&\Phi logY_0 - \Sigma_j(logY_j)\lambda_j \leq 0\end{aligned} \tag{2.9}$$

$$\Sigma_j(logX_j)\lambda_j \leq logX_0$$
$$\lambda \geq 0, \quad \Phi \text{ unconstrained}$$

where Φ is the dual to the normalizing constraint $\mu logY_0 = 1$ and each λ_j, $j = 1, 2, \ldots, n$ is the dual to the constraint, $-\mu logY_j + \nu logX_j \geq 0$. The dual Φ will subsequently be referred to as the "expansion factor." The duals λ are the virtual weights of the peers forming best practice. The purpose of program (2.9) is to seek the greatest possible factor of equiproportional expansion of the goals. The first set of constraints $\Phi logY_0 - \Sigma_j(logY_j)\lambda_j$ states that the equiproportionate expansion of the goals $\Phi logY_0$ should be carried out to a point not exceeding best practice $\Sigma_j(logY_j)\lambda_j$. The second set of constraints states that best practice use of each policy instrument cannot exceed the actual use.

The effectiveness rating of a country then equals the inverse of the maximal possible factor of equiproportional expansion of all goals. To see this, note that the duality theorem of linear programming yields

$$\nu^* logX_0 = \Phi^* \tag{2.10}$$

or, which is the same

$$\mu^* logY_0/\nu^* logX_0 = 1/\Phi^*. \tag{2.11}$$

If $\Phi^* = 1$, the goal achievements are maximal in the sense that no equiproportional increase of them is possible. But if Φ^* comes out as greater than 1, some equiproportional expansion of the goals is indeed possible. The country is rated as ineffective. A numerical example: Assume that the calculations for one particular country has produced an effectiveness rating of 0.96. Then it should be possible, using the same instruments of policy, to increase the achievements of every single goal by 4.2% (note that $1/0.96 = 1.042$).

Finally, the concept of *slack* is important. Even if the expansion factor Φ comes out as equal to one, there may still exist one or several goals that fall short of the best practice goal, *i.e.*, there is positive slack in one or several of the constraints $logY_0 - \Sigma_j(logY_j)\lambda_j \leq 0$. Similarly, there may also exist one or several policy instruments for which best practice falls short of actual use, *i.e.*, there is positive slack in one or several of the constraints $\Sigma_j(logX_j)\lambda_j \leq logX_0$. For a country to be rated as effective, however, we shall not permit any such positive slack. An effective country, then, needs to fulfill two conditions:

- The effectiveness rating equals one;
- The country exhibits no positive deviations from best practice (neither a goal slack nor a policy instrument slack).

Only then will we have made certain that the country is actually located on the envelope itself.

The account now provided should suffice to enable the reader to understand the calculations to be undertaken in this book. For additional details, please refer to Appendix 1.

The account now provided should suffice to enable the reader to understand the calculations to be undertaken in this book. For additional details, please refer to Appendix 1.

Chapter 3

The Beginnings

The work reported in the present volume represents the culmination of efforts initiated several years ago, in one way or another springing from the research environment around the IC^2 Institute (Innovation, Creativity, and Capital) at The University of Texas at Austin.

3.1 The Discovery of DEA

One may debate whether the original work on data envelopment analysis [Charnes, Cooper, Rhodes, 1978] was a "discovery" or an "invention." What is clear is that it was a milestone in the development of major techniques of operations research, placing it alongside other techniques such as linear programming, game theory, and network analysis. Whereas earlier pioneering analytical tools belonged to the classical age of the emergence of operations research as a science of its own in the 1940s and 1950s, two more decades were to pass before DEA arrived on the scene. Today, with the benefit of 35 years of hindsight, one may speculate whether it perhaps also was the last of those major developments.

What is also clear is that Charnes and Cooper immediately realized the potential of DEA. (See also the biographical comments offered in Part III of this book.) They belonged to that rare group of scholars who had created operations research in the first place, and they felt thoroughly at home taking the lead in disseminating the new breakthrough to the operations research community. Quite significantly, they chose the term "data envelopment analysis" to indicate the virtually open-ended field of possible applications of the new optimizing technique. It was a method of calculating the envelope to a scatter of observations — yes, but it was also something more: beyond economics it was a blueprint for processing all sorts of social data, military data, business data, and financial data. Similarly, they chose the term "decision making unit (DMU)" to identify the broad scope of units that were being ranked. In that first DEA work [*ibid.*], the DMUs were school districts, but they were soon followed in other papers by fighter wings, hospitals, banks, football teams, even Chinese cities — there seems to be no end to the possible applications.

The present book takes one step further, treating the nations of the world as DMUs. More to the point, we shall also use the term "policymaking units" (with the acronym PMU).

3.2 Productive Efficiency under Capitalism and State Socialism

Early work applying the ideas of DEA to the ranking of nations includes the examination by Land, Lovell, and Thore [1992; 1993; 1994] of productive efficiency under capitalism and state socialism.

Those who write the economic history of the 20th century will need to confront the strange web of misinformation regarding the economic performance of the Soviet Union and other socialist states. Even during the period of *perestroika* and the gradual unraveling of the Soviet economy, Western economists refused to see any systematic difference between the performance of capitalism and state socialism. The ruling dogmas of Western economies, including Keynesian theory, were transplanted to the "markets" of the controlled economies. Huge econometric Keynesian-type models were estimated using Soviet data. The Soviet economists, on their part, were quick to point out that the purpose of the work of the GOSPLAN was only to compute and set the prices in the economy that would otherwise have formed under perfect competition; indeed the price solution arrived in the Soviet Union was claimed to be superior to the erratically functioning market system in the West.

Proposing to compare the economic performance of capitalism and state socialism using the (then brand new) DEA technique, Land, Lovell and Thore decided to identify the decision making unit of data envelopment analysis with an entire economy, organized either along the lines of Western market capitalism or the central planning agency in the former Soviet Union or its satellite states in Eastern Europe. To effect the desired comparison, the authors extended the scope of standard DEA to include an explicit treatment of the different nature of uncertainty facing planners under the two systems. Under market capitalism, new technological uncertainties and new market uncertainties are continuously encountered as producers are engaged in product development and innovation. Under state socialism, production of mainly known technologies is delegated to state monopolies. But state socialism generates its own uncertainties. Plant managers learn to reckon with abrupt changes in production targets, and with uncertainties in the allocations of raw materials, labor and other inputs. In brief, whereas the manager under capitalism faces market uncertainty, the manager of the state socialist firm faces bureaucratic uncertainty.

To deal with these matters, the Land, Lovell, and Thore [1992] paper proposed a variant form of data envelopment analysis termed "chance-constrained DEA." The necessary mathematical developments were presented in 1993 [Land, Lovell & Thore], and they proceeded in Land, Lovell, and Thore [1994] to effect the desired comparison of the two competing systems. Data were collected for 17 market-oriented West European economies and 7 planned East European economies, observed annually for each of the three years 1978, 1979, and 1980. Two input variables were used: aggregate energy usage per worker and aggregate net capital stock per worker. The single output was real GDP per worker.

Results were presented for both standard DEA and chance-constrained DEA. With standard DEA, the only countries exhibiting efficiency (with an efficiency score = 100%) were Western countries. Their average efficiency rating over all years came out as 0.906. The East European countries were all sub-efficient; the average of all planned economies all years was only 0.580. The score of the Soviet Union was the lowest in every year. The peers of the Soviet Union (that is, the "role models" defining best practice) were Malta in 1978 and Turkey in 1979.

Employing the chance-constrained version instead, the difference between the Western and East European countries became even more pronounced. The average rating for market economies was then 0.992, the average rating for the planned economies was 0.550. The chance-constrained version features the presence of optimal buffers of output held as a contingency against stochastic variability. In the planned economies, only negative buffers are held: an expected shortage of goods. The calculations showed that shortages would occur in every country of state capitalism, every year. The constant shortages of consumer goods in socialist countries seem to indicate that the central planning agency did not even attempt to meet demand. The shortages take the form of a net exhaustion of available stocks — empty shelves and prospective customers lining up outside the store waiting for the next truck arriving from the warehouse.

The results were originally scheduled to be presented at the 47th Congress of the International Institute of Public Finance at St. Petersburg in August 1991. Finally, the superiority of the market economy in achieving productive efficiency would be demonstrated! But, alas, it was too late to resort to academic discussion. As a political reality, the Soviet Union collapsed only a couple of days before the scheduled event, and the congress was canceled. (The papers accepted for presentation at the congress were published a year later.)

3.3 Ranking the Economic and Social Performance of Nations

In a series of joint publications Golany and Thore [1997a; 1997b; 1997c] explored the use of standard data envelopment analysis to evaluate and rank the economic and social performance of nations.

Rather curiously, this collaboration got under way protesting some brilliant but rather outlandish views published by the future Nobelist Paul Krugman, who already then was known as the *enfant terrible* of the economics profession. In an article in *Foreign Affairs* titled, "Competitiveness: A dangerous obsession," Krugman [1994] had argued that the concept of "competitiveness" was meaningless since no single criterion will suffice to define the many aspects of competitiveness.

In contrast to terms like productivity or terms of trade, which have relatively clear and accepted definitions, the term competitiveness has many dimensions and has been invoked in many different economic contexts. But one idea seems to be common to these various interpretations: the idea of a "race" in the international marketplace, where some nations are forging ahead, pushing forward a frontier of maximal performance, while others are falling behind. The very idea of such a race Krugman labelled "dangerous."

The first paper by Golany and Thore, printed in a *Festschrift* dedicated to George Kozmetsky, used data collected by the US Council on

Competitiveness. They used DEA to calculate the "international competitiveness" of seven advanced industrialized nations, the so-called G-7 nations. The mathematical technique of DEA was developed precisely to effect a comparison and ranking of the performance of entities or decision making units when their performance is measured by several criteria rather than a single criterion. Employing a standard list of inputs and outputs, the authors measured the international competetiveness of a nation by its DEA efficiency score.

The paper used data compiled by the US Council of Competitiveness for the 21-year period 1972–1992. The calculations thus made use of a pooling of both cross-section data (for a given year) and time series data. Three variables were used as inputs: investment in plant and equipment, investment in civilian R&D, and investment in education. Similarly, there were three outputs: standard of living, exports, and manufacturing productivity. The calculations yielded the following results:

- Italy and Japan systematically outperformed the other countries; the United States belonged to a second tier also comprising France, Germany, and the United Kingdom. Canada obtained the lowest scores. Furthermore, although all countries displayed considerable erratic variation in their rankings, they tended to maintain their relative positions over time. No single country gained or lost in its competitiveness relative to the others.
- The competitiveness ratings of all seven nations had been systematically declining over the last twenty years. But, looking at developments since 1985 alone, no significant trend was evident.
- Rather than sounding alarms over the deterioration of US competitiveness (at least relative to these countries), the authors expressed concern that the performance of the entire group of G-7 nations had deteriorated over time. They suggested that if they had extended their rankings to include other countries as well — in particular the Far Eastern countries then known as the Asian Tigers — the results would have been different.

In their next joint work, Golany and Thore extended the criteria of ranking to take account of social variables such as education, health, and social welfare. This time they also ranked a much larger set of nations, 72 nations in all, including developing and poor nations from all continents [Golany and Thore, 1997b].

A comparison focusing on strictly economic or financial variables might easily be viewed as skewed or stacked in favor of industrialized nations. Depending upon the political hue of government, wider social goals may, in many countries, actually overshadow the strictly commercial goals of national economic policy. In rating the overall performance of a wide spectrum of different nations, then, one needs to identify a set of measures that imposes no *a priori* value judgment but incorporates a broad list of possible goals of national policy.

As long as the rankings are limited to a comparison of GNP and its determinants, the mathematical envelopment procedure in effect amounts to estimating a piecewise linear production function of conventional form. But, when nations are ranked on the basis of a broad array of social performance indicators including mortality rates and school enrollment in secondary education, the theoretical contact with an underlying production function becomes moot or even hypothetical. Instead, one is led to consider an economic and social performance "function" in a much wider sense.

The novelty embodied in such an extension rests with the fact that such generalized production relationships for an entire nation are no longer determined by some inherent input-output mechanisms but rather by economic policy. There exists no natural trade-off for a nation between productivity and, say, social policy. If such a trade-off does exist, it is all a matter of economic politics, the legislative bodies in the nation ascribing higher priorities to social policy than to productivity policy (being willing, say, to expand the social safety network of workers even if it would have to be paid for by lowering real wages).

The data used for the study were drawn from a database assembled by the US National Bureau of Economic Research. The following goal variables were distinguished:

- growth rate of GDP *per capita*,
- 1 minus infant mortality rate ages 0 to 1,
- enrollment ratio for secondary education,
- ratio of social insurance and welfare payments to GDP.

The policy parameters employed were the ratio of domestic investment to GDP, the ratio of government expenditure on education to GDP, and the ratio of government consumption expenditure net of education expenditure to GDP. The general idea behind this selection of variables was that as a country develops technologically and economically, it will also advance along a socioeconomic scale — offering better social benefits to its citizens (more social insurance, better health, better education, *etc.*)

The information now mentioned was compiled for 74 countries including poor, developing, and developed countries from various regions and continents. The data referred to the time period 1970–1985. The calculations showed that 23 countries were located at the frontier, scoring an efficiency rating of 100% and exhibiting constant returns to scale. The remaining countries were sub-efficient, scoring less than 100%. These countries could be divided into two groups:

(1) *Sub-efficient countries with* decreasing *returns to scale.* In such countries, there will no doubt be calls for improved productivity, industry modernization, and improved organization of education and health systems. But inefficiency is often deeply embedded in existing economic and social structures through weak entrepreneurial spirit, poor functioning of capital markets, disincentives created by tax codes, lack of modern health care equipment, poor nutrition, *etc.* Such structures are difficult to change and may only be subject to indirect government control.

The authors characterized such countries as being "mature." The list included the United Kingdom and the Scandinavian countries that have often been admired for their educational system and extensive social welfare. Yet the efficiency ratings of some of these countries turned out to be quite low. On the other side of the globe, Australia and New Zealand did not fare any better. It should not come as a surprise that in all these countries there had, for some time, been strong political pressure to halt the growth of the welfare state.

Some very poor countries also belonged to the same category, such as Botswana, Burma, Panama, Guyana, Fiji, and New Guinea. It is unfortunate enough that these countries display low policy efficiency ratings. Even more discouragingly, they also exhibit falling returns to scale. These countries desperately need improved educational resources and a social welfare net.

And yet, such an expansion of educational and welfare policy would only offer, at least in the short-term, falling returns.

(2) *Sub-efficient countries with* increasing *returns to scale*. For these countries, the authors assumed that there would be political pressure to step up the growth in government spending on education, health, and social welfare. Such spending would then presumably be seen as sound investment in a productive workforce and in human capital. Motivated in this fashion, the country would follow a path of fiscal activism. The government sector would grow, and expansion would be seen as economically sound. The authors characterized countries in this position as being "young." They all turned out to be developing nations and the list included including major Sub-Saharan countries and Latin American countries as well as three European countries: Greece, Iceland, and Turkey.

Chapter 4

Decent Work

To demonstrate the use of envelopment analysis to rate country achievements in economic and social policy, we begin with a study of Decent Work. Our work in this respect builds upon the extensive efforts by the International Labour Organization, both in defining Decent Work as a key goal of employment policy and in its exhortations to measure the possible Decent Work Deficit.

4.1 The Work by the International Labour Organization

In the report titled, *Decent Work* submitted by the director-general of the ILO to the International Labour Conference in 1999 [ILO, 1999], the primary goal for the organization was stated as that of "securing Decent Work for women and men everywhere" [*ibid.*, p. 3]. Expanding on the theme, the report goes on to say:

> The primary goal of the ILO today is to promote opportunities for women and men to obtain decent and productive work, in conditions of freedom, equity, security, and human dignity.

and it adds:

> This is the main purpose of the Organization today. Decent Work is the converging focus of all its four strategic objectives: the promotion of rights at work; employment; social protection; and social dialogue.

The concept of Decent Work struck a chord of immediate response within the community of international organizations. Already one year later it found its way into the *United Nations Millennium Declaration* [UN,

2000b]. Under the heading "Development and poverty eradication," the Declaration states:

> We also resolve: To promote gender equality and the empowerment of women as effective ways to combat poverty, hunger, and disease and to stimulate development that is truly sustainable . . . . To develop and implement strategies that give young people everywhere a real chance to find decent and productive work.

In many ways, the Millennium Declaration continues and expands the aims of Decent Work as earlier formulated by the ILO.[2] In a 2001 report titled, *Reducing the Decent Work Deficit: a global challenge* [ILO, 2001b], the director-general of the ILO took the next logical step. Statistics on inputs and outputs and goals are not enough. To promote the goal of Decent Work for all, the ILO must be able to measure and monitor progress and deficits of Decent Work, and to respond to the demands of constituents and the general public for information about these issues [*ibid.,* p. 66]. The "Decent Work Deficit" has to be calculated. This is a formidable task. How does one calculate the shortcomings of actual performance from an array of idealized targets?

4.2 Goals and Policy Parameters

In February 2002 ILO established the World Commission on the Social Dimension of Globalization to examine the process of globalization and to respond to the needs of people as they cope with the challenges of globalization. The report of the commission titled, *A Fair Globalization: Creating Opportunities for All* [WCSDG, 2004a] recommends making Decent Work a global goal along with fairer rules to support development. The UN General Assembly in 2005 adopted a resolution recognizing the contribution of the World Commission's report to achieving a fully inclusive and equitable globalization [UN, 2005].

---

[2]On the details, the reader may want to consult the ILO Information Folder Decent Work and the Millennium Development Goals, 2005. The folder cites the ILO director-general who on the International Day for the Eradication of Poverty, 2004 stated that "efforts to fulfill our collective commitments to fight poverty will fall short unless we focus on increasing job opportunities and Decent Work." The ILO promotes poverty reduction at the policy level and in practice through its Decent Work Agenda.

We now turn to representing Decent Work as a formal social preference function *V(Y)*. Using the key goals mentioned in the same 2005 report, we write the column vector of goals

$$Y = (EMP, NOPOV, WOM) \tag{4.1}$$

where

- *EMP* represents the total gainful employment in a country,
- *NOPOV* (no poverty) is a measure of social protection,
- *WOM* is a measure of gender equality.

More precisely, the goal indicators will be defined as follows: *EMP* equals 1 minus the percentage unemployment rate, *NOPOV* is 100 minus the percentage of the population with an income below US $2 per day, and *WOM* is the percentage of the working population who are women.

All data are given as percentage points. In this fashion, there is no discrimination between small countries and large ones. Using absolute numbers would leave big Western nations as winners, with poor nations in Asia and Africa falling far behind the frontiers spanned by the rich ones. Admittedly, using percentages is a very subjective choice of ours. But it illustrates a more basic circumstance: there exist no objective "real" or "true" numbers to be used for the calculations. We are not modelling here some objective engineering or technical production relationships; we are modelling a social decision-making situation. Whatever dimensions of that decision-making task we deem relevant are the "true" inputs (policy instruments) and outputs (policy goals).

Clearly, a low unemployment rate is one aspect of Decent Work. Gender equality and the absence of extreme poverty and hunger are others. Unfortunately, although widely used, unemployment figures are only the tip of the iceberg of the employment problems. Where open unemployment is low, low-quality low-income work often takes its place, or large number of workers — usually women — are excluded from the statistics. Gender is a ubiquitous source of labor market inequality. Women form the majority of unpaid, atypical, or discouraged workers [ILO, 1999, p. 21 and 28].

Social protection and social dialogue constitute two of the strategic objectives of the ILO. Social protection involves helping workers to maintain their incomes and ensures adequate access to medical care and social services. The ILO has been involved in strategies designed to raise the production capabilities in small urban and rural enterprises, and local development initiatives [*ibid.*, p. 29]. The purpose of such initiatives is to lower poverty.

Form the Cobb-Douglas generalized social preference function

$$V(Y) = EMP^{\mu_1} NOPOV^{\mu_2} WOM^{\mu_3} \tag{4.2}$$

where the coefficients μ_1, μ_2, μ_3 are the elasticities of V with respect to the three goals. If $\mu_1 + \mu_2 + \mu_3 = 1$, the preference function exhibits constant returns to scale. If at an optimum $\mu_1 + \mu_2 + \mu_3 < 1$ there are decreasing returns to scale in the country being evaluated, and if $\mu_1 + \mu_2 + \mu_3 > 1$ there are increasing returns to scale.

Taking logarithms

$$log\ V(Y) = \mu_1 logEMP + \mu_2 logNOPOV + \mu_3 logWOM \tag{4.3}$$

Turning now to the policy background, we shall use the column vector of policy parameters ("instruments")

$$X = (EXP, FDI, TARIFF, SUB) \tag{4.4}$$

where

- *EXP* is exports of goods and services, as a percentage of GDP,
- *FDI* is foreign direct investment, net inflows, as a percentage of GDP,
- *TARIFF* represents taxes and tariffs on international trade, as a percentage of total government revenue,
- *SUB* denotes subsidies and other transfers, as a percentage of total government expenditure.

These policy parameters were chosen to illustrate both the treatment of conventional macroeconomic variables and national and international policy parameters. *EXP* and *FDI* are two core reference indicators of economic globalization listed in the handbook by OECD [2005]. They measure the extent and intensity of economic globalization and the increased dependence of the national economy on its international partners. Globalization promotes export opportunities and offers opportunities for foreign direct investment. These factors were chosen to illustrate both the treatment of conventional macroeconomic variables and national and international policy parameters. *EXP* and *FDI* are two core reference indicators of economic globalization defined by OECD. Trade and investment liberalization can be a powerful force for fostering job creation and poverty reduction. But tariffs may also be used to protect local agriculture and industry, shielding domestic workers from foreign competition. If structured wisely, subsidies could support not only domestic employment but also the quality of work.

TARIFFs represent taxes on international trade and include import duties, export duties, profits of export or import monopolies, exchange profits, and exchange taxes. Import tariffs are often used to protect local agriculture and industry, thus shielding domestic workers from foreign competition. Presumably, such measures enhance the quantity and quality of work within the domestic agricultural sector. *SUB* represent subsidies and other government transfers and constitute a powerful and immediate control variable of central governments (the figures that we shall employ includes all unrequited, nonrepayable transfers on current account to private and public enterprises, social security, social assistance benefits and employer social benefits in cash and in kind, also grants to foreign governments and international organizations.)

The policy parameters are collected into the generalized social policy cost function, also of the Cobb-Douglas type

$$U(X) = EXP^{\nu_1} FDI^{\nu_2} TARIFF^{\nu_3} SUB^{\nu_4} \tag{4.5}$$

where ν_1, ν_2, ν_3, and ν_4 are the elasticities with respect to the four policy factors. There are social policy costs attached to the increased use of each of these policy factors ("instruments"). Just mentioning a few of these social costs, note the following. Government export promotion and assistance is universally accepted economic policy. But when one government becomes more heavily involved in industrial policy with an eye on furthering exports, other countries will often respond "competitively." Also, stimulating the influx of foreign capital may provoke organized labor. On the international scene, raising duties on imported goods and subsidizing domestic producers will cause an outcry from the World Trade Organization. In all these cases, the "cost" is not one in monetary units but in political terms.

Taking logarithms

$$logU(X) = \nu_1 logEXP + \nu_2 logFDI + \nu_3 logTARIFF + \nu_4 logSUB \tag{4.6}$$

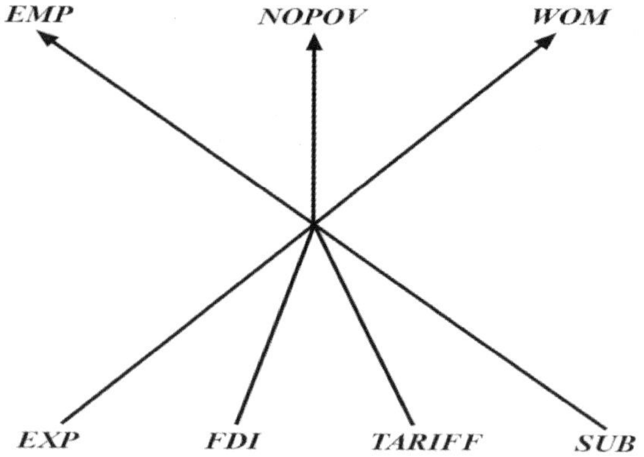

Figure 4.1 Decent Work, causes and effects.

The optimal ratio between expressions (4.4) and (4.6) is the desired measure of the effectiveness of Decent Work policy for the country currently rated.

Figure 4.1 above traces the causal relations between the variables explaining Decent Work. The effects are the indicators of Decent Work.

4.3 Empirical Results: The Effectiveness Frontier

Here and in Chapters 5 and 6 we report on the results for a selection of 102 countries for which we were able to find data of acceptable quality and with no data missing. (This data set is not only much more recent than the data used in our earlier publications, it is also almost twice as large.) Most data used are averages for the years 2000 through 2010. For the detailed definition of each variable and the data sources, see Appendix 2.

Remembering the call by the ILO for the calculation of the "Decent Work Deficit," and as has been explained in detail in Chapter 2, we find it natural to employ the goal-oriented ("output-oriented") version of envelopment. This will yield a numerical estimate for each participating country of the possible improvement in the attainment of the Decent Work goals, given the same use of policy parameters.

The countries that form the envelope (an effectiveness rating equal to one and no slacks) will then set an international standard for a successful Decent Work policy, making an effective use of the instruments at hand to achieve maximal goal achievements. But for countries falling below the envelope (effectiveness ratings less than one), there will indeed be present a

Decent Work deficit. Maintaining an unchanged use of policy instruments, it should be possible to increase the goal performance. The deficit of each goal (as measured as the difference between "best practice" and actual performance) will be calculated numerically.

For the numerical work, we chose the linear programming version (2.9) which now reads

$$
\begin{aligned}
&\max \Phi \qquad (4.7)\\
&\text{subject to}\\
&\Phi logEMP_0 - \Sigma(logEMP_j)\lambda_j \le 0\\
&\Phi logNOPOV_0 - \Sigma(logNOPOV_j)\lambda_j \le 0\\
&\Phi logWOM_0 - \Sigma(logWOM_j)\lambda_j \le 0\\
&\Sigma(logEXP_j)\lambda_j \le logEXP_0\\
&\Sigma(logFDI_j)\lambda_j \le logFDI_0\\
&\Sigma(logTARIFF_j)\lambda_j \le logTARIFF_0\\
&\Sigma(logSUB_j)\lambda_j \le logSUB_0\\
&\lambda \ge 0,\ \ \Phi \text{ unconstrained}
\end{aligned}
$$

In addition, all slacks were minimized (see Appendix 1). For the numerical solution we used the "Frontier Analyst Professional" version of Banxia Frontier Analyst 3.

4.3.1 *Initial examination of data*

Special attention needs to be paid to the possibility that one of the logarithms appearing in (4.7) turns out to be negative. In seven instances (Bangladesh, Greece, Indonesia, Japan, Kenya, Korea, and Nepal the statistical figure for *FDI* comes out as less than *e*, which generates a negative value for *logFDI*. There exists no ideal way of dealing mathematically with such cases. Economic and trade policy in these countries has resulted in international isolation in the sense that foreign direct investment is almost nonexistent. Hence, Decent Work, to the extent that it exists in these countries, depends almost entirely upon domestic circumstances.

The possibility of a mathematical "correction" of negative data in DEA was discussed by Lovell and Pastor in 1995. First they show that no standard

DEA model is scale invariant. Unfortunately, nor is the logarithmic DEA model scale invariant — this kills the solution that we proposed in our earlier work, converting all percentage points (%) to pro mille points (‰) instead. Next they discuss a possible linear translation of the data. But additive translations are not invariant in the CCR-model.

So, in the end, and with a heavy heart, we eliminated Bangladesh, Greece, Indonesia, Japan, Kenya, Korea, and Nepal from the data set. Our preliminary inspection of the data revealed another difficulty. For Luxembourg, the recorded *FDI* as a percentage of GDP is 364 — more than three times GDP. So here the shoe is on the other foot: the trouble is not that the figure is too small but that it is far too large. No other country matches this situation (Belgium is the runner-up with a *FDI* ratio of 25%). The reality behind the Luxembourg figure is of course that the country serves as a kind of financial hub for the European Union. But it would certainly not be fair to rate the performance of other countries in relation to that of Luxembourg. (If included, it comes out as effective and as a peer to almost all other observations). So, we decided to treat Luxembourg as an outlier, and eliminated it from the calculations.

The total number of countries for which we were able to gather complete data was 110. We thus ended up with $110 - 7 - 1 = 102$ countries, as already stated.

4.3.2 *The envelope*

We begin by reporting the countries lying on the effectiveness envelope. Table 4.1 lists sixteen countries that obtained an efficiency rating of 100%. Since the instruments slacks and goals slacks of these countries all are equal to zero, these countries are rated as effective. The actual observations of the goals then coincide with the optimal targets along the effectiveness frontier. Given their use of policy instruments, they achieve maximal goals. As we shall see, they serve as "role-models" (peers) for ineffective countries.

Inspecting the list, we recognize several Western countries with a strong social profile (Denmark, Norway, France, Portugal, the United Kingdom, and the United States). The list also includes some very poor countries which nevertheless are doing well in this context: Lao PDR, Maldives, Burkina Faso. The list includes the remote kingdom of Bhutan, whose

Table 4.1 Decent Work. List of 16 effective countries.

	Policy instruments, in%				Goals, in%		
	EXP	*FDI*	*TARIFF*	*SUB*	*EMP*	*NOPOV*	*WOM*
Denmark	48.42	4.06	2.64	25.03	95.58	100.00	94.63
United States	10.91	1.65	3.29	62.80	94.63	100.00	94.63
Burkina Faso	9.68	1.14	12.55	9.78	93.69	23.10	98.49
Jamaica	35.87	6.05	10.28	5.58	87.36	93.69	83.10
El Salvador	26.05	1.28	5.53	16.28	93.69	81.45	95.58
Norway	43.82	2.23	2.48	68.72	96.54	100.00	96.54
Maldives	62.80	4.90	21.33	2.75	91.84	100.00	86.49
Portugal	29.08	2.59	2.64	47.94	93.69	100.00	92.76
Niger	16.12	3.86	13.60	6.62	98.49	24.78	99.48
Italy	26.31	1.03	2.64	62.80	91.84	100.00	89.12
Iran	27.11	1.12	24.29	31.50	89.12	91.84	81.45
Lao PDR	32.14	3.10	8.00	9.30	98.49	28.50	98.49
United Kingdom	27.11	4.48	2.64	53.52	94.63	100.00	95.58
France	26.58	2.80	2.64	57.40	90.92	100.00	90.02
Turkey	22.87	1.55	3.00	42.10	90.02	92.76	90.02
Bhutan	40.04	1.67	20.09	6.30	97.51	60.34	96.54

former monarch framed a policy of "gross national happiness" supposedly reflecting the true and holistic quality of life.

4.4 Empirical Results: Decent Work Deficits

The author of *Reducing the Decent Work* laments:

> Although Decent Work is an attractive goal, the deficits we see around us show how difficult it is to make it a reality for all... There are many people for whom Decent Work is a reality; but worldwide these workers are a minority [ILO, 2001a].

As we have seen, 16 countries of 102 obtained an effectiveness rating of 100% and were recognized as being effective. The remaining countries are ineffective, which means that they score less than 100% or that they feature positive slacks in their use of policy instruments or in their goal achievements. For a look at some of the detailed results turn to Table 4.2 listing the ten countries that top the performance of the non-effective countries. They obtained an effectiveness rating greater than 96.5% (but

Table 4.2 Decent Work. Ten runner-up countries: top performers of the ineffective countries. Actual and frontier goal achievements. All data in %.

Country	Rating $1/\Phi$	Actual goal achievements			Frontier goals		
		EMP	*NOPOV*	*WOM*	*EMP*	*NOPOV*	*WOM*
Spain	99.91	88.23	100.00	83.93	91.84	100.48	90.02
Romania	99.20	92.76	91.84	93.69	96.54	102.51	97.51
Qatar	99.09	98.49	100.00	93.69	102.51	106.70	101.49
Cyprus	99.07	95.58	100.00	94.63	99.48	104.58	98.49
Ireland	98.71	94.63	100.00	95.58	102.51	107.77	101.49
Cameroon	97.58	94.63	68.72	94.63	105.64	75.94	107.77
Poland	97.45	85.63	99.48	83.93	103.54	112.17	102.51
Slovenia	97.36	93.69	99.48	93.69	107.77	114.43	105.64
Sweden	97.07	93.69	100.00	93.69	109.95	115.58	108.85
Latvia	96.84	89.12	99.48	90.02	109.95	115.58	108.85

did not reach 100%). For each country, the effectiveness score $1/\phi$ is listed together with its actual goal achievements and frontier goals, all expressed in percentages.

Admittedly, using those percentages is a very subjective choice of ours. But it illustrates a more basic circumstance: there exist no objective "real" or "true" numbers to be used for the calculations. We are not modelling here some objective engineering or technical production relationships — we are modeling a social decision-making situation. Whatever dimensions of that decision making task we deem relevant, are the "true" inputs (policy instruments) and outputs (policy goals).

To illustrate, Table 4.2 tells us that Spain, obtaining an overall performance score of 99.91%, faced two Decent Work deficits: an employment deficit of 3.61% (being the difference between the two numbers 91.84% and 88.23)%, and a deficit of female employment equal to 6.09% (the difference between 90.02% and 83.93%). The result for the NOPOV variable here and elsewhere in the table should not distract us; frontier values obviously cannot be greater than 100%. (Actually, we could clearly have included an upper bound of 100% on all unknowns (4.1) appearing in the programming problem (4.7), but we felt it to be more attractive to exhibit these super-100% numbers explicitly, thus indicating the nature and the size of the disequilibrium situation.)

Table 4.3 Decent Work. Peers of the ten ineffective countries listed in Table 4.2, and their weights.

Country	The peers and their weights
Spain	0.99 × Italy + 0.01 × Norway
Romania	0.2 × Denmark + 0.06 × Norway + 0.74 × United Kingdom
Qatar	0.76 × Denmark + 0.08 × El Salvador + 0.17 × Maldives
Cyprus	0.82 × Denmark + 0.15 × Norway + 0.04 × Portugal
Ireland	0.78 × Denmark + 0.23 × Norway
Cameroon	0.16 × Burkina Faso + 0.77 × El Salvador +0.03 × Maldives +0.07 × United States
Poland	0.38 × France + 0.26 × Italy + 0.39 × Norway
Slovenia	0.22 × Denmark + 0.36 × Italy + 0.45 × Norway
Sweden	0.39 × Denmark + 0.49 × Norway + 0.15 × Portugal
Latvia	0.21 × Denmark + 0.49 × Norway + 0.33 × Portugal

Table 4.3 lists the peers of the same ten countries, together with their weights. To a policymaker the peers can serve as benchmarks to be used for a possible improvement of the performance of the country. For instance, Romania, Ireland, and Latvia would apparently benefit from looking at and adopting a mixture of the policies of Denmark and Norway. Cameroon would do well looking at the performance of Burkina Faso and El Salvador (with a glance at the Maldives and the United States). And so on.

In Table 4.3 Denmark and Norway serve as peers quite often. As a matter of fact, Denmark happens to be the country that serves as a peer to others more often than any other country (in 56 instances). The United States serves as a peer in 51 instances. Two effective countries never serve as a peer to anybody: Turkey and Bhutan.

In the spirit of the CCR-model, no assumption is made that the weights in Table 4.3 necessarily add up to unity. This means that the composite country of best practice (2.2) is not necessarily a point on the convex hull to the observations (2.1) but could also be a point inside the convex hull (with its sum of weights being less than one) or a point outside the hull (the sum of weights being greater than one). For effective countries the sum is indeed equal to unity — the weight of a country itself is one and the weights of all other countries are zero. For all countries listed in Table 4.3, the sum of weights of the peers happens to be greater than one, indicating that the best practice point on the frontier not only involves a convex combination of the observations but also a radial expansion.[3]

Finally, let us take a look at the bottom of the ranking list. Fourteen countries in the entire sample obtained an effectiveness rating of less than 80%. Some of these economies were clearly dysfunctional, suffering from recent or present military strife or internal political upheavals, like Belarus, Ghana, Tajikistan, and Ukraine.

There exists a perfectly rational explanation of such low ratings. Countries far from equilibrium and at the "edge of chaos" can display "order" (see the discussion of Prigogine in Chapter 8 and in Part III of this book). Order is not equilibrium. Order can arise out of the dynamics of disequilibrium. In several publications one of us [Thore, 1996; 1999] has discussed the low efficiency ratings of some of the most rapidly growing computer companies in the United States (like Apple, Cray, Microsoft, and Sun during the opening phases of their life cycles during the 1980s). Sustained supergrowth — when one finds it — seems characteristically to be associated with wildly divergent disequilibrium processes.

Consider the performance of India (with an effectiveness rating of 80.22%), the Russian Federation (81.17%), China (75.59%). How can that be? As these countries went through an explosive phase of technological and social upheaval, they sacrificed short-term effectiveness in order to achieve rapid long-term growth. For further discussion of disequilibrium situations, see Chapter 5.

4.5 Decent Work and Policy Parameters

We have already mentioned the first two reports of the ILO director-general [ILO, 1999] and [ILO, 2001b]. In his third report [ILO, 2003] he discussed the "Decent Work dividends" that can accrue to families and societies as a whole through a concerted effort to attack poverty. In a concluding chapter, the following economic and social policy measures are discussed:

- employment and enterprise development,
- social protection,

[3] For a more detailed discussion, see Golany and Thore [1997, p. 197].

- rights and labor law reform,
- social dialogue,
- gender,
- partnerships between the ILO and its constituents and other international agencies.

How can those parameters of economic and social policy be controlled to enhance Decent Work? In the present context we can only answer those questions within the framework of the current list of policy inputs: *FDI*, *EXP*, *SUB*, and *TARIFF*. To begin with, remember the constraints

$$\Sigma(logEXP_j)\lambda_j \leq logEXP_0 \tag{4.8}$$
$$\Sigma(logFDI_j)\lambda_j \leq logFDI_0$$
$$\Sigma(logTARIFF_j)\lambda_j \leq logTARIFF_0$$
$$\Sigma(logSUB_j)\lambda_j \leq logSUB_0$$

that were included in the program formulation (4.7). They state that the optimal use of each policy inputs cannot exceed the actual use. But it is perfectly possible that the optimal use of one or several inputs equals actual use (zero instrument slack) or falls short of it (positive instrument slack).

The latter possibility (a positive instrument slack) can be dismissed right away. The outlook for instrument policy would then not look good — why should a policymaker increase the use of a policy input that is already in excessive use? Turning to the former case (zero instrument slack), we need to calculate the shadow prices (*i.e.*, the duals) of the input constraints (4.8). Each such shadow price will tell us the amount of improvement of the effectiveness rating that a marginal increase of the policy instrument would generate. To this end, consider again model (4.7) and its corresponding dual program. It determines multipliers of the inputs and the outputs that can be interpreted as weights of relative importance on the efficiency score. Denoting the (row vectors) of the virtual multipliers of the outputs and inputs by the letters μ and ν, respectively, our interest now rests with the duals

ν_{EXP} = the impact upon the effectiveness rating obtained by marginal increase of *logEXP*
ν_{FDI} = the impact upon the effectiveness rating obtained by a marginal increase of *logFDI*

Table 4.4 Impact upon the effectiveness rating obtained by a marginal increase of the logarithms of the policy instruments. Ten runner-up countries.

Country	(Duals) ν_{EXP} *EXP*	ν_{FDI} *FDI*	ν_{TARIFF} *TARIFF*	ν_{SUB} *SUB*
Spain	0.41	ε	2.35	ε
Romania	0.28	ε	2.03	0.21
Qatar	ε	0.20	0.69	0.95
Cyprus	0.27	ε	2.09	0.20
Ireland	ε	ε	2.70	0.24
Cameroon	0.90	0.30	ε	0.61
Poland	0.39	ε	2.28	0.04
Slovenia	ε	0.21	2.12	0.36
Sweden	0.27	ε	2.09	0.20
Latvia	0.27	ε	2.10	0.20

ν_{TARIFF} = the impact upon the effectiveness rating obtained by a marginal increase of *logTARIFF*

ν_{SUB} = the impact upon the effectiveness rating obtained by a marginal increase *logSUB*

The virtual multipliers represent the change in the optimal ϕ obtained for each marginal adjustment of exports, foreign direct investments, tariffs, and subsidies.

Table 4.4 shows the multipliers for those ten runner-up countries listed in Table 4.2. As demonstrated by the figures in the next but last column, the effect of tariff policy would in most cases be rather potent. Increased protectionism would be helpful to promote Decent Work. Obviously, this cannot be the full story. Yes, increased protectionism would stimulate employment in imports-competing industries. It would facilitate the fight against poverty. But there is more to the story than what is told by the goals and policy instruments now considered. Inflows of direct foreign investments would dry up, with negative consequences on growth and employment. Shutting the doors to the powerful waves of globalization and new technology arriving from abroad is a risky strategy.

Decent Work is not just a matter of domestic policy. It is also very much a matter of management of international relations. The causal framework that we have outlined in the present chapter is too narrow. We need to face the subject and problems of globalization head-on, as we shall do in the two next chapters.

In several cells in Table 4.4, the value of the dual variable is entered as ε (signifying a very small positive number). This indicates the presence of a horizontal slope (*i.e.*, constant goals) of the effectiveness facet. Points along such a facet are non-Paretoan — additional increases of inputs do not generate any increase of output.

In other words, one has reached the borderline of the Pareto-optimal locus. Any further increase of the policy inputs cannot be optimally sustained — a characteristic possibility along piecewise linear relationships with discontinuous slope coefficients.

Chapter 5

A Fair Globalization

The World Commission on the Social Dimension of Globalization, established by the International Labour Office in 2002, was to examine the process of globalization and to respond to the needs of people as they cope with the challenges of globalization. In its report *A Fair Globalization: Creating Opportunities for All* [WCSDG, 2004a], the commission formulated the goal of achieving "A Fair Globalization," tempering the presumed harsh effects of globalization by good political governance based on a democratic political system, respect for human rights, the rule of law, and social equity.

The Commission aimed at shifting the perspective on globalization from a preoccupation with markets to a preoccupation with people. It stressed the social dimensions of globalization — jobs, health, education, and the totality of the aspirations of people for democratic participation and material prosperity. The report states that if wisely managed, globalization can play a positive role in the fight against poverty and unsustainable development. It acknowledges the importance of domestic institutions and national policies and macroeconomic factors, and it recognizes the central role of a continuous social policy dialogue.

The main body of the report deals with the asymmetric effects of globalization on rich and poor countries [*ibid.*, pp. 80 *ff.*]. The Commission stresses the need to develop rules of the global economy that benefit the rights, livelihoods, security, and opportunities of people around the world. The functioning of the free markets needs to be complemented by environmental, social, and cultural considerations. In its concluding sections, the report of the Commission enters the subject of research, arguing for a stronger, up-to-date knowledge base on globalization. "What is measured is acted upon," [*ibid.*, p. 137]. It is argued that reliable and regular information, disaggregated by gender, is required on the social impact of globalization and the distribution of its benefits. On December 2, 2004, the UN General Assembly adopted a resolution recognizing the contribution of the World Commission's report in aiming for a fully inclusive and equitable globalization.

The Marrakesh Roundtable on Results [UN DESA, 2002] had endorsed a coherent framework for development effectiveness. The Marrakesh principles include a dialogue on results at all phases of the development process, managing by results, in which performance information is used for improved decision making, including progress monitoring and outcome evaluation. It calls for a need to move to a results management agenda entailing a shift in institutional practices — with a new effort to develop a common performance management system and integrating Management for Development Results into the practices of the multilateral development banks. This requires deepening efforts to systematically and transparently monitor performance indicators and defining the set of instruments that link behavior to performance outcomes [World Bank and IMF, 2006].

5.1 Goals

According to the World Commission, the main characteristics of globalization are the following indicators of the openness of the borders of the country [*ibid.*, p. 24].

- the liberalization of international trade,
- the expansion of foreign direct investments,
- the emergence of massive cross-border financial flows.

The Commission also pointed at the impact of new technology, especially in information and communications. Obviously, this list of dimensions may be viewed as the outputs of a generalized input-output relationship, using human and natural resources and variables of economic and social policy as inputs.

The Commission devoted an entire chapter to the subject matter of how countries can introduce fairer rules of competition, redressing inequities in terms of market access in international trade. In the present chapter we shall put the *equality or skewness of the vertical income distribution* in focus. The increased exports and in-flows of foreign capital that go together with an open economy builds profits — profits in the export industry, and in new ventures initiated from abroad. Swelling corporate profits tend, *ceteris paribus*, to make the vertical income distribution more unequal. The indicator of social fairness to be used subsequently will be the equality of the vertical income distribution.

How do these indicators interact with each other? In the short run, increased exports build profits and expand employment in the export industries. An increased influx of foreign capital brings in new risk capital and new management expertise. There will be increased profits, increased dividends, and increased wages being paid in the expanding sectors. Later, a process of "trickle down" may ensue, along the lines of the familiar Keynesian multiplier. But other sectors of the economy are shielded from competition from abroad and will experience little change. Even in the intermediate run, the net effect will typically be an increased inequality of the vertical income distribution.

This is not the end of the story, however. At the same time, powerful economic and social processes that redistribute income may have been put in motion by the introduction of new technical knowledge. Consider the arrival of new computer technology that enters the classroom and revolutionizes education. Or, consider new drugs and new health technology that benefits the less advantaged in the economy.

Continuing this line of thought, one may define A Fair Globalization for a given country as the maximal level of trade openness that is compatible with some given and ruling skewness of the income distribution (a more precise definition follows immediately below). As standard indicators of the openness and level of globalization in a given country, we shall choose:

- exports of goods and services as a percentage of GDP (*EXP*),
- net foreign direct investment as a percentage of gross capital formation (*FDI*).

Furthermore, we shall use the familiar Gini index as a measure of the inequality of the vertical income distribution:

- as a fairness index, we select a measure of the equality of the vertical income distribution, calculated as 100% minus the Gini index (*EQUAL*).

Clearly, no fast and robust conclusions can be drawn regarding the net effects of globalization on the Gini index. Instead, we will simply use *EQUAL* as a piece of statistical evidence, shedding light on the economic and social fairness (or absence of fairness) in each country.

We have already encountered the two variables *EXP* and *FDI* as policy instruments in Chapter 4. As often occurs in multi-criteria applications in the economic and social field, the concept of causality can be difficult and cross-currents of causal mechanisms can sometimes be recognized (such as during an export-led expansion where exports are the cause rather than the effect). So, variables indicating the openness of an economy may actually figure as *causes* to "Decent Work" but *effect variables* of "A Fair Globalization." The column vector of goals is now

$$Y = (EXP, FDI, EQUAL) \tag{5.1}$$

Form the Cobb-Douglas generalized social preference function

$$V(Y) = EXP^{\mu_1} FDI^{\mu_2} EQUAL^{\mu_3} \tag{5.2}$$

In order not to drown the reader with too many mathematical symbols, we are using here the same notation as in the social preference function (4.2) used to estimate Decent Work. No misunderstanding should arise.

The coefficients μ_1, μ_2, μ_3 are the elasticities of V with respect to the three goals. If $\mu_1 + \mu_2 + \mu_3 = 1$, the preference function exhibits constant returns to scale. If at an optimum $\mu_1 + \mu_2 + \mu_3 < 1$, there are decreasing returns to scale in the country being evaluated, and if $\mu_1 + \mu_2 + \mu_3 > 1$, there are increasing returns to scale.

Taking logarithms

$$log V(Y) = \mu_1 log EXP + \mu_2 log FDI + \mu_3 log EQUAL \tag{5.3}$$

5.2 Tracing the Causes of Globalization: The Policy Parameters

It is generally agreed that the roots of globalization lie with increased communication — in particular electronic communication — and transfer of knowledge in the modern world. Here we shall take these advances as given, and instead ask ourselves why the degree of exposure to such influence varies from country to country. Some countries are more receptive to change than others. The following three factors obviously facilitate the introduction of new communication techniques:

- The annual growth of GDP, measured as current GDP as a percentage of last year's GDP (*GROWTH*);
- The degree of monetization of the economy, measured as 1 minus the informal economy as a percentage of GDP (*FORMAL*);
- The degree of trade liberalization, measured as 1 minus the proportion of government revenues collected as trade duties (1–*TARIFF*).

Note in particular the definition of *GROWTH*: it is calculated as 100 plus the annual growth rate. A growth rate of 5% is entered as 105, a growth rate of −2% is entered as 98. This stratagem will maintain the same dimensionality of all the variables (annual number divided by annual number), and also avoid the problem of negative observations. The vector of the causes of globalization will thus be written

$$X = (GROWTH, FORMAL, 1 - TARIFF) \qquad (5.4)$$

These factors illustrate the role played by conventional macroeconomic variables (*GROWTH*), social conditions (*FORMAL*), and national and international policy parameters (1-*TARIFF*). An economy experiencing rapid *GROWTH* is better placed to reap the fruits of globalization, and also to suffer the iniquities and environmental disturbances that may accompany it. There are many examples of the rapid global transfer of recent advances in high technology and communication, building regional growth centers, attracting foreign capital, and boosting national exports — India's IT industry is a case in point. Rapid *GROWTH,* then, goes together with an export boom; at the same time, the high rate of return on real capital stimulates the influx of foreign investments.

Globalization essentially is a phenomenon of markets — local shielded markets being opened up to international competition. But many developing countries have huge non-monetized, non-market sectors that change little in the face of the communications and information explosion. These sectors constitute the "informal economy" where products and services are produced and consumed locally, without the intermediating role of market transaction. Only the *FORMAL* economy transmits the forces of globalization.

TARIFF represents taxes on international trade and includes import duties, export duties, profits of export or import monopolies, exchange profits, and exchange taxes. Government revenues are calculated as cash receipts from taxes, social contributions, and other revenues such as fines, fees, rent, and income from property and sales. The variable is obviously a powerful policy instrument.

The variables *GROWTH* and *FORMAL* are not policy instruments. Their role is indirect, acting as conduits transmitting actions of policy. They are treated as mitigating or enabling causal factors explaining globalization, characterizing the receptiveness of the nation to new technology and new ideas. (It is perfectly possible to argue, of course, that *GROWTH* also responds as an effect of globalization. As we shall subsequently argue more fully, all sorts of crisscrossing causal dependencies between variables are possible. At the moment, however, our task is to identify some of the more powerful *drivers* of globalization and the efforts of national policy to manage those drivers as effectively as possible.) To illustrate how *GROWTH* and *FORMAL* might be explicitly earmarked for the transmission of policy promoting the forces of globalization, consider the following measures of industrial policy:

- Promoting high tech start-ups by preferential allocation of credit and other support to new entrepreneurs, thus stimulating *GROWTH*;
- Promoting computer training courses for unemployed and socially alienated youth, thus extending the *FORMAL* sector of the economy.

Our three causal factors are collected into the generalized social cost function

$$U(X) = GROWTH^{\nu_1} FORMAL^{\nu_2} (1 - TARIFF)^{\nu_3} \qquad (5.5)$$

where ν_1, ν_2, and ν_3 are the elasticities with respect to the three causal factors. Equation (5.5) spells out the social costs attached to the increased use of each of these factors. In particular, note:

- Government export promotion and assistance is universally accepted economic policy. But when one government becomes more heavily involved in industrial policy with an eye on furthering exports, other countries will often respond "competitively."

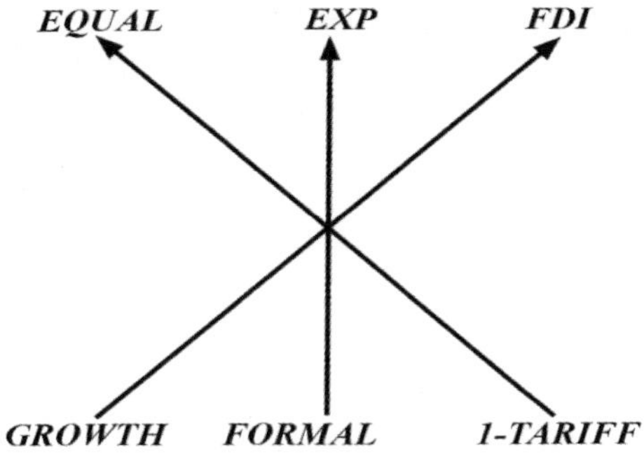

Figure 5.1 A Fair Globalization, causes and effects.

- Stimulating the influx of foreign capital may provoke organized labor.
- Raising duties on imported goods and subsidizing domestic producers will cause an outcry from the World Trade Organization.

In all these cases, the "cost" is not one in monetary units but in political terms. Taking logarithms

$$logU(X) = \nu_1 logGROWTH + \nu_2 logFORMAL + \nu_3 log(1-TARIFF) \tag{5.6}$$

The optimal ratio between expressions (5.3) and (5.6) is the desired measure of the effectiveness of the Fair Globalization policy for the country currently rated. Figure 5.1 above illustrates the causal links between the causes and effects of A Fair Globalization.

5.3 Empirical Results: The Effectiveness Frontier

The numerical calculations were carried out in the same manner as for Decent Work (Chapter 4) and for the same selection of 102 countries. As before, all input and output data are averages for 2000–2010. For detailed definitions of variables and data sources see Appendix 2. This time as well we used the linear programming version (2.9) which now reads

$$\max \Phi \tag{5.7}$$

subject to

$$\Phi logEXP_0 - \Sigma(logEXP_j)\lambda_j \leq 0$$

Table 5.1 A Fair Globalization. List of 18 effective countries.

Country	*FORMAL*	*GROWTH*	*1-TARIFF*	*EXP*	*FDI*	*EQUAL*
Liberia	55.7	101.5	84.8	27.4	24.1	61.6
Belgium	78.3	101.5	97.5	77.5	25.0	67.4
Panama	36.6	103.5	92.8	72.2	7.1	45.2
Malaysia	69.4	103.5	92.8	110.0	3.2	56.8
Georgia	34.1	105.6	95.6	29.1	8.2	59.2
Ireland	83.9	102.5	97.5	88.2	8.1	66.1
Maldives	70.8	105.6	78.3	62.8	4.9	62.8
Belarus	53.5	107.8	91.8	61.6	2.1	71.5
Hungary	75.9	102.5	97.5	72.2	10.4	71.5
Slovak Republic	82.3	104.6	97.5	75.9	4.1	72.2
Ethiopia	61.6	105.6	81.5	12.7	2.5	70.1
Denmark	82.3	100.5	97.5	48.4	4.1	75.2
Azerbaijan	42.1	113.3	90.9	50.9	10.3	64.7
Czech Republic	81.5	102.5	97.5	69.4	6.2	74.4
Sweden	81.5	102.5	97.5	47.9	6.3	75.2
Egypt	65.4	103.5	77.5	23.8	3.5	68.0
Ukraine	50.4	104.6	94.6	52.5	4.1	71.5
Thailand	49.4	103.5	87.4	68.7	3.6	58.0

$$\Phi logFDI_0 - \Sigma(logFDI_j)\lambda_j \leq 0$$
$$\Phi logEQUAL_0 - \Sigma(logEQUAL_j)\lambda_j \leq 0$$
$$\Sigma(logGROWTH_j)\lambda_j \leq logGROWTH_0$$
$$\Sigma(logFORMAL_j)\lambda_j \leq logFORMAL_0$$
$$\Sigma(log(1-TARIFF_j)\lambda_j \leq log(1-TARIFF)_0$$
$$\lambda \geq 0$$
$$\Phi \text{ unconstrained.}$$

As before, all slacks were minimized.

Eighteen countries span the effectiveness envelope, obtaining an effectiveness rating of 100% (see Table 5.1). The instruments slacks and goals slacks of these countries are all zero. These are the effective countries. The actual observations of the goals then coincide with the optimal targets. Excepting Belgium, Denmark, Ireland, and Sweden, they are all developing or formerly communist nations. Note that the list includes a few countries

Table 5.2 A Fair Globalization. Twelve countries with bottom effectiveness ratings (less than 92.1%). Actual and frontier goal achievements. All data in %.

		Actual data			Frontier values		
Country	Score	*EXP*	*FDI*	*EQUAL*	*EXP*	*FDI*	*EQUAL*
Lesotho	92.0	50.4	6.4	47.5	70.8	7.5	66.7
El Salvador	92.0	26.1	1.3	50.4	50.4	4.0	70.8
Costa Rica	91.8	45.6	4.5	50.9	64.1	5.2	72.2
Argentina	91.7	20.9	2.8	50.4	34.1	3.8	71.5
Dominican Rep.	91.6	32.1	4.1	49.9	44.3	4.7	71.5
Paraguay	90.9	46.5	1.3	45.6	68.0	2.9	66.7
Chile	89.9	38.5	7.0	46.5	58.0	8.8	71.5
Guatemala	89.2	24.5	1.5	43.8	50.4	4.0	69.4
Brazil	88.2	12.9	2.9	42.5	24.3	3.3	70.1
Colombia	87.9	16.8	3.2	42.1	29.4	3.7	70.8
Namibia	85.9	43.8	2.4	36.2	81.5	4.7	65.4
South Africa	84.6	29.1	1.7	37.3	53.5	4.4	72.2

with some very considerable inequalities in their income distributions. Panama is one such country; its score of $EQUAL = 45.2$ is actually one of the three lowest in the world. (The bottom score is for Namibia with the equality 42.1.) So, how can Panama still be ranked as effective? The answer is that Panama was, nevertheless, doing well compared to a few other poor countries with low inputs and low outputs.

The results for Malaysia are noteworthy: Malaysia (together with Ireland) tops the list of great exporters, the beneficiary of a huge wave of outsourcing of production from Western countries. The figures for the two other goals are not impressive, but the outstanding export results alone suffice to place Malaysia among the 18 international winners.

The remaining countries are ineffective which means that they score less than 100% or that they feature positive slacks in their use of policy instruments or in their goal achievements. For a look at the results turn to Table 5.2, which lists eleven countries at the bottom of the ranking list, obtaining an effectiveness rating of 92.1% or less. For each country, the effectiveness score $1/\Phi$ is listed together with its actual goal achievements and frontier goals, all expressed in percentage points.

The table reveals some very large deficits. The exports of South Africa was only 29.1% of GDP. Ideally, the country should be able to almost double the figure. Obviously, this result reflects the lack of internationalization of the South African economy. For all the countries in Table 5.2, the results for the *EQUAL* variable also spell out some very considerable deficits. To compensate for the strong winds of globalization, these countries would all need some huge doses of additional "fairness" — increased income equality.

5.4 Globalization and Turbulence

The methods outlined in this book describe how it is possible to identify those countries that maximize their achievements of their policy goals. Together, they span the upper envelope or frontier of goal achievements. Their policy effectiveness rating is one. Countries falling below the frontier obtain ratings less than one.

Within the framework of conventional economic equilibrium theory, countries on the frontier will all be Pareto-optimal. They are optimally adjusted to prices clearing all markets. But here the interpretation is much more subtle. Many or perhaps most of the goals of economic and social policy are not transacted on markets. For them, there are no prices. Consider the case of Decent Work, discussed in Chapter 4. There is no commodity or service called "female participation in the labor force." It has no price. Instead, it is determined through long-term and sometimes traumatic social processes like the formation of attitudes and opinions of the role of women in society and the education of women. An effectiveness rating less than one indicates that in the country currently evaluated, further emancipation and further progress of woman in the workplace should be possible, compared to what is being achieved in some other (peer) countries.

The work of the International Labour Office to create conditions of Decent Work in its member countries is reinforced by worldwide cultural trends toward greater equality in the workplace and the emancipation of women (with some notable exceptions in strict Muslim regimes). And so one might be permitted to posit that Decent Work frontier countries too represent a kind of economic and cultural "equilibrium."

Unfortunately, we are not aware of any similar rationale for believing that "A Fair Globalization" should represent a position of equilibrium in the social and economic policy dynamics of a nation. Certainly "A Fair Globalization" as outlined by the ILO is a worthy goal for nations. But are there any economic or social or even cultural mechanisms that tend to push a nation toward the frontier?

There is the optimistic view of the benevolent wisdom of policymakers responding to the wishes of their electorate. Free trade and international mobility of capital as practiced in the West seemed to "work," generating the rapid economic growth and dispersion of wealth in Europe and North America during the nineteenth and twentieth centuries. Other observers would be more pessimistic, seeing poverty-stricken nations all over the world succumbing to the power-grabs of tyrants or plutocrats gobbling up ever more of the nation's riches. To the citizens of these nations, A Fair Globalization is only a chimera.

A look at the data is helpful. We have already seen (in Table 5.1) that those eighteen countries that span the envelope have *EQUAL* ratios (equal to 1 — the Gini coefficient) ranging from the 70s (led by Denmark and Sweden at 75.19) to the 50s (with the exception of Panama dipping into the 40s). Not surprisingly, the lowest *EQUAL* rankings are found among countries which also obtain very low effectiveness rankings. Rankings in the 40s and even in the 30s dominate the bottom of effectiveness list. A surprising array of Latin American countries belong to this group: Peru, Honduras, the Dominican Republic, Paraguay, Guatemala, Chile, Brazil, and Colombia all get *EQUAL* rankings in the 40s and are found among the fifteen lowest performers in terms of their effectiveness ratings. Clearly, these nations are still today fighting a heritage of inequality imposed upon them by their former Iberian colonial masters. Conclusion: to construct a theory of the income distribution — and its dynamics — one needs to weave together economic, cultural, and historical factors.

Just as companies may be managed effectively or less effectively, economic and social policy in nations may be managed more or less effectively and successfully. What determines if one country reaches the Fair Globalization frontier and another does not? A conjunction of factors representing the policy efforts of men and women motivated in many very different ways. One way of describing this dynamic is by way of mathematical chaos theory, as we will discuss in Chapter 8.

Chapter 6

Nested Decision Trees

This chapter widens the search for causal relations between policy instruments and goals in social and economic policy to large hierarchical structures featuring a multitude of layers of single causalities. "Goals" may, in their turn, be subject to policymakers' efforts to reach even more ultimate objectives. Policy "instruments" may be controlled only indirectly via the actual parameters of action at hand. In other cases the distinction between goals and policy instruments may be obscure, with causal links operating in both directions.

Often there will exist no ultimate causal truth but only a causal model that may later be refined. The causal model is represented by a *decision tree* with each branch of the tree illustrating a partial causality. For an illustration of the main idea, Figure 6.1 depicts some key steps in tracing the causality links of factors related to social and economic policy. This is only one example of a great number of possible alternatives but should suffice to convey the complexity and difficulty of the task at hand.

Most variables depicted in the diagram are effects of one or several underlying factors, while at the same time they serve as causes to one or several overarching factors (the detailed arrangements of causal links is here suppressed and only indicated summarily by a single arrow pointing from each lower layer of factors to the next one).

Causal networks are well known in statistical multi-criteria analysis, and standard multivariate procedures are available to trace and test the presence and strength of the individual causal relationships in a given set of observations. A widely used computer-based technique for generating the

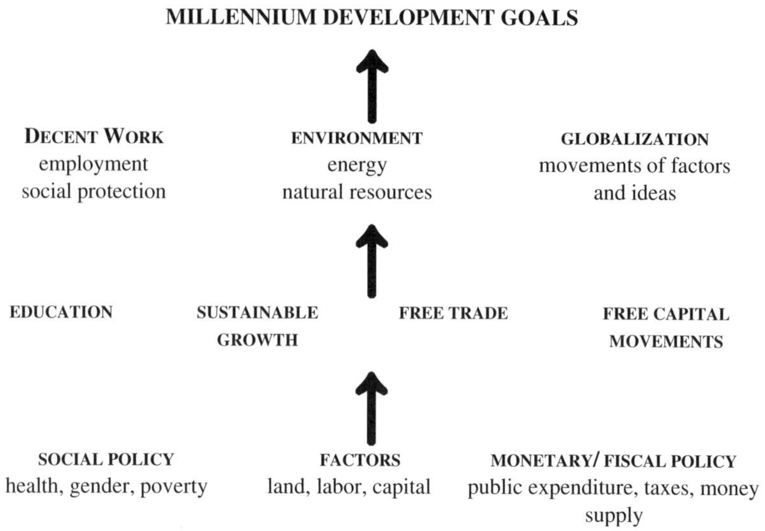

Figure 6.1 Decision tree featuring policy instruments and goals in social and economic policy.

decision tree is MACBETH (Measuring Attractiveness by a Category-Based Evaluation Technique) [Bana e Costa, *et al.* 2012].

In earlier chapters we have discussed Decent Work (appearing in the upper left hand corner of Figure 6.1) and Globalization (the upper right hand corner). We now face the challenge to integrate the two earlier separate causal frameworks to form a joint overarching causal structure. As we shall see, this immediately brings up the possibility of causal conflict. Is it possible to overcome the disruptive consequences of free trade and free capital movements and yet promote Decent Work?

6.1 Reconciling Twin Goals: Decent Work and A Fair Globalization

Any meaningful discussion of Decent Work needs to relate the conditions in labor markets to the effects of globalization. After having presented his two initial reports on Decent Work and the Decent Work Deficit in 1999 and 2001 respectively, the director-general of the International Labour Organization (ILO) three years later submitted the report *A Fair Globalization: The Role of ILO* [WCSDG, 2004]. At some length this publication develops the theme that:

> . . . in order to achieve A Fair Globalization that creates opportunities for all, Decent Work should become a global goal to be pursued by every country and the international community," [*ibid.*, p.3].

International organizations such as the United Nations (UN), the Organisation for Economic Co-operation and Development (OECD), the World Trade Organization (WTO), and the World Health Organisation (WHO) regularly stress the importance of achieving acceptable work conditions (Decent Work) and shielding vulnerable sectors of the economy from negative effects of globalization. For instance, the director-general of the WTO in January 2006 called for creation of a "new" Geneva Consensus:

> We need to "reform globalization" with a clear view to enhancing the development of social, economic, and ecological aspects of humanity. This is also in line with the millennium development goals that can be achieved through a "reform of globalization" from within and for development [WTO, 2006].

In the same vein, on its Internet "home page" WHO states:

> We are working to ensure that trade and globalization work to improve the health of the poor and disadvantaged populations. The overall goal is to achieve greater coherence between international trade and health policy so that international and multilateral trade rules maximize health benefits and minimize health risks especially for poor and vulnerable populations [WHO, 2013].

While the principles of policy development may be common across countries, the achievement of social-economic goals depend on national situations and political priorities attached to individual policies. The director-general of the ILO has stated:

> Each country has different deficits and needs, but there is a common idea that they need to be addressed with a package of mutually reinforcing action [ILO, 2001, p. 37].

A 2004 report by World Commission on The Social Dimension of Globalization [WCSDG, 2004b] expressed the hope to bend the market forces of globalization to generate some degree of fairness, and to deliver "unprecedented material progress, generate more productive and better jobs for all, and contribute significantly to reducing world poverty" [*ibid.*]. This, in its turn, would hopefully open the door for the possibility of creating more "Decent Work." But the authors also recognized that

> . . . the current process of globalization is generating unbalanced outcomes, both between and within countries. Wealth is being created, but too many countries and people are not sharing in its benefits.

These quotations express the well-meaning wish that some kind of reconciliation between the twin goals of A Fair Globalization and Decent Work can be worked out. This may indeed be possible sometimes, but, as we shall now see, the two goals can in some instances be at loggerheads with each other, being competing rather than supporting each other. This may be referred to as the "classical dilemma of trade policy."

Public discussions on the current wave of globalization are increasingly focusing on its development impact with new views emerging. There are ample precedents to support the hypothesis that trade can have both negative and positive effects on individuals, households, regions, companies and industries and the economy as a whole. Trade and investment liberalization based on principles of fair competition can be a powerful force for fostering job creation and poverty reduction. However, if not properly managed, they may lead to adverse social consequences accompanied by high unemployment and increased poverty that are very costly to overcome.

In many countries, the prevailing systems for decision making tend to separate economic, social, and environmental factors at policy, planning, and management levels. This has led to a widening of inequality, both at global and national levels. Making globalization serve all economic actors calls for careful sequencing of trade/investment liberalization reforms and the need to make social trade-offs where necessary. A strong political commitment and institutional capacity may be needed to redistribute the benefits of globalization.

6.2 Multi-Criteria Analysis: Nested Causality Trees

Figure 6.2 brings together the causal structures of Decent Work and of A Fair Globalization into a single diagram. As before, the directed links indicate causal relationships (from cause to effect). The top part represents Decent Work (*cf.* Figure 4.1), the bottom part A Fair Globalization (*cf.* Figure 5.1).

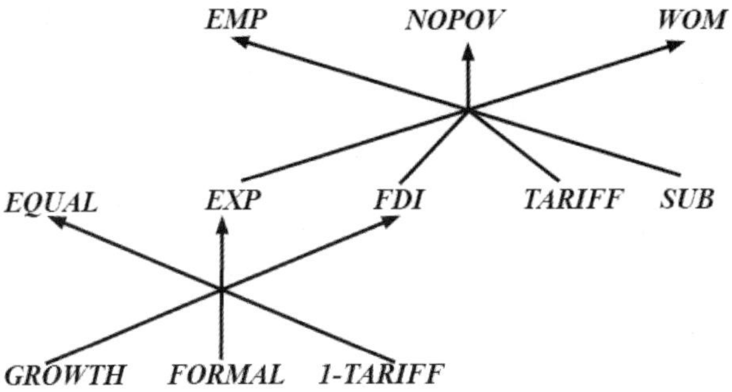

Figure 6.2 Decent work and a fair globalization: the causal tree.

This hierarchy implies the presence of two nested social utility functions. The top layer value function would be the utility function (4.1), describing Decent Work as a trade-off between employment, social protection, and the participation of women in the labor force. The second-layer value function represents the variables in utility function (5.1), describing A Fair Globalization as a trade-off between exports, foreign direct investments, and income equality. Symbols in the causal tree are the same as we have used before:

- *EMP*= total gainful employment,
- *NOPOV*= a measure of social protection,
- *WOM*= a measure of gender equality,
- *EQUAL*= 100% minus the Gini index,
- *EXP* = exports of goods and services,
- *FDI* = net foreign direct investment,
- *TARIFF* = proportion of GDP collected as trade duties,
- *SUB* = subsidies and other transfers as a proportion of total government expenditure,
- *GROWTH*= 100% plus annual growth rate of GDP,
- *FORMAL* = degree of monetization of economic transactions in a country, measured as 1 minus the informal economy as % of GDP.

The two variables *EXP* and *FDI* serve as causes in the upper part of the causal tree (Decent Work) and as effects in the lower part (A Fair Globalization). The variable *TARIFF* plays an interconnected role in the tree. On the one hand, *higher* tariffs may be used to shield domestic workers from foreign competition and would thus promote Decent Work. On the other hand, *lower* tariffs mean a more open economy and access to the fruits of Globalization. So, are lower tariffs good or bad? We shall return to this question in a moment.

6.3 A Nested Two-Stage Sequence of Effectiveness Ratings

To portray this cascading causal mechanism of the entire causal tree in Figure 6.2, we now outline a sequential process of effectiveness ratings. For each country, the ratings gauge the achievements of economic and social policy at each stage of the successive causal sub-hierarchies, joining them into an extended causal process. As we shall see, this integrated approach delivers much more forceful empirical results than the two isolated rating models by themselves. For each country, we shall now obtain not one but two effectiveness ratings: the effectiveness of the country in reaching the idealized conditions of Decent Work, and its effectiveness in reaching the goals of A Fair Globalization.

The effectiveness rating of a country in terms of Decent Work is calculated as the ratio between the social utility of the goals, and the social cost of the policy parameters is

$$V(EMP, NOPOV, WOM)/U(EXP, FDI, TARIFF, SUB) \tag{6.1}$$

Similarly, the rating of the country in terms of A Fair Globalization is calculated as

$$V(EXP, FDI, EQUAL)/U(GROWTH, FORMAL, 1-TARIFF) \tag{6.2}$$

In both cases, the calculation takes the form of solving a fractional programming problem, as described earlier.

One may refer to this sequential linkage of calculations as a *two-stage* or *hybrid* rating model. It accomplishes the need to gauge the policy achievements of each country at each stage of the causal tree. The *first stage* model is (6.2), solving for the A Fair Globalization (AFG) score; the *second stage* model is (6.1) solving for the Decent Work (DW) score. The two programs enable us to empirically determine a set of nested social preference and cost functions.

We have already listed the effective countries at each stage (see Tables 4.1 and 5.1). Only two countries turn out to be rated as effective at both stages: Denmark and the Maldives. Norway (with a DW score of 100 and a AFG score 99.8), Ireland (98.7 and 100, respectively), and Sweden (100 and 97.3, respectively) are close. So, a few countries have found it possible to design their economic and social policies reaching (or almost reaching) both sets of goals.

The example of Denmark is quite significant because for the Decent Work calculations, Denmark happens to serves as a peer to more than half of all the countries (to 57 of them, to be precise). And for the AFG calculations, Denmark serves as a peer to 42 countries in globalization. Denmark can be looked upon as a "role model" to half the world! Following the example set by Denmark, one would find the two sets of goals are perfectly doable.

Nevertheless, a large number of countries find it difficult to reconcile the two sets of goals. Figure 6.3 plots the scores of all the countries. As can readily be seen, there is no significant correlation between the two scores (the correlation coefficient is 0.04). A few countries that are adjusted optimally at the first stage (A Fair Globalization) obtain quite low scores for Decent Work (Azerbaijan 85.2, Panama 80.7, Ukraine 80.0, Thailand 77.1, and Belarus 75.9) The policy conclusion of such a combination of

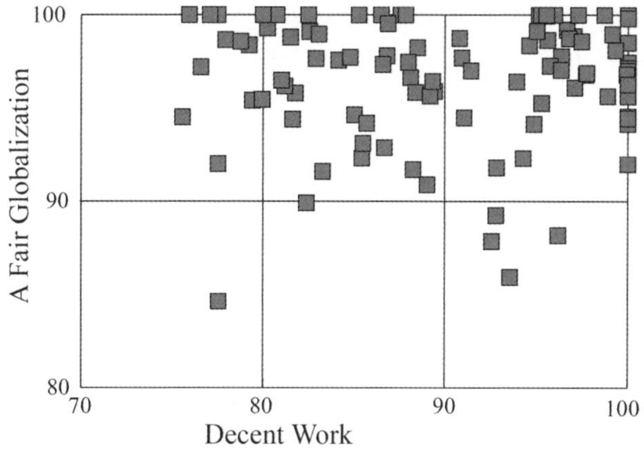

Figure 6.3 Scatter diagram of 102 countries.

Horizontal axis: Decent Work score; vertical axis: A Fair Globalization score.

ratings would seem to suggest putting more emphasis on the emancipation of women (boosting the figures for the *WOM* statistic).

Conversely, a number of countries that are doing well at the second stage (Decent Work) get quite low scores at the globalization stage. Examples are El Salvador, Jamaica and Turkey (all having globalization scores in the low 90s). The income distribution in these countries is quite uneven. The United States also belongs to this group: the United States got one of the lowest scores at the globalization stage but is 100% effective in terms of Decent Work, demonstrating the possibility that even a quite unfair globalization (huge income differences between rich and poor) can still entail Decent Work.

6.4 The Classical Dilemma: A Novel Approach

In theory, it would be perfectly possible to define A Fair Globalization to include all desired features of Decent Work. But in any empirical work, one would have to lay down a list of dimensions of each concept. If these dimensions are at least partly exclusive, the dilemma remains that countries may find globalization hurtful to work conditions. To examine these matters more carefully, consider now Table 6.1, which lists all countries that are listed as DW-effective (a DW score of 100%), or Table 6.2, listing all countries that are AFG-effective (a AFG score of 100%). The classical dilemma of trade policy amounts to understanding the problematic role of the variable *TARIFF* as it affects the calculations at the two stages of envelopment. *TARIFF* serves as a link between globalization and Decent Work. The variable *1-TARIFF* is an input into the first stage calculation (free trade stimulates globalization); see equation (6.2) above. Similarly, *TARIFF* is an input into the second stage (protection promotes the possibility of Decent Work); see equation (6.1).

In order to spell out numerically this role of the variable *TARIFF*, we now demonstrate a novel application of two-stage DEA, confronting the results from the first stage calculations directly with the results from the second stage. Switch the DEA calculations at both stages from an output formulation to an input-oriented one. The first stage will then reveal the scope for reducing 1-*TARIFF* and still reach the frontier of optimal Fair Globalization. And the second stage will reveal the scope for reducing

Table 6.1 List of countries that are rated 100% AFG-effective. Scores, actual *TARIFF* rate and target *TARIFF* rates; see main text.

Country	DW score	AFG score	Actual TARIFF	DW Target TARIFF	AFG Target TARIFF
Liberia	82.5	100	15.0	9.3	15.2
Belgium	95.1	100	2.6	2.5	2.5
Panama	80.7	100	7.6	5.2	7.2
Malaysia	77.5	100	6.8	4.4	7.2
Georgia	86.4	100	4.8	3.9	4.4
Ireland	98.7	100	2.6	2.6	2.5
Belarus	76.0	100	8.5	5.1	8.2
Hungary	96.0	100	2.6	2.5	2.5
Slovak Republic	95.5	100	2.6	2.5	2.5
Ethiopia	87.8	100	18.7	11.8	18.5
Azerbaijan	85.2	100	9.3	6.7	9.1
Ethiopia	95.2	100	2.6	2.5	2.5
Sweden	97.3	100	2.6	2.5	2.5
Egypt	87.5	100	22.4	5.6	22.5
Ukraine	80.0	100	5.2	3.7	5.4
Thailand	77.1	100	12.3	7.0	12.6

TARIFF while still reaching the frontier of optimal Decent Work. In other words, the calculations for each country will deliver an interval: a maximal *TARIFF* for which A Fair Globalization would obtain and at the same time a minimal *TARIFF* for which optimal Decent Work would obtain. If the gap is zero, both stages deliver optimality.

As is well known, switching from an input-oriented version to an output-oriented one, or vice versa, leaves the efficiency frontier unchanged. An observation will be characterized as effective with an output formulation (*i.e.*, located on the frontier) only if it is characterized as efficient with an input formulation. But for an inefficient observation, the projection onto the frontier can be different under the two formulations.

The peers (*i.e.*, the set of corner points of the facet in which the projection is located) will then also typically be different, as would the prescription for a possible improvement of current performance.

The observed *TARIFF* for all countries are listed in the fourth column in Table 6.1. The two last columns list the frontier values of the same variable, calculated from Decent Work and from A Fair Globalization, respectively.

Table 6.2 List of countries that are rated 100% DW-effective. Scores, actual *TARIFF* rate and target *TARIFF* rates; see main text.

Country	DW score	AFG score	Actual TARIFF	DW Target TARIFF	AFG Target TARIFF
Italy	100	96.7	2.6	2.6	4.4
Norway	100	99.8	2.5	2.5	2.5
Bhutan	100	96.7	20.1	20.1	20.2
Denmark	100	100.0	2.6	2.6	2.5
Maldives	100	100.0	21.3	21.3	21.7
France	100	97.5	2.6	2.6	2.5
El Salvador	100	92.0	5.5	5.5	6.3
Burkina Faso	100	96.4	12.6	12.6	12.6
Iran	100	98.5	24.3	24.3	24.1
United States	100	94.5	3.3	3.3	3.5
Ukraine	100	96.3	2.5	2.6	2.5
Portugal	100	95.6	2.6	2.6	3.5
Niger	100	97.0	13.6	13.6	13.5
Jamaica	100	94.2	10.3	10.3	10.0
Lao PDR	100	97.2	8.0	8.0	8.2
Turkey	100	94.6	3.0	3.0	3.5

Inspecting the results, the countries can be divided into four categories as listed below.

(i) Denmark and the Maldives are frontier corner points at both stages. For each of these countries, the observed *TARIFF* coincides with the optimal *TARIFF* and the observed 1-*TARIFF* coincides with the optimal *1-TARIFF* For these countries, then, fair globalization policy and Decent Work policy work hand in hand.

(ii) Sixteen countries are frontier corner points at the stage A Fair Globalization, but are off-frontier when estimating Decent Work. They are Azerbaijan, Belarus, Belgium, Czech Republic, Egypt, Ethiopia, Georgia, Hungary, Ireland, Liberia, Malaysia, Panama, Slovak Republic, Sweden, Thailand, and Ukraine. They are listed in Table 6.1 together with the observed *TARIFF* data and an interval of possible *TARIFF* reduction. The interval ranges from the optimal *TARIFF* at the first stage (the lower bound) to the optimal *TARIFF* at the second stage (the upper bound, coinciding with the observed *TARIFF*). These countries are all ineffective at the first stage (Decent Work) but they are effective at the second stage (A Fair Globalization). The policy recommendation would then be to engage in some moderate reduction of the *TARIFF* variable, thus trading off the (perfect) rating of A Fair Globalization against some improvement of the score in terms of Decent Work.

To illustrate: Egypt and Ethiopia both curtail contacts with the outside world, imposing a protective regimen involving *TARIFF* levels of 22.4% and 18.7%, respectively. These levels coincide with the frontier levels for the second stage, meaning that no reduction is possible while maintaining the current level toward A Fair Globalization. However, these high *TARIFF* rates are excessive in terms of Decent Work; it would actually be possible to lower them to 5.6% and 11.8%, respectively. Such a lowering of the trade barriers would of course not be without political opposition. Nevertheless, there is a strong argument for lowering *TARIFF*, and there is not really any contradiction between globalization policy and Decent Work policy. In the same manner a moderate amount of trade liberalization would be helpful for Azerbaijan, Belarus, Georgia, Liberia, Malaysia, Panama, Thailand, and Ukraine.

(iii) Next, turning to the opposite case, consider the fourteen countries that are 100% effective at the first stage (Decent Work) but ineffective at the second stage (A Fair Globalization): Bhutan, Burkina Faso, El Salvador, France, Italy, Iran, Jamaica, Lao PDR, Norway, Niger, Portugal, Turkey, the United Kingdom, and the United States. This time the interval between the lower bound and the upper bound of *TARIFF* ranges from the optimal *TARIFF* at the first stage (coinciding with the observed *TARIFF*) to the optimal *TARIFF* at the second stage. Whereas the variable *1-TARIFF* in general is assumed to enhance globalization, we see that for El Salvador, Portugal, and the United States it is actually excessive (the observed *TARIFF* falls short of the optimal value).

An instructive case is represented by Portugal. As in all European Union countries, there are few hindrances to free trade. The observed *TARIFF* rate was only 2.6%. This is also the optimal rate at the first stage of the calculations (Decent Work). But Portugal is off-frontier during the second stage. Hence, it should be possible to reduce the input variable *1-TARIFF* — that is, it should be possible to increase *TARIFF*. As shown in the table the *TARIFF* variable could theoretically be increased to 3.5%. A moderate increase in tariff levels, trading off the perfect rating of Decent Work for improvement toward A Fair Globalization, would obviously seem natural. Again, there is no clash between the goals of Decent Work and the goals of A Fair Globalization.

(iv) It remains to mention that all the other countries, being off-frontier at both DEA stages, present the "classical dilemma of trade policy." It is not necessary to discuss the details here. Suffice it to say that for most of these countries the observed *TARIFF* level is located inside the interval ranging from the Decent Work optimum to A Fair Globalization optimum. Hence any lowering of *TARIFF*, while being helpful to A Fair Globalization, would be detrimental to the level of Decent Work obtained. Conversely, any increase of *TARIFF*, while helpful to Decent Work, would inhibit the pace of A Fair Globalization.

6.5 A Generalized Format of Sequential Ratings

In conclusion, we briefly outline the general format of a two-step nested instruments/goals hierarchy (see Figure 6.4). At the top of the decision pyramid is the vector of ultimate goals $Y = (Y_1, Y_2, \ldots, Y_s)$. At the bottom the vector of policy inputs (instruments) $X = (X_1, X_2, \ldots, X_m)$. Between them we have entered a vector of "intermediate goals" $Z = (Z_1, Z_2, \ldots, Z_t)$ that are determined by the policy inputs X but at the same time serve as inputs to the ultimate goals Y. We previously encountered two such intermediate goals, *EXP* and *FDI*, which are outputs to A Fair Globalization and, at the same time, inputs to Decent Work.

Figure 6.4 Policy decision tree with intermediate goals.

Next define corresponding social preference and cost functions *V(Y), W(Z), U(X)* with their Cobb-Douglas counterparts

$$
\begin{aligned}
logV(Y) &= \mu logY \\
logW(Z) &= \pi logZ \\
logU(X) &= \nu logX
\end{aligned}
\tag{6.3}
$$

It is then possible to arrange two consecutive sets of fractional programming, as follows

$$
\begin{aligned}
&\max \pi logZ_0/\nu logX_0 \\
&\text{subject to} \\
&\pi logZi/\nu logXi \leq 1, \quad i = 1, 2, \ldots, n \\
&\pi, \nu \geq 0
\end{aligned}
\tag{6.4}
$$

$$
\begin{aligned}
&\max \mu logY_0/\pi logZ_0 \\
&\text{subject to} \\
&\mu logYi/\pi logZi \leq 1, \quad i = 1, 2, \ldots, n \\
&\mu, \pi \geq 0
\end{aligned}
\tag{6.5}
$$

Program (6.4) rates the effectiveness of the policymaking unit (PMU) $i = 0$ in reaching the intermediate goals Z; program (6.5) rates the effectiveness of the same PMU in reaching the ultimate goals Y. Taken together, they portray a cascading causal mechanism, joining together the successive sub-hierarchies into an extended causal process.

Empirical work will identify the set of PMUs that is effective in reaching the intermediate goals, producing a first stage effectiveness ratio equal to 1. Similarly, a second set of PMUs will be identified that is effective in reaching the ultimate goals, producing a second stage effectiveness ratio equal to 1. A few PMUs may actually turn out to be effective at both stages. As such they represent a *nested equilibrium.*

Chapter 7

Competitiveness

The ambitions of economic and social policy seem to increase over time. The reach of the New Deal of the 1930s looks impressive but rather modest today. Even the Swedish "welfare state" of the same era was eventually outdone in far-reaching measures instituted in modern economies. New goals are being formulated and slowly converted into practical policy. The millennium development goals seemed reasonable as we entered the new millennium, but would certainly have seemed a pie in the sky to earlier politicians.

One goal found in the headlines of newspapers these days is a nation's "competitiveness." The idea that a country could and should engage in competitiveness policy is certainly not a new one (we shall review some of the literature on the subject in a moment), but has gained momentum in the age of fiscal "austerity" in the Western world following the 2008 collapse of Lehman Brothers. As countries pursued a policy of spiraling internal devaluation through falling wages and rising unemployment, there seemed to be only one way out of their misery: boosting exports by increasing the competitiveness of the export sector.

So, what exactly does it take for a nation to become "competitive?" Living in an age of rapid innovation in computers and communication, it is natural that many would associate competitiveness with "creativity" and the development of new and revolutionary technology, and the explosive growth of a few darlings on the stock exchanges. International production and distribution patterns are aligned in response to new possibilities. At the same time, Schumpeter's "creative destruction" is at work, closing factories and laying off workers in stagnant companies or entire industries that are no longer competitive. The Economic Commission of the European Parliament and of the Council of the European Union [ECEP and CEU, 2006] put it this way:

> Competitiveness: the capacity of enterprises to adapt quickly to change, exploit their innovation potential and develop high-quality products.

This sounds reasonable, but how might one measure these things?

With a standard term, we want to construct an "index" of competitiveness. It would be constructed as some kind of weighted aggregate of the measures of the various indications or manifestations of competitiveness. That is, one would have to agree on a list of reasonable indicators and collect statistics measuring them, say Y_r, $r = 1, 2, \ldots, s$. Also, one would have to agree on the weights to be attached to each such indicator, μ_r, $r = 1, 2, \ldots, s$. The resulting index would then be

$$\sum_r \mu_r Y_r \tag{7.1}$$

Another approach of considerable interest is to focus on the causal factors presumably explaining competitiveness, that is, on the *inputs* into the competitiveness process rather than the outputs. Again, a list of such inputs $i = 1, 2, \ldots, m$ need to be generated and the weights of each input vi, $i = 1, 2, \ldots, m$ to be determined. One then arrives at the index

$$\sum_i \nu_i X_i \tag{7.2}$$

We shall quote ambitious instances of both index calculations (1) and (2) below. The enumeration of a reasonable list of inputs and outputs is fairly straight-forward. The great difficulty is assessing the weights. Pursuing the general argument of the present book, the obvious alternative is to calculate the *optimal* weights by envelopment analysis. Using conventional linear data envelopment analysis, one would then maximize the ratio

$$\left(\sum_r \mu_r Y_r\right) \Big/ \left(\sum_i \nu_i X_i\right) \tag{7.3}$$

For an effective country, the ratio will equal unity so that the output index equals the input index. But for ineffective countries, using the "output-oriented" formulation of DEA, the ratio exceeds unity — the output index exceeds the input index. Numerical examples will be provided in due course.

The corresponding logarithmic formulation to (7.3) as developed in the earlier chapters of the present book will not be invoked here. Firstly, it is not immediately obvious that the list of all outputs can be identified as policy goals and the list of inputs as policy instruments. In particular, the causes of competitiveness certainly will include factors like natural endowments (oil, say) that are not subject to policy control. Secondly, there would seem to exist no immediate objection to an assumption of constant marginal rates of substitution between the output variables or between the input variables (the main reason for the logarithmic formulations being that such an assumption seemed unrealistic).

The present chapter thus illustrates that logarithmic envelopment is no panacea to the evaluation of economic and social policy. When the outputs under consideration are not all pure goal variables and when the inputs are not all policy instruments controlled by a national policymaker, standard linear envelopment is to be recommended.

7.1 The Manifestations of Competitiveness

The US Council on Competitiveness located in Washington, DC, was founded during the Reagan administration in 1986. Its professed goal is to increase the economic competitiveness of the United States in the global marketplace. It sponsors conferences, seminars, and special events, and publishes annual reports of its findings. During its early years of operation, the US Council was very much influenced by the ideas of Harvard professor Michael Porter, author of two pioneering textbooks on business competitiveness [1980; 1985] that at the time more or less came to define the subject of business strategy in the MBA curriculum at leading business schools. Extending his analysis to the competitive position of entire countries, he published a couple of years later *The Competitive Advantage of Nations* [1990].[4]

Porter dismisses many commonly accepted indicators of competitiveness such as labor costs, exchange rates, economies of scale, or bountiful

[4]For a summary see his article with the same title, *Harvard Business Review*, March, April 1990.

natural resources. Instead he finds the true source of competitive advantage on the national level to be productivity (the value of the output produced by a unit of labor or capital). Productivity depends on both the quality and features of the output and the efficiency with which it is produced. Sustained productivity growth requires that an economy continually upgrade its productivity in existing industries by raising product quality, adding desirable features, improving product technology, or boosting production efficiency. The nation's productive units must develop the capability to compete in more and more sophisticated industry segments and in entirely new industries.[5]

Bela Balassa (1928–1991) was a widely read foreign-trade economist who, in his writings, repeatedly returned to the distinction between inward-oriented and outward-oriented development policies (*Comparative Advantage, Trade Policy and Economic Development,* Harvester Wheatsheaf 1989 and *New Directions in the World Economy*, Macmillan 1989.) In the same spirit, we may distinguish between inward-oriented productivity growth that increases the productivity of import-competing domestic industries, and outward-oriented growth enhancing the productivity of export industries.

Two examples will illustrate. Book and newspaper publishing is a domestic/inward-oriented industry that is currently being shaken by dramatic technological change as new written media are being invented and mass-marketed through the Internet. Established publishing houses are losing competitiveness; they lay off workers and shrink production. New online publishing ventures expand rapidly with distribution of daily newspapers, magazines, and books via so-called tablets; they enjoy a competitive edge. An example of outward-oriented productivity growth is the production and exporting of nursery-raised salmon in countries like Norway, Canada, and Chile. As the price of wild fish skyrockets in the face of depleting ocean stocks, the price of nursery-raised salmon is now within reach of everybody. Salmon is competitive, cod is not.

---

[5]Attempts to nail down the meaning of productivity by calculating the so-called "total factor productivity" remain inconclusive as it cannot be measured directly. (It is obtained as a statistical residual accounting for effects in total output not caused by the measured amounts of labor and capital.) "Competitiveness" is a multi-dimensional concept and so is "productivity" and conventional economics does not know how to handle them.

Inward-oriented competitiveness manifests itself in rapidly increasing real income and real standard of living. Outward-oriented competitiveness manifests itself in growing exports. During its early years of operation, the US Council on Competitiveness collected statistics for a number of countries on three indicators of competitive performance:

(1) the annual growth rate of the real standard of living,
(2) the annual growth rate of real exports (manufactured goods),
(3) exports divided by real manufacturing productivity.

The third of these indicators is a bit more sophisticated than the first two. Considering a given level of manufacturing productivity, one country can still have a competitive edge on another if its manufacturing output possesses superior attributes so that it is more attractive to buyers. Most competition in the modern world is not price-driven, but quality-driven.

Commemorating its two first decades of operations, the US Council [2006] issued the report *The Competitiveness Index: Where the US Stands*, 2006. Porter's influence is still recognizable (he wrote the foreword to the report) but now a new kind of argument is presented:

> Over the past two decades, the nature of global trade has changed in important ways, where goods crossing borders is no longer the only — or even a useful — measure of where value is created. Twenty-first century value creation is linked less to production, exports, and employment — the traditional metrics of industrial competitiveness. [*ibid.*, p. 29.]

Instead, the report argues, value is created through intangible assets flowing through constantly shifting global networks. When a US company ships a half-finished manufactured product to a foreign affiliate for further processing and ultimate sale abroad, it is difficult to determine exactly where the value is being created. The competitiveness of the company is certainly not measured by its contribution to US exports as measured by the official trade statistics.

7.2 Causal Factors of Competitiveness: The World Economic Forum

The World Economic Forum based in Geneva started the calculations of its *Global Competitiveness Index* in 1979 (see the annual *Global*

Competitiveness Reports issued by the Forum). It recognizes twelve "pillars" or causative factors that influence competitiveness:

(1) institutions,
(2) infrastructure,
(3) macroeconomic environment,
(4) health and primary education,
(5) higher education and training,
(6) goods market efficiency,
(7) labor market efficiency,
(8) financial market development,
(9) technological readiness,
(10) market size,
(11) business sophistication,
(12) innovation;

with each of these categories broken down into a large number of subgroups. We shall also refer to these pillars as competitiveness "facilitators." A panel of World Economic Forum advisors in each country affix a competitiveness "value" (on a 1 to 7 scale) to each subgroup, and a constant weight (the weights are the same for all countries, adding to one). The value X_i for each pillar, $i = 1, 2, \ldots, 12$ thus is obtained as the arithmetic weighted average of the values of the subgroups. Finally, using constant weights for each pillar as well, an overall competitiveness index (CI) for the entire country is calculated.

Briefly, the World Economic Forum breaks down the concept of competitiveness into its smallest component causal factors, calculating an overall index as an arithmetic weighted average of the values of the factors. Most of the statistics are drawn from standard international sources like the World Bank, the OECD, the WTO, and the IMF.

7.3 Ranking the Competitive Performance of Nations: DEA

In the remainder of this chapter, we shall present the calculation of an international *competitiveness effectiveness rating* for a large number of countries, applying the classic CCR-model of data envelopment analysis [Charnes, Cooper & Rhodes, 1978]. To facilitate a comparison with the work of the US Council on Competitiveness and the World Economic Forum, we opt to follow the approach and the data employed by these institutions as closely as possible. Thus, we shall define the effectiveness rating as the ratio between a "competitiveness indicator index" (the virtual output of DEA) calculated along the lines of the US Council, and a "competitiveness facilitator index" (the virtual input) calculated along the lines of the World Competitiveness Index of the Forum. Adopting the notation outlined in section 7.1, we shall form the competitiveness indicator index as $\sum_r \mu_r Y_r$ where the indicators $r = 1, 2, 3$ are:

- the annual growth rate of GDP,
- the annual growth rate of exports of goods and services,
- GDP per person employed, in 1990 US dollar equivalents (purchasing power parity).

Comparing with our earlier list, note the following:

- The growth of GDP obviously is not quite the same as the growth in the real standard of living (which presumably should be price-adjusted and measured *per capita*). However, the necessary statistical corrections would have severely limited our country coverage, losing most African and Asian countries.
- Limiting the growth of exports to manufactured goods seems these days no longer to be a valid restriction. International manufacturing has become so intricately bound together with shipments and reshipments of half-finished products between various locations all over the globe that it is almost impossible to discern what are exports of manufactured goods. Also, competitiveness is increasingly manifested, not only in manufacturing, but in the export of services.
- Measuring productivity as GDP per person employed rather than GDP per hours worked is an approximation that again was forced upon us by the unavailability of data. (The difference in coverage is a minor thing compared to other huge problems: What sort of employment are we talking about? In some developing countries, the main male employment is being a soldier engaged in perennial warfare, and government purchases of weaponry for them is counted as government consumption adding to GDP.)

One technical detail: in order to avoid the possibility of negative figures, the two growth rates Y_r, $r = 2, 3$ will be measured as 100 times the annual growth rate in percentage points. Similarly, we form the competitiveness facilitation index $\sum_i \nu_i X_i$ where the facilitators $i = 1, 2, \ldots, 12$ are the twelve World Economic Forum pillars. Given data for $j = 1, 2, \ldots, n$ countries, write the observations of country j as (Y_{rj}, X_{ij}). The two indices as calculated for country j are then $\sum_r \mu_r Y_{rj}$ and $\sum_i \nu_i X_{ij}$, respectively. Next, using the original ratio model of DEA to determine the effectiveness rating for one particular country $j = 0$, consider the fractional programming problem

$$\max \left(\sum_r \mu_r Y_{r0}\right) \Big/ \left(\sum_i \nu_i X_{i0}\right) \tag{7.4}$$

subject to

$$\left(\sum_r \mu_r Y_{rj} \Big/ \sum_i \nu_i X_{ij}\right) \le 1, \quad j = 1, 2, \ldots, n$$

The unknowns in program (7.4) are the virtual weights of the competitiveness indicators $r = 1, 2, 3$ and the virtual weights of the competitiveness facilitators $i = 1, 2, \ldots, 12$. The program maximizes the effectiveness ratio for country $j = 0$, given that the effectiveness ratio for all other countries stays well-defined (less than or equal to one). Choosing the output-oriented version of DEA, one adjoins to (7.4) the norming condition

$$\sum_r \mu_r Y_{r0} = 1. \tag{7.5}$$

In words, the competitiveness facilitator index is by definition set equal to one. The optimal rating of a country then equals the inverted value of virtual input, that is, $1/(\sum_i \nu_i X_{i0})$. If this optimal value is one, the country is said to be "effective." The virtual value of the twelve facilitator pillars then exactly exhausts the virtual value of the three productivity indicators. But if the value of the program is less than one, the value of the indicators falls short of the total value of the pillars and the country is "ineffective."

In the usual manner of DEA, the effective countries together trace a "frontier" of best performance. Ineffective countries lie behind the frontier. Projecting an ineffective country onto the frontier, one finds the improvement in performance of each indicator that should optimally have been possible, thus delivering a diagnostic of the possible shortcomings of each indicator and the scope for improvement necessary to reach effectiveness.

The not least interesting result is the solution values of the virtual weights. In forming its World Competitiveness Index $\sum_i \nu_i X_i$, the World Economic Forum assumes *a priori* known and given weights $\nu_i, i = 1, 2, \ldots, 12$. Here we instead *solve* for the *optimal* weights. Our calculations thus will serve as a check on the realism of the postulated weights applied by the Forum.

7.4 Empirical Results

We report on the results for the output-oriented DEA model with constant returns to scale (the so-called CCR-model based on the Charnes, Cooper and Rhodes pioneering 1978 work). For the outputs $Y_r, r = 1, 2, 3$ we turned to the World Development Index published by the World Bank. Selecting the year 2011 for our study, we obtained satisfactory output data for 91 countries. In order to avoid the possibility of negative numbers, all growth rates were converted to 100+ annual percentage growth rate. For the inputs, The World Economic Forum kindly agreed to share its extensive database with our Swiss foundation The Geneva Consensus. In this manner we obtained the raw (unrounded) data on the inputs ($X_i, i = 1, 2, \ldots, 12$) for the same 91 countries. Most of these data refer to the year 2011 (when recent statistics are not available the WEF uses the most recent data available).

After a number of difficult years, the world economy in 2011 was experiencing a fragile although very unequally distributed recovery:

> ... much of the developing world is still seeing relatively strong growth, despite some risk of overheating, while most advanced economies continue to experience sluggish recovery, persistent unemployment, and financial vulnerability, with no clear horizon for improvement [*ibid*, p. xiii].

We should, therefore, not be surprised to discover that statistics for this year display considerable turmoil on the international scene. All in all 42 countries turned out to be effective (effectiveness rating = 100), a remarkably high number considering the pronounced disparity between

Table 7.1 Competitiveness: Partial list of peers.

Country	Y_1 GDP	Y_2 Exports Growth	(US$ thousands) Y_3 GDP per person employed
Ireland	101.43	105.06	56.75
Angola	103.92	93.65	2.88
Malawi	104.35	104.63	1.84
Moldova	118.65	141.77	14.65
United States	101.80	106.68	68.16
Bangladesh	106.71	129.34	3.97
Italy	100.37	105.90	45.17
Kyrgyz Republic	105.96	115.72	7.22
France	102.03	105.40	52.86
Tanzania	106.45	127.49	1.70

them. Ten of them are listed in Table 7.1. To DEA, these countries are equally "good;" there is no winner among them and no loser.

The list in Table 7.1 includes countries that are both very rich (the United States, France, and Italy) and very poor (Malawi and Tanzania). Yet they all belong to the exclusive group of countries that will serve as "peers" to one or more ineffective countries. Even poor countries can serve as role models (to other countries that may be even poorer)! For instance, Malawi serves as a role model to Senegal which is ineffective.

Turning next to the ineffective countries (49 countries in all), a number of Western European countries turn out to be ineffective: the United Kingdom, Germany, Switzerland, the Netherlands. These are countries clearly suffering from the current financial and economic malaise in the Western world. Several of the most rapidly growing countries in the world are also ineffective: China, Korea, Brazil, India. They demonstrate the birth pangs of chaotic growth.

Table 7.2 presents the output data for the six countries at the top of the list of ineffectiveness, and the six countries at the bottom of it. For each output variable, the table lists both the actual observed value and the projection onto the envelope — the target value representing "best practice." For all countries the target is larger than the actual performance. Such an improvement is indeed possible precisely because the country has been rated as ineffective. Note that the target annual growth of GDP for several

Table 7.2 Competitiveness. Ineffective countries (top and bottom entries of entire list).

Country	Effectiveness rating	Y_1 GDP growth	Y_1 Target	Y_2 Exports growth	Y_2 Target	Y_3 GDP per person employed	Y_3 Target
Pakistan	99.9	102.96	103.03	102.38	105.67	8.30	8.31
Slovenia	99.6	100.71	101.23	106.97	107.44	37.11	37.27
Germany	99.5	103.03	104.86	107.82	108.38	43.28	43.50
Morocco	99.0	104.99	106.05	102.12	106.96	11.22	13.43
Canada	98.8	102.53	103.73	104.58	105.81	49.54	50.12
Japan	98.8	99.43	100.62	99.64	104.12	44.57	47.09
...	...	...	...	...	...	...	...
Kenya	87.2	104.38	119.72	106.62	127.59	2.48	5.83
Hungary	86.1	101.65	118.06	106.34	123.51	20.89	24.26
Peru	85.9	106.86	124.47	108.77	134.22	15.71	18.30
Bulgaria	85.8	101.84	118.70	112.28	130.87	19.20	22.38
Philippines	84.0	103.64	123.40	97.20	130.10	8.60	10.24
Czech Rep.	83.2	101.89	122.45	109.55	131.65	26.70	32.09

countries at the bottom of the table exceeds 120%. How can that be possible when the fastest growth rate of all countries was 118.7%? The answer is that "best performance" is not a simple arithmetic average of results for peer countries. For instance, Kenya's peers with their weights are Angola (0.21), Ghana (0.50), Venezuela (0.09) and Zimbabwe (0.28). Ghana and Zimbabwe are the most important peers but the total of the weights adds up to 1.08, that is, a number exceeding 1.00. This indicates that the projection of Kenya onto the frontier involves not only forming an arithmetic average of the corner points of the optimal facet of the envelope (read: its peers) but also a radial expansion. This kind of result is typical when we estimate the constant-rate-of-scale CCR-model.

Additional detail is provided in Table 7.3, listing the two most important peers for the same countries. Two peers occur more often than the others: Venezuela (six times), Zimbabwe (4 times). This is not because they in any sense were more successful than other peers (they are all rated 100% effective) but because the observations for them are more extreme than the others and thus place them at conspicuous corner points of the envelope. (Although being one of poorest countries in the world, Zimbabwe reported

Table 7.3 Same countries as in Table 7.2, with two most important peers and their weights.

Country	Effectiveness rating	Most important peer and its weight	Second most important peer and its weight
Pakistan	99.9	Mozambique (0.33)	Zimbabwe (0.22)
Slovenia	99.6	Estonia (0.30)	Venezuela (0.25)
Germany	99.5	Sweden (0.42)	Uruguay (0.26)
Morocco	99.0	Ethiopia (0.62)	Zimbabwe (0.17)
Canada	98.8	Ireland (0.34)	New Zealand (0.27)
Japan	98.8	Ireland (0.64)	New Zealand (0.27)
...	...	...	...
Kenya	87.2	Ghana (0.50)	Zimbabwe (0.28)
Hungary	86.1	Venezuela (0.37)	Iceland (0.15)
Peru	85.9	Burkina Faso (0.29)	Venezuela (0.27)
Bulgaria	85.8	Estonia (0.26)	Venezuela (0.26)
Philippines	84.0	Zimbabwe (0.77)	Venezuela (0.23)
Czech Republic	83.2	Venezuela (0.37)	Burkina Faso (0.29)

a growth of 9.4% annual growth of its GDP and a 17.7% annual growth of its exports.[6])

7.5 Competitiveness: Concluding Remarks

We have in this chapter presented yet another example of measuring and ranking the priorities and achievements of economic and social policy, this time looking at the efforts of nations to enhance their international "competitiveness." The effectiveness metric is again formed as the ratio between the social preference of the goals of policy laid down, and the imputed social cost of policy. Our goals of national competitiveness policy were all variations on the concept of productivity; the instruments of policy have all been carefully listed and documented by the World Economic Forum. In the present instance the social preference function and the social

[6]We accepted at face value all statistics provided in the World Development Index published by the World Bank.

cost function were all taken to be linear aggregates, simply multiplying each goal and each policy instrument by a social weight. As in earlier chapters, the weights were determined for each nation by a fractional programming problem maximizing its effectiveness score. Using an "output-oriented" approach, the weights were normalized so that the weighted goal sum equals unity.

We realize that our approach will be viewed by many with skepticism. Two large international organizations, one on each side of the North Atlantic, have for many years been engaged in serious studies of international competitiveness, each one apparently with little contact with the other. The US Council on Competitiveness, drawing on the pathbreaking work of Michael Porter, identifies the goals of competitiveness in terms of the various dimensions of national productivity. The World Economic Forum based in Geneva has assembled an impressive database on twelve "pillars" of factors motivating or promoting competitiveness, here interpreted as potential instruments of competitiveness policy. In our view, these two schools should not be seen as competitive but rather as complementary; they are both equally necessary. A true measure of competitiveness must consider both goals achieved *and* policy instruments employed.

Identifying three dimensions of the productivity goal (output growth, export growth, and GDP per employee), social preference was determined as a weighted amalgam of them. The weights are determined individually for each country in order to maximize its effectiveness rating. Similarly, identifying the twelve dimensions of policy instruments (the World Economic Forum "pillars"), the weighted amalgam of total policy costs selects individual and characteristic weights for each country. This is a far cry from the procedures of the World Economic Forum which assumes the weights of each pillar to be set *a priori* and equal and the same for all countries.

It would of course be possible to analyze our results in greater depth, but at this stage we think it is prudent to limit our report to the general principles of the new metric and leave the details to the future. As we have seen, competitiveness can be analyzed in many ways. The metric proposed here should not be felt intimidating by anybody, it simply identifies a set of nations that have reached optimum and another set of nations that fall short of the demands of equilibrium theory. For each of these latter nations a small group of "peers" is identified which together determine the hypothetical improvements of goal achievements that should be feasible. The peers are not necessarily the masters of the world, but they feature some goal achievements that would be instructive and helpful to others. We believe that such advice would be more helpful than the "take it or leave it" worldwide rankings that the World Economic Forum delivers.

Chapter 8

Disequilibrium and Chaos

While Tinbergen in the early 1950s wrote his pathbreaking treatises on economic policy, a consolidation of the inherited economic theory occurred — the codification of neoclassical theory. A generation of young mathematical economists such as Paul Samuelson, Ken Arrow, Gerard Debreu and Tjalling Koopmans were to formalize the building-blocks of an impressive mathematical idealization of a free market economy. The economic agents in the neoclassical economy are abstract consumers and producers, suspended in time, making the rational decisions of "economic man." Markets are in equilibrium. And, Tinbergen would say, economic policymakers make optimal decisions.

While this theory dominated the economics profession as the 20th century was drawing to its close, a set of revolutionary ideas were promoted by a few dissenting voices, clamoring for greater realism in economics such as evidenced by path-dependency, disequilibrium, and chaos. Here we discuss some of these ideas: how they apply to a theory of economic and social policy, and how the presence of disequilibrium can be demonstrated empirically by envelopment analysis.

The discovery of disequilibrium and the explicit introduction of time (the "arrow of time") in real-world processes of change occurred first in physics and thermodynamics. Economists, too, eventually realized that the processes they study are inherently irreversible. The world changes and we change with it. We cannot go back to the economic conditions ruling in the 1920s or even in the 1960s. New technology is developed. Consumer preferences evolve. Tropical rainforests are razed. The stratosphere becomes polluted with greenhouse gases.

8.1 Path-dependency, Lock-in, Evolution, Creative Destruction

The Santa Fe Institute is an offshoot from the nuclear weapons laboratories and computer laboratories at nearby Los Alamos, offering an opportunity for hard-core physicists and computer jocks to mix with scholars in "soft sciences" like economics and social sciences. The institute has become renowned for its work in the study of complex behavior in mathematical, physical, and living systems.

Discarding the standard notions of equilibrium, economists working at Santa Fe developed a new kind of economic system with "positive feedback," like real estate booms and stock market crashes. Once such systems get rolling, they keep snowballing and feed themselves, up to a point. Positive feedback arises in an economy when there are increasing returns to scale. If the average productions of some firms fall with increasing output, the managers of these firms will find it profitable to expand their scale of operations. Outputs and market shares of individual firms will embark upon a dynamic path of growth.

Examples of positive feedback in economic and social policy can be found in most of the pressing economic and social agenda of the present day. The scramble to develop new green technology is leading to a rapid buildup of both wind and solar power. Once some particular technology, like offshore wind turbines, has been demonstrated as viable, there is a rush to develop these possibilities. The average cost of manufacturing solar cells is falling rapidly; as a result the solar cell industry in China is growing dramatically, and companies and private persons around the world are turning to this new medium of energy generation. There is a wind turbine boom and there is a solar power boom.

Powerful mechanisms often reinforce the positive feedback among a pack of competing firms. There is synergy in the development of high technology. Corporations learn not only from their own experience but also from their competitors. Each manufacturer does not have to invent the wheel all over again. One can climb on others' shoulders, adapt existing technical designs, and take note of what seems to sell for competitors and what does not sell.

Product development is one of the most important occupations of firms in the high technology age. Sometimes product development takes the form of a discrete jump in technology, a Schumpeterian "innovation," but more commonly it is about improving the technological characteristics or the marketing appeal of an already existing product. Modern products are almost invariably multidimensional, that is, they have an entire vector of attributes. Product development enhances the attributes of an existing product or it adds new attributes.

The adoption of a novel technology sets the stage for subsequent product development and innovation. Any one given vintage of technology will eventually be superseded by even more advanced technology. Consider, for instance, the technology chain: dial telephone, touch tone telephone, cordless telephone, mobile phone, "smart" phone (with access to the Internet). The graph of the network buds as new links and new nodes are added hierarchically.

In the short run, budding in the network involves mainly growth at the top hierarchical layer of the network. The network grows at its periphery. But in the long run, as the network expands, what was once the periphery may eventually become the core of entire families of novel technologies. Choices of technology that were once marginal may define the fundamentals of the technologies of the future. As a consequence, choices that once seemed insignificant may eventually turn out be crucial. Technologies become "locked in." As an example, Santa Fe economist B. Arthur [1989] quotes the competition between steam and the internal combustion engine for the propulsion of motor vehicles at the end of the nineteenth century. Once the Otto engine had been chosen, the stage was set for the development of successor technologies like the Daimler engine, the spray carburetor, the honeycomb radiator, the self-starter and so forth. The steam alternative was never pursued.

When self-reinforcing mechanisms are at play, there is little reason to expect the resulting growth path to be orderly and linear. Companies and government entities will scramble to exploit emerging opportunities. New startup companies will enter the fray. Arthur suggested that the resulting dynamic economic system can possess a multiplicity of solutions, that is, a multiplicity of alternative future courses. Many candidates for long term self-reinforcement may exist; the accumulation of small random events early on pushes the dynamics into the orbit of one of these and thus selects a time path that the system eventually settles on.

These technological webs can undergo bursts of evolutionary creativity and massive extinction events, just like biological ecosystems. Consider the invention of the automobile, replacing an older technology, the horse. Along with the horse go the smithy, the Pony Express, the watering troughs, the stables, the people who curried horses, and so on. The whole subnetwork of technologies that depended upon the horse suddenly collapses in what the economist Joseph Schumpeter once called "the gale of creative destruction." It is "creative" because in its wake whole new subnetworks of goods and services would appear, paved roads, gas stations, fast food restaurants, motels, traffic courts, traffic cops, and traffic lights. [Waldrop, 1992, interviewing W. B. Arthur.]

Evolution of new goods and services (and their eventual obsolescence) occurs not only for industrial products but for medical, educational, and government services that are the subject to economic and social policy. New hospital wards built to accommodate the latest medical progress, will eventually need to be refashioned entirely. Entire hospitals are closed down (as happened with most of the tuberculosis sanatoriums one hundred years ago). New university research facilities are being built, but will ultimately need to be refitted to pursue entirely new lines of research. New commercial airports are being built and others are closed down. (When the downtown airport of Oslo closed its doors, a hectic phase of creative destruction set in, building a new high tech city on land formerly occupied by runways.) What will happen to the NASA installations when the private sector takes over all space flight?

Still keeping Tinbergen's policy optimization problem in mind, there is the added difficulty that — not only are the various technologies of generating economic and social services in modern society subject to rapid development — the *political evaluation* of the urgency of these services is also in a continuous path-dependent flux. Scientific knowledge increases — medical breakthroughs occur, genetic engineering leads to new farming opportunities, seismic probes reveal the presence of untapped reserves of oil and gas, improved engineering designs lead to more energy-efficient transport. But the political will to translate such progress into government policy (the willingness to fund extensive inoculation programs in Africa, to permit the sale of genetically modified foodstuffs, to open up arctic waters to oil and gas exploration, to impose mandatory rules on the fuel efficiency of cars sold to the general public) is often hotly debated, and sometimes changes dramatically over time. In language that Tinbergen would have understood: the overall social utility function itself shifts over time. It, too, is path-dependent.

8.2 Diffusion, Self-organization and Chaos

The theory of diffusion in economics has been pursued most energetically in marketing. Marketing economists try to assess and forecast the degree of acceptance by customers of a new product and the level of new product sales. Most diffusion models have their roots and analogies in models of epidemics or in biology and ecology. One of the underlying behavioral premises is that new product acceptance is an imitation process or process of social interdependence. The basic tool of diffusion theory is the diffusion curve. It can be employed to portray the growth of sales of a product over time, such as the annual sales of motor vehicles in the United States. The curve starts out growing quite rapidly, at an approximately exponential rate. Eventually the rate of increase of annual sales tapers off. The market becomes saturated.

To explain rapid growth, one might first try the mathematical hypothesis that the rate of growth of sales stays constant over time. This assumption leads to exponential growth. The diffusion curve is obtained by a simple modification of this argument. In the real world, sales cannot grow without limit. There exists some maximal or potential sales volume at which market saturation occurs. Assume no longer that the rate of growth of sales is constant, but rather that it is proportional to the potential sales volume still left unsatisfied. The solution is the diffusion curve: it begins at an exponential rate, but eventually flattens out (at the saturation level). The curve has a characteristic Sshape. See Figure 8.1.

Use the notation

$$\begin{aligned} t &= \text{time} \\ x_t &= \text{sales (volume at time } t) \\ A &= \text{saturation level} \\ F_t &= \text{the fraction } x_t/A \text{ of the total saturation value reached so far} \end{aligned}$$

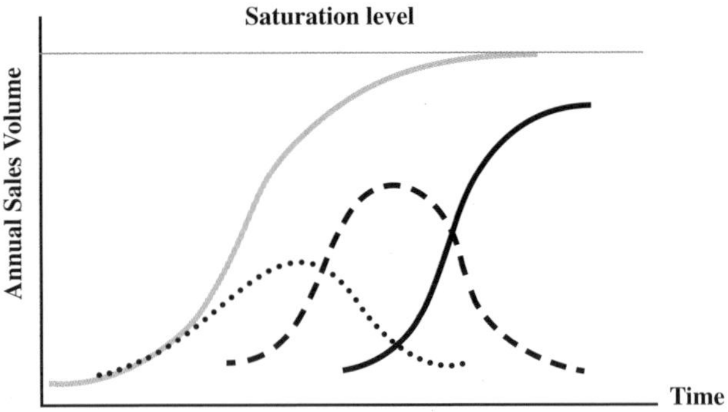

Figure 8.1 The life cycles of successive technology generations.

and the equation of the diffusion equation is

$$F_t/(1 - F_t) = e^{\alpha t} \quad (8.1)$$

where the left hand side is the ratio between current sales and the remaining sales potential. The equation states that this ratio grows exponentially over time, with the growth rate α. Differentiating (1) one gets Verhulst's equation of population growth:

$$dF/dt = \alpha F(1 - F) \quad (8.2)$$

stating that the rate of growth of a population is directly proportional to the current population and the available "food." Inserting $F = x/A$, equation (8.2) can alternatively be written

$$dx/dt = \beta x(A - x) \quad (8.3)$$

where $\beta = A\alpha$. Subtracting a "death term" kx reflecting the gradual obsolescence of a product over time, the same equation reads

$$dx/dt = \beta x(A - x) - kx \quad (8.4)$$

The diffusion curve is formed by a succession of life cycles or "vintages" of individual technologies. As illustrated in Figure 8.1, new waves of product cycles carry the diffusion curve upwards. During the upswing phase of the diffusion curve, new product cycles rapidly enter the market. During the maturing phase, they arrive at a slower pace.

The most well-known model of innovation diffusion is credited to Frank Bass [1969]. Bass divided potential customers for a new product into two classes: innovators and imitators. Sales to innovators grow at their briskest pace when the product is new, but more slowly when adoption becomes more common. Sales to imitators follow the diffusion curve. The Bass paper made a forecast of the timing and magnitude of the peak of sales for color television sets, when only three years of data were available. It proved to be extremely accurate.

The general idea that evolution takes the form of a succession of generations of "species," be it economic species or biological species, is as old as the concept of evolution itself. In the marketplace, a novel and attractive product will capture ("steal") market share that would otherwise have belonged to competitors selling outmoded product designs. The buyers face the opportunity of switching from an earlier product generation to a later one. The same phenomenon occurs in the biological world when dandelions and crabgrass take over a lawn. The capture occurs as a crowding out, the taking of potential living space.

The mathematics of successive generations of species was developed in the 1930s by the Italian mathematician Vito Volterra. His classical treatise is titled, *Lecons sur la Theorie Mathematique de la Lutte pour la Vie (Lessons on the Mathematical Theory of the Struggle for Life).* Here one finds the origin of the modern nonlinear mathematical theory of evolution. Biological evolution occurs among plants and animals, as new species compete for living space. It is irreversible in time. Many of the laws describing the growth, decay, and interaction of biological populations can also be applied to social, economic, and financial systems. Evolution is not always orderly. It can take the form of sudden invasions of new species and the extinction of others.

In 1975, the mathematician J. Yorke was working with a diffusion curve programmed on a computer, examining its development over time. Using a continuous time variable in the mathematical formulation, the standard diffusion curve appeared on the screen, rising quickly at first, and then slowly approaching its saturation level. Replacing continuous time by discrete time (cutting up the time dimension in a series of still segments), equation (8.4) above then reads

$$x_{t+1} - x_t = \beta x_t(A - x_t) - kx_t \tag{8.5}$$

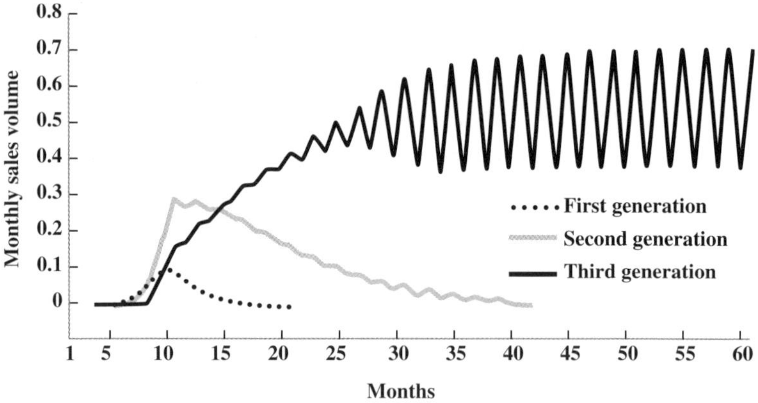

Figure 8.2[7] The possibility of bifurcation: sales statistics for three consecutive product generations. The third generation product starts bifurcating in month 29.

The discrete time path of the diffusion curve converges toward the continuous path. It may temporarily overshoot the saturation level, but eventually zooms in toward the equilibrium value.

The coefficient β turns out to regulate the "boom-and-bustiness" of the dynamic course of events. Changing the parameters of his numerical model slightly, Yorke made a startling discovery. The curve became jittery and "bifurcated" (it split into two). The annual sales volume ended up oscillating between two alternative values, one greater saturation level and another smaller saturation level (Figure 8.2).

Bifurcation indicates that the sales statistics are poised at the "edge of chaos." It is a balancing act between order and full-blown chaos. It is a fleeting moment before the system takes the plunge into disorder. It is the sudden appearance of alternative futures, a forking point along the road of technological advance, such as two competing product designs.

If the parameter of boom-and-bust was increased even further, the discrete path broke up into chaos. It looks unorganized and random. A wild

[7]The diagrams in Figures 8.2 and 8.3 were first presented in Thore [1995]. The computer simulation in Figure 8.2. was set up as follows: Let X be the sales of the first generation, Y the sales of the second generation and Z the sales of the third generation. The initial values were put at X = 0.001, Y = 0.0001, Z = 0.00001 Furthermore, sales in any subsequent month (denoted +1) was assumed to be related to sales in the previous month by the equations X+1=2X(1−X−Y−Z)-0.1X, Y+1=3Y(1−X−Y−Z)−0.25Y, and Z+1=3.75Z(1−X−Y−Z)−0.4Z.

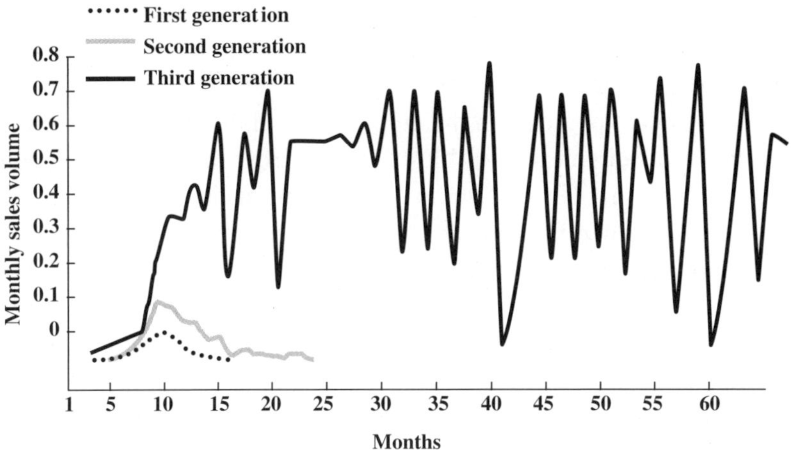

Figure 8.3 Chaos: sales statistics for three consecutive product generations. Sales of the third generation product turn chaotic in months 10–11.[8]

dance. See Figure 8.3. And yet, it has been generated from a very simple and deterministic mathematical rule. Yorke's paper was published in a mathematical journal in 1975. A new science had been born.

Is chaos the same thing as randomness? In our computer simulation, chaos is produced by a few simple nonlinear mathematical equations. The path of the chaotic process over time is determined, point by point, by an exact mathematical formula. It is "deterministic." Randomness, on the other hand, is the result of probability drawings, like the random throw of dice. Chaos looks random but there is order hidden behind the apparent whimsicality.

The concepts of bifurcation and chaos have above been illustrated with examples from the marketing of new products. Clearly, they also extend to social and economic policy and the competitive battle between alternative "vintages" of policy. Consider education policy as formulated by Western pedagogy and the educational alternatives offered (or rather not offered) by militant Muslims, closing schools to all female students. In parts of Afghanistan, Pakistan, and many Muslim countries in Africa, the girl in the classroom is seen as an abomination. As local militia expands their control,

[8]The numerical assumptions are the same as those for Figure 8.2, but the sales for the third generation product have this time been set at $Z+1 = 4.35Z(1 - X - Y - Z) - 0.4Z$.

female students are dismissed and chased home. As the legal government reasserts itself, they are welcome again. A bifurcation of two competing worldviews of educational policy.

The tumultuous events in the euro market in the fall of 2011 provide an instructive example of full-blown chaos. How does a country within the euro zone formulate an "optimal" policy of managing its government debt portfolio, when the cost of issuing Treasury bonds denominated in euros is not only unknown, but swings from the attractive to the prohibitive within seconds? Some of the largest commercial banks in Western Europe were willing to enter into wildly speculative positions — at one moment confident that their own government would bail them out if they collapsed, the next moment struck with fright that the entire euro system would cave in. The disequilibrium processes that swept through the markets were not only irrational but bordered on panic.

8.3 Dissipative Processes and Disequilibrium

Ilya Prigogine was awarded the 1977 Nobel Prize in chemistry for his contributions to nonequilibrium thermodynamics, particularly for his theory of dissipative structures. (See Chapter 3.) He has emerged as the proponent of an evolutionary conception of the world, replacing the Newtonian mechanistic paradigm. He has shown that the behavior of matter under nonequilibrium conditions can be radically different from its behavior at, or near, equilibrium. This difference introduces multiple choices, self-organization, and complex dynamics.

Close to equilibrium, a description of the temporal evolution of a system can be expressed by linear equations. Far from equilibrium, one deals with nonlinear equations, which may lead to bifurcations and to the spontaneous evolution of organized states of matter and the appearance of dissipative structures. As an example of a dissipative structure, consider a pan of liquid heated from below. When the temperature is low, heat passes through the liquid by conduction. As the heat is intensified, regular convection cells appear spontaneously. The liquid boils. Energy is transferred from thermal motion to convection currents. The boiling dissipative structure is radically different from the equilibrium structure of the liquid. It can be maintained in far-from-equilibrium conditions only through a sufficient flow of energy. Yet, it represents order — order at the edge of chaos.

Dissipative structures can be found also in man-made systems such as social and economic policy. Consider the "Arab Spring" of 2011 — virtually every Muslim country suddenly faced waves of social discontent and unrest — as the ruling power elite was challenged by explosive demands for free expression and assembly. Why did these local "convection cells" appear at the same time, causing the entire Middle East to boil? What was the nature of the "energy" that sustained it?

In the book *Self-Organization in Nonequilibrium Systems: From Dissipative Structures to Order through Fluctuations*, G. Nicolis and I. Prigogine [1977] discuss the evolution of ecosystems such as insect societies where each species occupies a niche. The authors draw curves similar to Figures 8.2 and 8.3 above, illustrating that new generations of species (arriving through genetic mutations) are able to exploit the environment ever more effectively. The increasing effectiveness to exploit each resource provides a basis for understanding the notion of "the survival of the fittest" familiar from Darwin's theory.

As in Figure 8.2, the resulting evolution may admit two steady states, simulating the observed regularity of variation in the construction of actual termite nests [*ibid.,* 454–55]. There is ordered behavior (but not equilibrium): self-organization and order through fluctuations.

How do these developments impact on economic theory? For one thing, they show that economists need to consider the arrow of time, irreversible processes, and the possibility of far-from-equilibrium positions. The Newtonian theory of mechanistic and timeless equilibrium theory is not dead, it just needs to be imbedded in an irreversible and evolutionary setting. Similarly, the great achievements of neoclassical economic theory are not dead, but need to imbedded in a setting of technological and financial innovations, increasing returns to scale, path dependency, and the possibility of far-from-equilibrium processes. Economists need to construct a new theory of market formation, where the actors — producers and consumers — are imperfectly adjusted to their theoretical equilibrium. In extreme cases, they may be pursuing individual orbits of hypergrowth, or orbits of eventual extinction. Just as in a dissipative process of boiling water, the actors of the market may collectively form a far-from-equilibrium state of dynamic swarming of the individual cells but maintaining unchanging macro properties — the edge of chaos.

Part I

Appendices

Appendix 1. Numerical Solution: Fractional Programming Model[9]

Explaining the envelopment procedure in the main text of Chapter 2, we arrived at the fractional programming model

$$\begin{aligned}
&\max\ \mu logY_0/\nu logX_0 \qquad\qquad (A.1)\\
&\text{subject to}\\
&\mu logY_j/\nu logX_j \leq 1, \quad j = 1, 2, \ldots, n\\
&\mu, \nu \geq 0
\end{aligned}$$

The purpose of the present appendix is to convert this program into a simple linear program that can be solved with a standard numerical code. We shall also look at the corresponding dual program, in this way obtaining an attractive alternative interpretation of the numerical value of the effectiveness rating of a country. The rating turns out to equal one divided by the factor of possible equiproportional expansion all goal achievements, given the use of policy parameters. All this is contained in Theorems A1 and A2 as expressed below.

In Chapter 2 two different modes of constructing the envelope were explained: the policy-oriented version and the goal-oriented version. Adopting here (and throughout this book) the goal-oriented version, we

[9]To make the present appendix suitable for independent reading, some material already covered in Chapter 2 is duplicated here.

normalize the virtual weights of the goals μ to meet the condition

$$\mu log Y_0 = 1. \tag{A.2}$$

The entire programming problem then reads

$$\begin{aligned} &\min \ \nu log X_0 \\ &\text{subject to} \\ &\mu log Y_j / \nu log X_j \leq 1, \quad j = 1, 2, \ldots, n \\ &\mu log Y_0 = 1 \\ &\mu, \nu \geq 0 \end{aligned} \tag{A.3}$$

A linear programming equivalent is immediately obtained as

$$\begin{aligned} &\min \ \nu log X_0 \\ &\text{subject to} \\ &-\mu log Y_j + \nu log X_j \geq 0, \quad j = 1, 2, \ldots, n \\ &\mu log Y_0 = 1 \\ &\mu, \nu \geq 0 \end{aligned} \tag{A.4}$$

Notice that program (A.4) instructs us to minimize the cost of social policy $U(X)$subject to constraints. We also note that the program delivers an effectiveness rating of the PMU currently being rated that is less than or equal to one (the set of linear inequalities in (A.4) is $\mu log Y_j / \nu log X_j \leq 1$, $j = 1, 2, \ldots, n$; hence, in particular $\mu log Y_0 / \nu log X_0 \leq 1$). But there is no guarantee that program (A.4) generates an effectiveness rating $= 1$. In other words, there is no guarantee that the solution to (A.4) is a position of policy optimum. The imputed value of all goals may fall short of the imputed value of all policy costs.

As illustrated in Figure 2.4, the fractional programming problem (A.4) has a simple and attractive geometrical interpretation. It solves for a point on the effectiveness upper *frontier or envelope* to all given observations $(log X_j, log Y_j)$, $j = 1, 2, \ldots, n$. More precisely, we are in this book concerned with the *upper conical hull* to the given observations, insisting (in the spirit of the original CCR-model, see Chapter 2) that the envelope display constant returns to scale throughout.

Consider now the collection of all the given PMUs plotted in logarithmic space and form the weighted average or *composite* PMU

$$[\Sigma_j(logX_j)\lambda_j,\ \Sigma_j(logY_j)\lambda_j], \tag{A.5}$$

where λ_j is a vector of nonnegative weights (one weight for each observation $j = 1, 2, \ldots, n$) summing to unity. Then any observed PMU with the coordinates $(logX_0, logY_0)$ lies on the *goal frontier or envelope* if there exists no composite PMU so that

$$\Sigma(logY_j)\lambda_j \geq logY_0 \tag{A.5a}$$

$$logX_0 - \Sigma(logX_j)\lambda_j \geq 0 \tag{A.5b}$$

$$\lambda \geq 0 \tag{A.5c}$$

Such a PMU can also be said to be goal-*undominated.* There exists no other composite PMU producing the same goals but using less or the same policy instruments. But if such a composite PMU exists, the observed PMU is *dominated* and it lies below the envelope. In Figure 2.4, point E is dominated. The point E″ uses the same policy instrument X to produce more of the goal Y. E″ is undominated and lies on the envelope.

Next, consider the dual to program (A.4)

$$\max\ \Phi \tag{A.6}$$

$$\text{subject to}$$

$$\Phi logY_0 - \Sigma_j(logY_j)\lambda_j \leq 0$$

$$\Sigma_j(logX_j)\lambda_j \leq logX_0$$

$$\lambda \geq 0$$

$$\Phi \text{ unconstrained}$$

where Φ is the dual to the normalizing constraint $\mu logY_0 = 1$ and each λ_j, $j = 1, 2, \ldots, n$ is the dual to the constraint $-\mu logY_j + \nu logX_j \geq 0$. The dual Φ is a number that may be referred to as the "expansion factor." The duals λ are the virtual weights of the peers forming best practice.

Program (A6) seeks the greatest possible factor of equiproportional expansion of the goals; the first set of constraints $\Phi logY_0 - \Sigma(logY_j)\lambda_j \leq 0$ states that the equiproportionate expansion of the goals $\Phi logY_0$ should be carried out to a point not exceeding best practice $\Sigma(logY_j)\lambda_j$. The second set of constraints states that best practice use of each policy instruments cannot exceed the actual use. This equiproportional scaling up may be thought of as projecting the vector of observed goals onto the envelope.

THEOREM A1. *The effectiveness rating of a country equals the inverse of the maximal possible factor of equiproportional expansion of all goals.*

Proof: By the duality theorem of linear programming (the asterisk indicates the optimal value)

$$\nu^* logX_0 = \Phi^* \tag{A.7}$$

or, which is the same

$$\mu^* logY_0/\nu^* logX_0 = 1/\Phi^* \tag{A.8}$$

where the asterisk in the common fashion denotes the optimal value,

Q.E.D.

Now, if the current observation lies *on* the envelope, no equiproportional expansion of the goal outputs is required. Then $\Phi^* = 1$ and the effectiveness rating of the observation is $= 1$. The observation is effective. But if the observation lies off and below the envelope, some equiproportional expansion $\Phi^* > 1$ of the goals is indeed possible and the effectiveness rating is < 1. The observation is ineffective. This is:

THEOREM A2. *The effectiveness rating* $(A.2)$ *of any instruments-goals observation along the envelope equals 1. Furthermore, using the goal-oriented version program* $(A.3)$*, the rating of all observations lying below the envelope will be less than 1.*

A1.1 *Non-Archimedean infinitesimals*

The careful reader will have noticed a small loophole in the preceding analysis. We have defined the envelope as the locus of undominated points. But the optimal solution to program (A.6) does not necessarily deliver an undominated or effective point. It just solves for the largest possible equiproportional expansion of the goals.

To see what is involved, consider the goal slacks (the slacks between the expanded goals of the PMU currently examined and the hypothetical goal of the composite PMU)

$$s = \Sigma_j(logY_j)\lambda_j - \Phi logY_0 \geq 0 \tag{A.9}$$

and the instrument slacks (the slack between the instrument uses of the actual instrument use of the PMU currently examined and the use of the composite PMU)

$$t = logX_0 - \Sigma_j(logX_j)\lambda_j \geq 0 \tag{A.10}$$

A positive goal slack (A.9) means that there exists a composite best practice PMU generating at least one goal exceeding the maximally expanded goal $\Phi logY_0$. A positive instrument slack (A.10) means that there exists a best practice PMU using a smaller quantity of at least one instrument than the given set of instruments $logX_0$. In either case, the observed PMU is not undominated. Hence, to make sure that the solution to (A.4) is effective one also needs to require all the slacks (A.9) and (A.10) vanish, $s = t = 0$.

To sum up, two conditions need to be fulfilled to make sure that an observed PMU is *effective*, that is, constituting an envelope or frontier point: (i) the efficiency rating $\Phi * = 1$ and (ii) the slacks (A.9-10) vanish. To find out whether it is possible to drive the slacks down to zero, one replaces program (A.4) by

$$\begin{aligned} &\max\ \Phi + \epsilon(s+t) \\ &\text{subject to} \\ &\Phi logY_0 - \Sigma_j(logY_j)\lambda_j + s = 0 \\ &\Sigma_j(logX_j)\lambda_j + t = logX_0 \\ &\lambda, s, t \geq 0 \\ &\Phi \text{ unconstrained} \end{aligned} \tag{A.11}$$

where ϵ is an arbitrarily small positive constant (a so-called non-Archimedean number).[10] The presence of the non-Archimedean constant in the objective function effectively allows the maximization over Φ to preempt the optimization involving the slacks.

[10]The mathematical trick involved here, taking recourse to non-Archimedean infinitesimals, is of course one of the hallmarks of the work of A. Charnes, which he originated in his famous 1952 paper on the possibility of degeneracy in linear programming.

Appendix 2. Data Definitions

EMP: One minus unemployment rate (% of total labor force). Definition: Unemployment refers to the share of the labor force that is without work but available for and seeking employment. Definitions of labor force and unemployment differ by country.

EQUAL: A measure of the equality of the vertical income distribution. Definition: 100% minus the Gini index.

EXP: Exports of goods and services (% of GDP). Definition: of goods and services represent the value of all goods and other market services provided to the rest of the world. They include the value of merchandise, freight, insurance, transport, travel, royalties, license fees, and other services, such as communication, construction, financial, information, business, personal, and government services. They exclude labor and property income (formerly called factor services) as well as transfer payments.

FDI: Foreign direct investment, net inflows (% of GDP). Definition: Foreign direct investments are the net inflows of investment to acquire a lasting management interest (10% or more of voting stock) in an enterprise operating in an economy other than that of the investor. It is the sum of equity capital, reinvestment of earnings, other long-term capital, and short-term capital as shown in the balance of payments. This series shows net inflows in the reporting economy and is divided by GDP.

FORMAL: The degree of monetization of the economy. Definition: Measured as one minus the shadow economy as a percentage of GDP.

GDP and *GROWTH:* Gross domestic product and the annual growth rate of same. growth calculated as current GDP divided by last year's GDP, in percent.

NOPOV: Non-poverty headcount ratio at $2 a day. (% of population). Definition: Population above $2 a day is the percentage of the population living on less than $2.15 a day at 1993 international prices. As a result of revisions in PPP exchange rates, poverty rates cannot be compared with poverty rates reported previously for individual countries. The figure 2.0 signifies a poverty rate of less than 2.0%.

SUB: Subsidies and other transfers (% of government expenditure). Definition: Subsidies, grants, and other social benefits include all unrequited, nonrepayable transfers on current account to private and public enterprises; grants to foreign governments, international organizations, and other government units; and social security, social assistance benefits, and employer social benefits in cash and in kind.

TARIFF: Taxes on international trade (% of government revenue). Definition: Taxes on international trade include import duties, export duties, profits of export or import monopolies, exchange profits, and exchange taxes.

WOM: Women in paid employment as % of total employees. Definition: Paid employment includes persons above a specified age who performed any work at all, in the reference period, for pay or profit (or pay in kind), or were temporarily absent from a job for such reasons as illness, maternity or parental leave, holiday, training or industrial dispute. Unpaid family workers who work for at least one hour should be included in the count of employment, although many countries use a higher hour limit in their definition. Members of the armed forces are typically included among persons employed; however, some countries restrict measurement to civilian employment.

Appendix 3. Data Sources

The World Bank World Development Indicators database: http://data.worldbank.org/ data-catalog/world-development-indicators.

EMP: International Labour Office, Key Indicators of the Labour Market database.

EQUAL: World Bank, Development Research Group. Data are based on primary household survey data obtained from government statistical agencies and World Bank country departments. Data for high-income economies are from the Luxembourg

Income Study database. For more information and methodology, see PovcalNet (http://iresearch.worldbank.org/PovcalNet/jsp/index.jsp)

EXP: World Bank national accounts data, and OECD National Accounts data files.

FDI: International Monetary Fund, International Financial Statistics and Balance of Payments databases, World Bank, Global Development Finance, and World Bank and OECD GDP estimates.

GDP: World Bank national accounts data, and OECD National Accounts data files

NOPOV: Nationally representative primary household surveys conducted by national statistical offices or by private agencies under the supervision of government or international agencies and obtained from government statistical offices and World Bank Group country departments.

SUB and *TARIFF:* International Monetary Fund, Government Finance Statistics Yearbook and data files.

WOM: International Labour Office, Key Indicators of the Labour Market database.

FORMAL: Friedrich Schneider, Andreas Buehn, Claudio E. Montenegro, "*Shadow Economies All over the World. New Estimates for 162 Countries from 1999 to 2007*," Policy Research Working Paper 5356, The World Bank Development Research Group Poverty and Inequality Team and Europe and Central Asia Region Human Development Economics Unit July 2010. In this paper the following more specific definition of the shadow economy is used: the shadow economy includes all market-based legal production of goods and services that are deliberately concealed from public authorities for any of the following reasons: (1) to avoid payment of income, value added or other taxes, (2) to avoid payment of social security contributions, (3) to avoid having to meet certain legal labor market standards, such as minimum wages, maximum working hours, safety standards, *etc.*, (4) to avoid complying with certain administrative procedures, such as completing statistical questionnaires or other administrative forms.

Part II

A Geneva Consensus

by Ruzanna Tarverdyan

Part II

Overview

William W. Cooper's centennial is an appropriate occasion to recall his achievements, recognize his contributions to operations research, and reconsider the powerful potential of data envelopment analysis (DEA). The present volume demonstrates how this technique can serve to underpin transparent global governance aiming at sustainable development goals in an age of globalization.

Bill passed away on June 20, 2012, in Texas. On the same day world leaders gathered in Rio de Janeiro for the Rio +20 conference, accompanied by a crowd of both peaceful citizens and militants, all in their own way affirming their commitment to sustainable development goals. The outcome document, *The Future We Want,* [UN, 2012b] laid the foundation for a new era of partnership for development cooperation. Global deliberations on post-2015 development agenda call for forging a political consensus to fight poverty, inequality, and hunger — along with attaining other global sustainable development goals.

Good strategies for sustainable development integrate and balance many goals where possible, and provide trade-offs between them where necessary. Past strategies have not always succeeded in this respect, even when sustainable development and poverty reduction were the objectives. There is a new consensus among major development partners to move away from input-oriented impact monitoring to output and outcome-based approaches that help shift the emphasis of development programs to development priorities and results.

An integrated analysis of policy goal trade-offs involves a multiple-input and -output framework. Traditional analysis fails to adequately capture the multidimensional character of the problem. Fortunately, data envelopment analysis is ideally suited for the purpose, delivering a metric that ranks the performance of nations or regions according to their ability to marshal economic and social policy to attain a spectrum of desired goals.

Why "Geneva Consensus?" Clearly, the international frameworks for sustainable development are poorly developed. Attaining sustainable development is conditional on the ability to form multidisciplinary and crosscutting global partnerships, tapping into the knowledge and commitment of the international development community — particularly the WTO, ITC, UNCTAD, UNEP, ILO, UNECE, and other UN Agencies and international organizations based in Geneva. In partnership with the World Bank, IMF, OECD, and other multilateral international organizations, Geneva is best-placed for providing a new forum where Global Decision Makers may dialogue on key policy issues and monitor the performance of nations toward agreed international agendas.

The term "consensus" is derived from the Latin *cōnsentiō* (feel together; agree), a fusion of *cōn-* (together) and *sentiō* (sense; perceive; feel) — with *neutrality* being prerequisite. Switzerland has historically been a global center for accommodating fair, neutral outcomes of the most sophisticated political decisions, in the spirit of solidarity. Neutrality is a foreign policy norm for Swiss authorities and it has served as a model for others. What is commonly considered as *risk* is the impact of the environment within the system's thinking and its reciprocal influence on the system. Within that context, Switzerland's neutrality liberates any global decision-making from such risk.

I should like to conclude with the words of Jean Jacques Rousseau. In his *Discourse on the Origin and Foundation of Inequality Among Mankind* which he dedicated to the state of Geneva in 1755, he wrote:

> It is, perhaps, in the power of the city of Geneva alone, to produce the edifying example of so perfect an union subsisting between its clergy and men of letters. And it is in great degree, on their wisdom, their known moderation, and on their zeal for the prosperity of the State that I build my hopes of its constant and perpetual tranquility.

Chapter 9

Beyond GDP

> A country's economic growth may be defined as a long-term rise in capacity to supply increasingly diverse economic goods to its population, this growing capacity based on advancing technology and the institutional and ideological adjustments that it demands. All three components of the definition are important.
>
> *Simon Kuznets*, Nobel Memorial Lecture, 1971

9.1 Recognizing the Limitations of GDP

Since the inception of macroeconomic theory in the 1930s, Gross Domestic Product (GDP) has played the role of one of the most important statistical indicators of societal performance in national accounts. Even while developing the concept and definition of GDP, in a 1934 report to the US Congress, Simon Kuznets cautioned that it did not measure "welfare." Again, in his 1971 Nobel memorial lecture, he reiterated that "the welfare of a nation can scarcely be inferred from a measurement of national income." Yet, while the limitations of were quickly recognized, it has been widely used as a measure of national welfare in proxy for other non-measured phenomena reflecting overall societal progress. Thus, the challenge to measure societal progress beyond economic and financial indicators such as the GDP has been at the center of various national and international studies for many years.

Kuznets listed the following six characteristics of modern economic growth based on conventional measures of national product and its components, population, labor force, *etc.*

Aggregate growth rates

- The high rates of growth of *per capita* output and of population in developed countries—both being large multiples of the previous rates observable in these countries and of those in the rest of the world.
- The rate of rise in productivity, *i.e.*,of output per unit of all inputs, is high, even when we include among inputs other factors in addition to labor, the major productive factor.

Structural transformation

- Major aspects of structural change include the shift ... to non-agricultural pursuits and, recently, away from industry to services; a change in the scale of productive units, and a related shift from personal enterprise to impersonal organization of economic firms, with a corresponding change in the occupational status of labor.
- The closely related and extremely important structures of society and its ideology have also changed rapidly. Urbanization and secularization come easily to mind as components of what sociologists term the process of modernization.

International spread

- The economically developed countries, by means of the increased power of technology ... have the propensity to reach out to the rest of the world — thus making for one world in the sense in which this was not true in any pre-modern epoch.
- The spread of modern economic growth, despite its worldwide partial effects, is limited in that the economic performance in countries accounting for three-quarters of world population still falls far short of the minimum levels feasible with the potential of modern technology.

This list foreshadows a larger search for metrics with a wider coverage than Gross Domestic Product (GDP), which will be reviewed in a moment. Discussing structural change, Kuznets further pointed out that "the continuous disturbance of pre-existing relative positions of... economic groups is pregnant with conflict — despite the rises in absolute income or product common to all groups." He hoped for a flexible political and social framework to help accommodate rapid structural change and resolve the conflicts that it generates, while encouraging the growth-promoting groups in society. He also reflected on the social impact of modern economic growth, stating that "many of these effects are of particular interest, because they are not reflected in the current measures of economic growth."

Stakeholders in economic development acknowledge both the strengths and weaknesses of GDP. As a key indicator of the economic performance of the market economy, it is of essential use to conduct economic policy; yet it cannot be used to measure societal progress. Indicators for non-economic dimensions of development — such as poverty and social exclusion, risks and sustainability, and care for the environment — must complement GDP to avoid policy missteps. Alternative concepts have been tested and are increasingly used for policymaking at regional, national, and international levels.

9.2 The Search for a More Meaningful Metric

To address the distributional shortcomings of GDP, the idea of social accounting was suggested already in the 1960s. In the following decade, several initiatives were launched aimed at correcting national accounts aggregates for environmental and other non-market factors. This also meant raising concern from the national level to the global arena:

- 1972: The Club of Rome published its report, *Limits to Growth,* presenting a Malthusian confrontation between limited resources and the growing population [Meadows, *et al.*, 1972].
- 1972: Participants of the UN Conference on the Human Environment held in Stockholm declared that economic development and environmental quality must be managed in a mutually beneficial way.
- 1973: Nordhaus and Tobin developed their Measure of Economic Well-being (MEW).
- 1974: Hueting proposed the Sustainable National Income (SNI) measure.

There is universal acknowledgment that GDP as a measure of production does not reflect issues such as environmental sustainability and social inclusion. It is perfectly natural within any statistical system that a metric developed for one particular purpose will be ill suited for another. Confusion might then easily occur. The basic question is: What do analysts and policymakers want to measure? While GDP is useful to measure the levels of market activity, it is not a measure of well-being. Clearly, a set of indicators to measure social and environmental progress (distinct from economic performance) requires tools that reflect the multidimensional nature of the notion of "progress." Typically, collections of indicators to measure "progress" describe average conditions of people living in different countries and regions. The timing of measurement is also important, *i.e.*, the given interval (such as a year) for measuring flows or changes in those flows.

The concept of "progress" made an international breakthrough with The Brundtland Report, *Our Common Future* [UNWCED, 1987], which refined the conceptualization of sustainable development and widened it beyond environmental concerns to include social aspects at national and international levels. At the same time, consideration of environmental problems led to a review of the naturally acidified environment and its effect on health. The timely availability of social and environmental indicators is still a major concern, and these efforts have not yet been incorporated into commonly accepted macro indicators.

9.2.1 *The human development index and beyond*

In 1990, another major milestone was realized in the search for alternatives or complements to GDP when the UN created the "human development index" (HDI). While it is a quite simple index that synthesizes only a limited amount of information, the HDI has remained one of the few regularly compiled indexes used by international organizations for systematic cross-country comparisons. To balance comparisons based on GDP per capita in PPP (purchasing power parities), HDI extends the analysis to include two major dimensions of development and progress — a nation's *health* and its *educational achievement*. Health is measured by life expectancy at birth; educational achievement is measured through the average adult literacy rate (with the weight 2/3) and the student enrollment rate (weight 1/3). The three dimensions (economic prosperity as GDP, health, and education) are then given equal weights in the overall index. Since its first publication, possible modifications to these variables have been widely discussed.

The UNDP is committed to further develop the HDI as a general index of sustainable human development, and the experience gained from constructing the HDI has played an important role in raising international awareness of essential non-economic dimensions of the quality of life. This set the stage for the UN summit held in Rio de Janeiro in 1992 to introduce the notion of sustainable development into the policy debate ("Agenda 21"). The need for statistical documentation also became clear. Today, an updated version of the HDI now includes measures of the harmonious or consistent human development of a nation beyond longevity, knowledge, and the standard of living.

Since the 1992 summit, international and supranational organizations such as the European Union, the European Commission (Eurostat), the Organisation for Economic Cooperation and Development (OECD), and the World Bank have launched large-scale projects to measure sustainable development or societal progress. A list of major international initiatives undertaken to measure sustainable development and related concepts is presented below:

- 1992: Commission for Sustainable Development (UN)
- 2001: European Union Strategy for Sustainable Development (EC)
- 2005: Working Group on Statistics for Sustainable Development UNE CE-OECD-Eurostat)
- 2007: GDP and Beyond (EC)
- 2008: Measurement work on sustainable development, well-being, and social progress (OECD)
- 2009: Stiglitz-Sen-Fitoussi Report (France)
- 2010: Sponsorship group on measuring progress, well-being, and sustainable development (EC)
- 2011: BRAINPOoL (Bringing Alternative Indicators into Policy) consortium across Europe
- 2012: E-frame (EC)
- 2012: Rio +20 Conference (UN)

In 2001 the OECD first addressed measurement challenges in the field of sustainable development and well-being. A report titled, *Sustainable Development — Critical Issues*, summarizes the results of a three-year project. In 2003 the OECD, with the UN, the EC, and the IMF published a *Handbook on Integrated Environmental and Economic Accounting,* proposing an accounting framework and methodologies for correcting national accounts for environmental degradation and resource depletion. In 2006, a further OECD report, *Alternative Measures of Well-being,* discussed the limits of GDP as a welfare matrix. The OECD also organized a series of conferences on "Statistics, Knowledge, and Policies" (at Palermo in 2004, Busan in 2009, and New Delhi in 2012) aiming to shape a global consensus on the need to strengthen statistical work in this field. Following a 2007 forum in Istanbul, the OECD-hosted "Global Project on Measuring the Progress of Societies" was established.

In November 2007, the European Commission jointly with the European Parliament, the Club of Rome, the Worldwide Fund for Nature and the OECD organized the "Beyond GDP Conference" with the participation of the major stakeholders in the EU institutions, its member states, the research community, statistical offices, and civil society — where a consensus was reached on the need for more adequate metrics.

9.2.2 *The Sarkozy commission*

With the increasing integration and globalization of national economies as manifested by large inward foreign direct investments, capital and trade flows, and intensified labor mobility, the adjustments of GDP for the relations of a nation with the rest of the world have become an important issue. In February 2008, French president Nicholas Sarkozy asked J. Stiglitz, A. Sen, and J. P. Fitoussi to head a commission to address the prevailing dissatisfaction with the present state of statistical information about the economy and society. This "Commission on the Measurement of Economic Performance and Social Progress" or Sarkozy Commission, was charged to identify the limits of GDP as an indicator of economic performance and social progress, examine the problems in measuring GDP, and consider which additional information might deliver more relevant indicators of social progress.

According to the Sarkozy commission, the conventional measure of the value-added produced by resident units (or GDP per capita) is an imperfect proxy of the income at their disposal, indicating instead, how much economic agents can consume immediately or invest in the future. In countries employing a large community of migrant workers who transfer their wages to their respective homelands, GDP and gross national income can differ substantially. The same applies to property income, dividends, and interest arising from domestic production that is then transferred to non-resident owners of the domestic productive units.

Calculations of gross national income (GNI) and gross disposable income (GDI) of an economy can also be problematic. Formally, GNI is defined as GDP minus net taxes on production and imports, and compensation of employees and property income payable to the rest of the world, plus the corresponding items receivable from the rest of the world. To adequately reflect the gross disposable income of the economy, other current transfers to and from the rest of the world should also be taken into account, including the payments of taxes on income and property, social contributions, and social benefits.

In its report, the Sarkozy commission presented the strengths and weaknesses of the current definition of GDP. As noted by the commission, the inadequacy of GDP as a welfare indicator and as an index for measuring socioeconomic progress has commonly been referred to in the public debate. There is a widespread acknowledgment that GDP suffers from two major weaknesses [Afsa, *et al.*, 2008]:

- Being a monetary aggregate, GDP pays little or no attention to distributional issues, elements of human activity, or well-being (for which no direct or indirect market valuation is available).
- GDP measures productive flows and, as such, ignores the impact of productive activities on stocks, including stocks of natural resources.

9.3 Recent Progress

The UN has regularly reviewed a *system of national accounts* (SNA) — a consideration of acknowledged national strengths and weaknesses — and drawing on research, practical experience, and international standards for business and public accounting. The improved "SNA 2008" standard has features that fall into five groups: assets, the financial sector, globalization and related issues, the general government and public sectors, and the informal sector. This standardized approach ensures comparability between countries for global research and analysis.

In 2009 the European Commission issued the document, *A Roadmap for Action: GDPand Beyond — Measuring Progress in a Changing World,* setting out short- and medium-term actions that might lead to the forming of indicators that complement GDP and provide the knowledge base for effective and coherent policymaking:

- *Action 1:* As GDP growth figures do not provide sufficient information about social and environmental outcomes, top-level indicators on environmental protection and quality-of-life should be developed.
- *Action 2:* For policymaking and public debate, complementary environmental and social indicators need to be available together with GDP; the timeliness of such indicators needs to be improved.
- *Action 3:* GDP per capita and its growth over time does not tell how economic benefits are shared within a society. To enable a debate on equity and fairness, it is necessary to know the distribution between regions and social groups of income, health, education, and environmental quality.
- *Action 4:* GDP growth rates do not indicate whether economic development is sustainable. Tools need to be developed to measure and communicate overall sustainability.
- *Action 5:* Traditional macro indicators such as GDP do not measure environmental or social outcomes. Current accounting should be expanded to include environmental and social issues.

In 2011 in the context of the OECD's 50th anniversary, the "OECD Better Life Initiative" was launched. Its main outputs were presented in a report, *How's Life?* that included a list of well-being indicators based on a framework structured around eleven dimensions (housing, income, jobs, education, environment, civic engagement, health, life satisfaction, safety, and work-life balance). A web-based interactive tool, *Your Better Life Index,* was launched at the same time. Further work to advance the measuring of well-being and green growth is underway under the auspices of the OECD Committee on Statistics.

On the academic side, economists have shown an interest in constructing measures of well-being, life satisfaction, and happiness. Recent literature on the subject recognizes that the relation between subjective well-being and monetary income is only partial. Current international initiatives include the OECD "Better Life" initiative (measuring well-being and societal progress), its "Green Growth" strategy, and the program "Toward a Green Economy." There is a World Health Organisation initiative on the "Measurement of and Target-setting for Well-being." In June 2012, the OECD, in collaboration with Eurostat and the European Statistical System, organized a European conference on "Measuring Well-being and Fostering the Progress of Societies." Some recent indicator sets cover the subject of sustainable development, even employing participatory approaches at the local level.

The fourth OECD World Forum on "Measuring Progress for Well-being and Development" in New Delhi in October 2012 similarly confirmed the desire to measure societal progress for people's sustainable well-being. Also in 2012, the UN Statistical Commission adopted the System of Environmental Economic Accounting as the international statistical standard — a multipurpose conceptual framework for understanding interactions between the economy and the environment, and for describing stocks and changes in stocks of environmental assets.

Thus the search for a more meaningful metric continues to move forward. A major outcome of the 2012 Rio +20 Conference was the launching of a process to develop a set of Sustainable Development Goals for the year 2015 and beyond, building upon the experience gained from the millennium development goals.[11] The document, *The Future We Want,* [UN, 2012b] summed up the results of the Rio +20 conference on sustainable growth and included a section *Beyond GDP*. Paragraph 38 addressed this message to the official statistical community:

> We recognize the need for broader measures of progress to complement gross domestic product in order to better inform policy decisions, and in this regard we request the United Nations Statistical Commission, in consultation with relevant United Nations system entities and other relevant organizations, to launch a program of work in this area, building on existing initiatives.

To meet this request, the UN Statistical Commission set up a "Friends of the Chair" group in February 2013. The commission is now initiating work on global-level indicators to complement GDP.

[11]The World Bank on the same occasion launched an initiative to account for the natural capital resources of the world.

9.4 An Indicator Pyramid

Indicators have traditionally been used as tools to monitor progress in economic, social and environmental areas and for informed policy target-setting. In the publication, *Communication on Europe 2020,* issued by the European Economic and Social Committee (EESC) in 2013, indicators are defined as "quantitative variables measured or calculated which, individually or as part of a set, allow obtaining as much valid empirical information as possible on a specific matter." Traditionally, the responsibility for indicator definition and use lies with the policymakers; the statistical system only guarantees the quality of the underlying data.

An indicator set consists of indicators showing the reality in all its complexity: the state of society, its social, economic, and ecological connections, and its development over time and space. When measuring an issue as broad and complex as societal progress, the EESC presents the indicator construction as a process involving various actors that necessarily cope with potentially conflicting goals of different disciplines: a balance must be struck between statistical measurability, scientific consistency, credibility/objectivity, and political relevance.

At the base of the indicator pyramid there are the *basic data* on selected specific topics, which are collected by subject-related surveys or — as in the case of the environment — physical measurements. The basic data can be used in many ways for specialized planning, research, and monitoring purposes. At the middle level of the pyramid are *indicators* that are more aggregated or more selective in terms of their subject matter; they may be integrated into sets of indicators, *e.g.*, indicators. The top of the data pyramid is occupied by *macro indicators* (sometimes referred to as summary indicators). Key aggregates and composite indicators at the top reflect specific statistical information.

9.5 Composite Indicators

Composite indicators can be useful for comprehensive analyses of trends of socioeconomic conditions within and between countries. A type of macro indicator, composite indicators are traditionally used to help measure multidimensional and complex phenomena — by replacing nonmeasurable phenomena with intermediate, but measurable, objectives.

A composite indicator is formed by aggregating several elementary indexes over a broad spectrum of dimensions describing the subject (whether human development, well-being, environmental sustainability, *etc.*) The component-indicators have no common unit of measurement and no obvious weighting method usually exists. The distinctive features of composite indicators relate to the domains covered, the normalization methodology used, and the weights used for aggregation.

The 2008 OECD *Handbook on Constructing Composite Indicators* provides detailed instructions for constructing composite indicators and discusses methodological approaches for constructing aggregate measures. For each step, decisions need to be made, based on expert judgment. The last two decades have seen remarkable advance in methodology and statistical work to measure sustainable development. A number of meaningful indicators have been developed by international institutions and non-government organizations. Composite indicators proposed in the academic literature also help place the measurement of sustainable development high on the agenda of national and international institutions. A recent inventory cataloged almost 300 composite indicators from the fields of economics, social studies, the environment, globalization, and technology. Some influential composite indicators are:

- 1989: Index of Sustainable Economic Welfare [Daly & Cobb]
- 1992: Ecological Footprint [Rees]
- 1993: Genuine Savings [Pearce & Atkinson]
- 1995: Genuine Progress Indicator [Cobb, *et al.*]
- 1999: Sustainable Net Benefit Indicator [Lawn & Sanders]
- 2002: Index of Economic Well-being [Osberg & Sharpe]
- 2005: Environmental Sustainability Index (ESI) and an Environmental Performance Index (EPI) [Esty, *et al.*]
- 2005: Living Planet Index (LPI) [Loh, *et al.*]
- 2008: Sustainable Society Index (SSI) [van der Kerk & Manuel]
- 2010: Happy Planet Index (HPI) [Marks]

To cope with existing differences, the UN Commission for Europe (acting through its statistical office Eurostat) and the OECD joined efforts to establish a task force to develop a harmonized conceptual framework to measure sustainable development. On May 27, 2013 the task force issued *A Framework and Suggested Indicators to Measure Sustainable Development* — a report that was endorsed the following month by the Conference of European Statisticians (a body representing about 60 countries). The proposed framework organizes a large number of indicators and presents the information in a concise manner for statistical experts, development practitioners, and policymakers.

While composite indicators are popular among academia and environmentalist groups, policymakers' opinions diverge between the use of indicator sets and the use of composite indicators to guide policies. The Commission task force underscored the importance of trans-boundary impacts at the current stage of globalization, stressing that relationships between countries are becoming more and more important. It stated that a major challenge in identifying an appropriate approach to measuring sustainable development lies in choosing between composite indicators and indicator sets. Except for the World Bank, which relies on composite monetary indicators in its research on sustainable development [World Bank, 2011], nearly all international organizations and national statistical offices currently use indicator sets.

9.6 Empirical Production/Transformation Functions

The use of aggregate production functions has been the major "hardware" in the theory of economic growth. The production function is an abstract mathematical relationship that describes the quantity of output as a function of the quantity of input, assuming technical efficiency — the maximum output possible for every feasible combination of inputs. It relates a nation's output of goods and services to the input of capital and labor, identifying the accumulation of physical capital, investment in human capital, and technological progress as the driving forces behind aggregate production.

Recent developments identify the important determinants of the productive process to include: management practices, geographical factors, protection of property rights, public policies toward market regulation and macroeconomic stabilization, social insurance, and conflict management. But while such institutional determinants shape the "rules of the game," they are not captured by the traditional production function. Beyond the notion of a production function, links of social factors to human well-being also need to be considered. A generalized and multidimensional "transformation function" would relate a nation's development outcomes to various inputs that go beyond capital and labor (management practice, institutions, *etc.*) Yet the exact functional relationship between such inputs and the outputs may be unknown, even while clear empirical evidence supports such transformation.

In conventional microeconomic theory the specification of a production function determines the nature of the input-output relationship in an organization. The underlying assumption is then the existence of a functional transformation technology that determines what maxi-mum amount of outputs can be produced from a given combination of inputs (or alternatively, the minimum combination of various inputs needed to produce a given level of outputs). However, as observed by Seiford and Thrall [1990], "This description of the production technology would be provided by the production function, if it were known." In reality the production/transformation function is not known.

A distinguishing feature of DEA is an absence of assumptions about the underlying functional form relating independent and dependent variables. No theoretical relationship is assumed for DEA. It is a "black-box" technique that can be used when there is insufficient knowledge or lack of consensus on the nature of causal relationships. Only data are needed — observations about the various inputs and their magnitudes and about the resulting output variables and their magnitudes. DEA constructs a piecewise empirical production frontier from the observed data. DEA can handle multiple inputs and outputs that are interacting in complex and unknown ways and may be measured in different units.

By "empirical" function [Charnes, *et al.,* 1983] we shall mean a vector function whose values are known at a definite number of points and whose values at other points in its domain are constructed by linear (usually convex) combinations of values at known points. The points in the domain are "inputs," the component values of the vector function "outputs."

9.7 Why DEA?

Data envelopment analysis sharpens the evaluative features of mathematical programming to assess actual accomplishments and deliver superior management information. DEA is an analytical system acclaimed to be "a leading-edge method of performance measurement that supports benchmarking, continuous improvement, and strategic analysis." One can only agree with Bouysou [1999] that "DEA can safely be considered as one of the recent success stories" in operations research.

For the purpose of DEA, observations are collected for a finite number of entities called decision making units (DMUs), such as private firms, hospitals, or (as in our case) entire countries. The construction of a typical DEA model will then involve the following steps:

- determining the input and output variables;
- choice of optimization orientation — input minimization or output maximization (in the present volume output maximization is usually assumed);
- possible weight restriction (see further below);
- the use of cross-section data or longitudinal data.

The list below enumerates reasons why DEA is well suited to be used for policy impact assessment at the national or even global level:

- DEA reveals frontier rather than central tendencies.
- DEA does not require explicit assumptions about functional forms or relative weights to obtain its results.
- DEA copes with information asymmetries; it is useful for uncovering relationships that would remain hidden from other methodologies.
- DEA can handle multiple non-commensurate socioeconomic variables interacting in complex and unknown ways, when there is insufficient knowledge of causal relationships or a lack of consensus on alternatives. DEA can be used to address managerial and economic issues providing useful results for conducting *ex-post* evaluations of the performance of the DMUs, and thus enable decision makers to agree upon *ex-ante* measures directed at improving their performance.
- DEA is an integrated approach to multiple criteria decision making. It establishes benchmarks, measures DMU performance compared to these benchmarks, and informs how benchmarks can best be reached.
- DEA will provide answers to the following questions:
  - Who are the best-in-class decision-makers managing to perform better under the same conditions?

— How well is a decision maker doing relative to the others — not relative to a theoretical maximum but in *real life*?
— Whom could a decision maker learn from?
— What would be its target levels of observed parameter values?
— Where and how much could it improve?

DEA is a benchmarking tool that evaluates a population of decision making units (countries in our case) in their performance in converting input to outputs. The purpose of the analysis is to identify the countries that most effectively transform their inputs to outputs. These units are located on the effectiveness frontier. The remaining units, falling behind the frontier, are deemed ineffective.

The efficiency score of DEA is 1.00 for frontier points; the virtual output then equals virtual input. It is less than one for subefficient points located behind the frontier (virtual output falling short of virtual input). The frontier (envelope) itself consists of the efficient observations (with scores equal to one) and the surface of the convex hull enveloping them. Frontier points are referred to as "best practice" or "benchmarks." Any best practice point can be written as a linear combination of its "reference" units or "peers" (*e.g.*,the corner points of the current frontier facet). For a country that falls behind the frontier, DEA calculates the additional output that the unit might have produced with best practice, which is the target for an inefficient unit — found by projecting the inefficient unit radially to the frontier (stepping up all outputs in the same proportion while using the same inputs). The peers identify "role models" from which a country should be able to learn how to improve its performance. DEA assumes that data are error free and that performance differences of the DMUs are due to different resource mixes and managerial effectiveness.

In conclusion, DEA's efficiency scores and the envelopment frontier are precise — based on real observation, rather than estimations. DEA calculations focus on individual observations in contrast to population averages, and they produce a single aggregate measure for each country in terms of its utilization of input factors (independent variables) to produce desired outputs (dependent variables). Other attractive features include:

- DEA can simultaneously utilize multiple outputs and multiple inputs, each being scaled in its own units;

- DEA can be adjusted for the presence of exogenous variables and it can incorporate categorical variables;
- DEA calculations are value-free and do not require specification or knowledge of any priory weights or prices for the inputs or outputs;
- DEA makes no assumptions regarding the functional form of production/transformation relationship;
- DEA can accommodate personal judgments when so desired.

Chapter 10

Beyond the Washington Consensus

> We need a new Geneva consensus ... for the opening up of trade that takes into account the resultant cost of adjustment ... . We need to reform globalization with a clear view to enhancing the development of social, economic and ecological aspects of humanity.... Trade opening is necessary, but it is not sufficient in itself.... Humanizing globalization means that we must take care of the victims of globalization. To achieve this, global solutions must be sought for addressing the negative impact of globalization at all levels — individual, community, and universal levels.
>
> *Pascal Lamy*, Director-General, WTO, Santiago 2006

10.1 The Washington Consensus

In world history the 1980s will remain the decade of three world leaders: Thatcher, Reagan, and Gorbachev. Together they demonstrated the importance of personal leadership for the future of nations and for humanity at large. The liberalization and deregulation policies they initiated and pursued launched a new course in international affairs: the era of globalization. With the collapse of the Soviet empire and the disintegration of the former Council for Mutual Economic Assistance that had been founded in 1949 as an alternative to the Marshall plan for the Soviet satellite states in Eastern Europe, the bankruptcy of the Soviet state-regulated socialist economic system became apparent to everybody. Under the aegis of the United Nations (UN), the newly liberated countries joined the large family of international institutions, embarking on a process of accession to the World Trade Organization's General Agreement on Tariffs and Trade (GATT) to be able to benefit from the fruits of open global markets. Inspired by the triumph of market-oriented economic theories over theories advocating government ownership or control, a widespread process of privatization, competition, and agreements to lower trade barriers commenced globally.

The relationship between globalization and development has been one of the most challenged issues in economic policy in recent decades. The Washington Consensus as formulated by the British economist John Williamson [1990] refers to a set of broadly free market economic ideas such as free trade, floating exchange rates, free markets and macroeconomic stability. At the time, the consensus expressed the general economic philosophy of prominent economists and international organizations in Washington DC including the IMF, the World Bank and the US Treasury. The underlying assumption of the consensus was that trade openness is beneficial and indeed essential for the growth and development of a developing country. In order to open such economies to favorable development, it was suggested that they liberalize their imports and orient production toward exports to ensure faster growth.

The term was coined in 1989 in a background paper presented by Williamson for a conference that the Institute for International Economics convened to examine the extent to which old prescriptions of development economics that had governed Latin American economic policy since the 1950s, were being swept aside by a new set of ideas that had long been deemed appropriate within the OECD. Williamson presented a list of ten groups of policy interventions (ten commandments) that he believed practically everyone in Washington agreed were needed to be implemented in Latin America. This, then, was the Washington Consensus. By implication, senior members of the Congress, the administration, the international financial institutions in Washington, the economic agencies of the US government, the Federal Reserve Board, and the think tanks would all subscribe to these ideas.

The policy reforms aimed at initiating industrialization and import substitution. According to Williamson, the original conception of the consensus was founded on three big ideas: a market economy, trade liberalization and openness to the world, and macroeconomic discipline. The ten reform agenda items are:

(1) fiscal discipline to eliminate public deficits;
(2) a change in the priorities of public spending: withdrawal of subsidies and increased spending on health and education;

(3) tax reform: broadening tax bases and reducing tax rates;
(4) positive real interest rates determined by the market;
(5) exchange rates determined by the market guaranteeing their effectiveness;
(6) liberalization of trade and opening of the economy (remarkably, however, Williamson did not include the liberalization of capital flows);
(7) no restrictions on foreign direct investment;
(8) privatization of public enterprises;
(9) deregulation of economic activity;
(10) a solid guarantee of property rights.

Elaborating on these points, Williamson later [2008] made the following additional observations:

- *Fiscal discipline.* At the time, almost all countries in Latin America had run large government deficits leading to balance of payments crises and high inflation. As a result, considerable capital flight to abroad was occurring, deepening domestic levels of poverty.
- *Reordering public expenditure priorities.* This suggested switching public spending patterns toward policy measures that would both stimulate growth and alleviate poverty, from non-merited subsidies to basic health care, education, and infrastructure.
- *Tax reform.* The aim would be a tax system combining a broad tax base with moderate marginal tax rates.
- *Liberalizing interest rates.* Recognizing the importance of financial liberalization but saying very little about the necessity for prudential supervision of banks and financial institutions.
- *Competitive exchange rates.* Asserting that exchange rates should be left free and without interventions from the central bank.
- *Trade liberalization.* This was clearly one of the key principles of the policy recommendations. Only scant attention was given to the issue of how quickly borders should be opened up and trade be liberalized.
- *Liberalization of inward foreign direct investment.* Under this heading Williamson never included comprehensive capital account liberalization, believing that it did not or should not command a consensus in Washington.

- *Privatization.* An originally neoliberal idea that at this time seemed to have won broad acceptance within the Washington community.
- *Deregulation.* This focused specifically on easing barriers to entry and exit, not on abolishing regulations designed for safety or environmental, nor to govern prices in a non-competitive industry.
- *Property rights.* This was primarily about providing the informal sector with the ability to gain property rights at acceptable cost.

The ten categories of recommendations of the Washington Consensus can be organized into two mutually reinforcing groups of policies: stability through fiscal adjustment and market orthodoxy (commandments i, ii, iii, x); and liberalization through a dramatic reduction of the role of the state in the economy (iv, v vi, vii, viii, ix).

10.2 The Washington Consensus Criticized

Since its inception, the term Washington Consensus has provoked ideological controversies. In 2008 Narcís Serra and Joseph Stiglitz edited a volume titled, *The Washington Consensus Reconsidered: Toward a New Global Governance.* The book discusses the relationship between the articles of the consensus and how the term has come to be widely understood. The team of authors provides a comprehensive discussion of the shortcomings of the suggested reforms. They conclude that both theory and evidence weigh heavily against what has come to be called the Washington Consensus.

The original intention of the Consensus was to formalize a set of development strategies that commanded a consensus in some significant parts of Washington. It was inspired by the liberalization policy instruments of the Bretton Woods institutions and the World Trade Organization. For many critics, however, it seemed to discount the role of government policy and move toward a global *laissez-faire* economy where the only thing that mattered would be the growth of GDP.

An early international development strategy of the 1970s expressed concerns with the environment and called for intensified national and international efforts, searching "to make the world, in its economic, and social aspects, a more just and rational home for mankind." As a result, in 1973 the UN initiated a system-wide project to study environmental aspects of the future world economy. In the UN General Assembly resolution 3201 (S-VI) of May 1, 1974, an alarming and growing gap between developed and developing countries was established, calling for corrections of inequalities and redressing existing injustices, with the aim of narrowing the gap and ensuring an acceleration of economic and social development and justice for present and future generation.

In 1977 the UN published a study titled, *The Future of the World Economy,* presenting the impact of prospective economic issues and policies on the International Development Strategy for the second UN Development Decade [Leontif, *et al.*]. The Washington Consensus, against this background, many considered it to have disregarded both the advantages of industrial policy and reasonable equity considerations (supporting an adequate legal and institutional safety net).

The Washington Consensus was predicated upon a strong faith in unfettered markets and aimed at reducing, or even minimizing, the role of government. To its critics, the Consensus has come to be associated with market fundamentalism — the view that markets solve most, if not all, economic problems by themselves. Already in the 1970s, however, advances in economic theory had shown that markets can fail due to imperfections in information, limitations in competition, and incompleteness. Markets do not always produce efficient outcomes by themselves, implying the necessity of a role for government intervention. According to Stiglitz, these advances in economic theory had already removed the intellectual foundations of market fundamentalism long before the Washington Consensus became fashionable.

The dividends of macroeconomic stability are still open to controversial interpretations. A broader view of macroeconomic stability would include not only price stability and sound fiscal policies but also the sustainability of the real economy. To its detractors, neither theory nor practice supported the plausibility of the Washington Consensus. Accordingly, it should not have come as much of a surprise that the Consensus prescriptions failed to work as promised. Disillusion with the Washington Consensus grew throughout the developing world. The agenda seemed to many neither necessary nor sufficient preconditions for sustainable growth, ultimately failing to deliver policies that would promote the advancement of developing countries.

In retrospect, Williamson concluded that there was no consensus around the Washington Consensus after all, but rather a convergence of opinion around key concepts. He suggested that it would have been more appropriate to label his list the Universal Convergence rather than a consensus, "since the extent of agreement is far short of consensus but runs far wider than Washington."

10.3 Post-Washington Consensus

In the aftermath of the Washington Consensus there is a general agreement about the nature of many of its shortcomings. The most important of these is a failure to consider local economic structures within developing countries, focusing on a too narrow set of objectives and on a too limited set of policy instruments. The development goals determining the policy framework should not be just an increase in GDP, but should regard the distributional impact of policies that would look to include equitable and sustainable increases in societal well-being.

The Washington Consensus clearly failed to adequately address the subject of governance — the role and character of public institutions that has later been placed at center stage, stressing not only the importance of governance of individual countries but also the issue of global governance. To many, the Consensus had confused ends with means, so that privatization and liberalization had become not means to an end, but ends in themselves. Major development goals such as reducing poverty, building equity, and sustaining the environment were not part of the Consensus protocol. Stiglitz identifies six elements of a post–Washington Consensus:

(1) a post–Washington Consensus cannot be arrived at simply within the confines of Washington;
(2) one-size-fits-all policies are doomed to fail;
(3) economic science has not yet provided sufficient evidence, sufficiently strong theory, or empirical evidence, to result in a broad consensus about what countries should do;
(4) a critical complementary role of government with markets associated with the developmental state;
(5) development requires strengthening of both market and state institutions;

(6) success is to be measured not just by an increase in GDP, but by a broader set of measures — including those that assess environmental and social sustainability.

10.4 The Barcelona Development Agenda

In response to widespread criticism of the Washington Consensus, the Universal Forum of Cultures met in Barcelona in September 2004 to consider the prospects for growth and development around the world. (The list of participants included both Williamson and Stiglitz.) The Forum proposed an alternative system of policies featuring seven general principles that were believed to offer more flexible approaches to development.

The Barcelona Development Agenda [UFC, 2004] spelled out a broader concern for equitable and sustainable development as reflected in long-term goals for macroeconomic policy, a wider range of economic policy instruments, a balanced role for markets and government, and the creation of a better system of global governance. The conference proposed reforms both at national levels and at the global level responding to two sets of questions: What can each country, individually, do to enhance sustainable, stable, equitable, and democratic development? and How should the global economic architecture be changed? There was agreement among the participants on seven "sets of lessons" that would serve as priorities for reform:

(1) *Institutional quality and market orientation matter.* The rule of law and property rights are a decisive precondition for successful development to occur. A country's history, culture, and other specific circumstances need to be respected.
(2) *Poor financial policies are barriers to development.* Developing nations that hope to prosper should pursue prudent financial, monetary, fiscal, and debt policies — as weak and maladjusted measures manifest in large debts, both public and private, while poorly regulated banks and loose monetary policies are serious threats and tend to inhibit development. Large public debt can burden governments with debt service obligations that consume a significant proportion of the GDP, and might result in financial crises that disproportionally affect low-income households.

(3) *Sustained growth cannot be guaranteed by a single set of policies.* To ignite sustained growth, international lending organizations and aid agencies should encourage countries' ownership over their development agenda and shall be free to experiment with policies that would suit their specific circumstances best. The most binding constraints to growth shall be identified and addressed through a combination of microeconomic, industrial, and macroeconomic policy mixes.

(4) *Multilateral trade negotiations should proceed in a manner that promotes development.* Since agricultural and textile protectionism in developed countries creates obstacles for market entry and expansion in developing countries, trade negotiations should include stakeholders from impacted states. Trade policies in developing countries should be examined to identify and correct those that limit growth. A successful conclusion of the Doha Round[12] will provide more opportunities for world growth, thereby creating more room for developing countries to pursue their own growth strategies.

(5) *Current international financial relationships are not working well.* The international financial arrangements should be reformed. Both private capital and development financial flows to middle income countries are highly volatile and delinked from economic fundamentals in the recipient countries. Developing nations are under-represented in the decision making bodies of the multilateral lending institutions. Their voting power is outdated, reflecting the relations of the past.

(6) *Asymmetric international arrangements on movements of capital and labor.* Current policies of international financial institutions and G7 governments generally favor the transfer of financial capital, but often discourage the movement of labor capital across borders. Both equity and efficiency considerations support allowing greater international migration. A set of international rules and institutions are needed to guide cross-border movements of people, improving the rights of migrants.

[12]The Doha Round is the latest round of trade negotiations among the WTO membership. Its aim is to achieve major reform of the international trading system through the introduction of lower trade barriers and revised trade rules.

(7) *The worsening of the environment, including problems of global warming, need to be tackled.* One billion human beings living in poverty should be a cause for unrelenting concern. AIDS and other epidemic diseases represent a tragedy for the least developed countries. Donor nations' commitment to increase aid levels to meet the MDGs remains largely unfulfilled.

There was also a recognition that the international community had to address effectively other important economic problems such as exchange rates instability, problems with the global reserve system, and the possibility of sovereign defaults.

The Barcelona agenda represents a major departure from the past, stressing the importance of a fair income distribution, poverty reduction, protection of the environment, as well as tailoring policies to country-specific situations. It recognizes that the complex relationship between globalization and sustainable development calls for an integrated multi-disciplinary analysis of the policy instruments with respect to timing, the consequences of reforms on the economic security of developing countries, and with due consideration of national sovereignty.

10.5 The Way Forward

The declaration of the *Rights of Man and of the Citizen* dating from the French revolution in 1789 has served as a founding stone in the history of universal human rights. It is valid at all times and in every place and it pertains to human nature itself. Transferring the concept of liberty to the sphere of economics, the idea of "economic liberalization" can only be ethically and politically defended provided that such liberty does not injure others (or at least minimizes possible negative impacts on others), that it applies to all members of society (or, failing this, that timely compensatory mechanisms are established), and that the limits of economic liberalization are defined by law or existing social and physical infrastructure. As a consequence, even a liberal economic regime needs institutional support and state regulations.

The Washington Consensus can best be characterized as a consensus for liberalization and globalization. It was not a consensus for equitable growth and sustainable development. Unfortunately, economic globalization has outpaced political globalization and global governance has not kept pace with the needs of the current version of a globalized world with universal equal rights for all. This calls for reform of multilateral arrangements toward a more coherent and just system.

Many feel that the international rules of the game are often unfair, and the international institutions have pushed one particular ideology — an ideology that has resulted in economic policies particularly ill-suited to many developing countries. Stiglitz points his finger at an undemocratic governance of the international institutions: existing voting structures do not reflect current economic standing of countries. Given such asymmetry in the governance structures, it is unsurprising that the decisions and actions made by international economic institutions reflect the ideology of advanced industrial countries, and even the interests of their multinational corporations and financial institutions.

In order to be effective, the International Monetary Fund must be seen as representing the interests of all its 188 member countries, and that its governance structure reflect the realities of today's world economy. In November 2010, the IMF agreed to wide-ranging governance reforms reflecting the increasing importance of emerging market countries. Currently IMF member states are in the process of ratifying this 2010 Quota and Governance Reform. The reforms will ensure that smaller developing countries can retain influence on the operations of IMF — a major achievement in enhancing the credibility, legitimacy, and effectiveness of the Fund. All EU member states have already fully ratified the Quota and Governance Reform.

In January 2013, the Executive Board of the IMF further formulated important building blocks for a revised quota formula and agreed on a review of the formula together with the 15th General Review of Quotas by January 2014. The review is expected to reflect the changing dynamics in the global world and will lead to further increases in the quota shares of emerging market economies, producing a combined shift of 9 percent of quota shares to these countries.

The World Bank governance reform process is less advanced. Some progress has been made on the subject of voting reform but more is needed in terms of finding an appropriate voting formula by 2015. With the aim of ending extreme poverty and promoting shared prosperity and environmental sustainability, the World Bank put forward a Development Committee paper titled, *A Common Vision for the World Bank Group,* outlining the proposed goals and principles for the future strategy of the World Bank Group [World Bank and IMF, 2013].

The *Oxford Handbook on Governance* [Levi-Faur, 2012] published in 2012, outlining formalized models of governance, highlights the importance of information gathering and information processing in governance. It acknowledges that information will often be politicized prior to being acted upon. Someone must consider the governance environment, react to information collected, make decisions, and then continue to consider the consequences of each round of governing.

The Rio +20 Conference, held in June 2012, in Rio de Janeiro, was an important milestone in initiating a process of strengthening the institutional framework for policies aiming at sustainable development goals. The document, *The Future We Want,* [UN, 2012b] stressed the growing recognition that we live on a single planet within explicit planetary boundaries, and in an increasingly interdependent global multi-dimensional system that goes well beyond the economic marketplace.

The framework of UN activities and its system-wide agenda for sustainable development is now integrated both with the work of the General Assembly and the deliberations of the Economic and Social Council (ECOSOC). This coordination has led to the replacement of the former Commission on Sustainable Development by a new High Level Political Forum (HLPF) on Sustainable Development representing a group of prominent political leaders devoted to the common cause of sustainable development. The HLPF is mandated to oversee the implementation of sustainable development commitments, provide political leadership and guidance, enhance integration of the dimensions of sustainable development within a single framework, improve cooperation and coordination within the UN system, and strengthen the science policy interface. There is a hope that working at a higher political level with regular meetings, the HLPF will contribute to enhancing coherence.

Chapter 11

Toward a Sustainable Globalization

> I support globalization and believe it can bring more benefits to the poor than its alternative. But it must be the right kind of globalization. To me, globalization is like a hundred-lane highway criss-crossing the world. If it is a free-for-all highway, its lanes will be taken over by the giant trucks from powerful economies. Bangladeshi rickshaw will be thrown off the highway. The rule of strongest takes it all must be replaced by rules that ensure that the poorest have a place and piece of the action, without being elbowed out by the strong.
>
> *Muhammad Yunus*, Nobel Memorial Lecture, 2006

11.1 Challenges of Globalization

The term globalization is used in many ways, but the underlying principal is the progressive integration of economies and societies within a common global framework. It is driven by the dissemination of new technologies, expansion of new economic relationships, and the interconnectedness of national and international policies engaging an ever-growing range of international actors including governments, business, labor, civil society, and scientific and religious organizations.

A rich literature defines the phenomenon of globalization — discussing the worldwide political, socioeconomic, environmental, and cultural interdependency and awareness — that has become a major driving force for change in today's world. This change is expressed in increasingly free cross-border flow of ideas, people, goods and services, and capital — as well as environmentally and biologically harmful substances.

Broadly speaking, there are *two* major aspects of globalization. *The first* refers to factors and institutions — such as trade, technology, multinational enterprises, and communications that bring societies and citizens closer together to shape a single global marketplace. Deregulation of markets, technological innovation, and cheaper communication have allowed investors to diversify their participation in competitive overseas markets. In consequence, a significant increase in cross-border financial movements, including direct foreign investment, has become a key factor in international economic integration.

The second refers to policies — such as trade and capital market liberalization, agreements on international property rights, technologies and communications that are pursued both at the national and the international level — enhancing the openness of and integration between countries. These policies hopefully inject fairness and accountability into international trading and financial systems aiming at a level playing field for all actors. From this perspective the existing pattern of globalization is not an inevitable trend. It is, at least in part, the product of policy choices and, sometimes, misuses of discretionary power in the interest of the few. While technical change is usually irreversible, government policy can be changed to accommodate societal needs. Actually, technological advance can by itself widen the policy choices available for the pursuit of sustainable development goals.

A global framework is needed to insure against political risks, covering both imports and exports. Unfortunately, the governance of globalization lags far behind the accomplishments of "hard" sciences, such as the advances in information and communication technology. Against the background of the unprecedented success of the Internet currently serving about 2.5 billion persons, there is still a long way to go before the potential benefits of the Globalization WAN (wide area networks) initiative will reach individual countries and their populations.

There are widely differing perceptions of the impact of globalization, especially concerning its possible favorable or destructive economic, social, and environmental consequences. This partly stems from its varying effects on different social groups and actors across the world. The wealth of individual countries and the well-being of their peoples increasingly depends on what happens outside their boundaries. Access to foreign markets, foreigners' access to their markets, and instability in exchange rates and capital markets create both opportunities and threats for sustainable development. People as global citizens form their perceptions of globalization partly based on the statistical record and also as part of the political discussion. Modern information and communication technology offers unprecedented opportunity for the global citizenship to express its voice in shaping policy choices. Policies can be fine-tuned, adjusted, and if necessary changed, by responsive policymakers to ensure their social legitimacy.

11.2 The Social Dimension of Globalization

Social problems such as poverty and inequality have their genesis in a pre-globalization era. Some argue that globalization has exacerbated these problems while others contend that globalization has contributed to a reduction in their incidence. In either case, these social problems clearly need to be addressed if globalization is to be politically viable, economically sustainable, and ethically acceptable.

To reduce inequality between and within countries and to ensure that the benefits of the global economy benefits reach working people and their families, the International Labour Organization (ILO) in November 2001 took the initiative of establishing the World Commission on the Social Dimension of Globalization. The Commission had 25 members and was co-chaired by president Tarja Halonen of Finland and president Benjamin Mkapa of Tanzania. The Commission was established to respond to the needs of people as they cope with the unprecedented changes that globalization has brought. The social dimension of globalization, as originally defined by the Commission, would embrace the impact of globalization on the life and work of people, on their families, and their societies. Concerns and issues are often raised about the impact of globalization on employment, working conditions, income, and social protection. Beyond the world of work, the social dimension encompasses security, culture and identity, inclusion or exclusion, and the cohesiveness of families and communities.

Recent decades have been remarkable by the measures taken by governments at the national level — and the serious attempts by international regulatory bodies, funds, and programs — and a growing number of multilateral initiatives to manage the social consequences of globalization. A number of international agreements and global treaties stress global commitment to eradicate poverty, address unemployment, and promote social integration. These efforts culminated in the recent landmark report, *A New Global Partnership: Eradicate Poverty and Transform Economies Through Sustainable Development,* [UN, 2013.] presented in May 2013 to the UN secretary-general by the High-level Panel on the Post-2015 Development Agenda. The panel is a 27-member group of high-ranking persons established in 2012 to provide recommendations on advancing the development framework beyond the target date for the UN Millennium Development Goals. Most of these challenges still need to be addressed and implementation mechanisms still need to be identified. There have been positive developments in reducing extreme poverty, decreasing mortality rates, progress in primary school enrollment, and achieving gender equality. Contrary to the hopes and expectations of many, however, markets have failed to deliver a steadily increasing number of productive jobs throughout the world.

11.3 Widening Inequalities

The past decade has revolutionized the spread of information and communication technologies, bridging differences in time and space. Widespread use of e-banking, e-commerce, and knowledge networks has decreased transaction costs and facilitated the process of acquisition and dissemination of knowledge. But it has also increased global inequalities, as the use of advanced information and communication technologies has enabled a small number of leading companies and individuals to capture a larger share of the market and thus to increase the gap between the market leaders and the followers. While modern IT has become an instrument for advancement for some economic actors, for others it has created a new kind of insecurity. Globalization reveals a growing global inequality of technological skills and know-how.

While the World Trade Organization (WTO) operates on the basis of a single vote for each country, key decisions are made by leading economic powers in closed meetings. The executive directors representing France, Germany, Japan, the Russian Federation, Saudi Arabia, the United Kingdom and the United States account for 46% of the voting rights in the World Bank and 48% in the International Monetary Fund. As a result, the

United States and the European Union are able to protect their agricultural industries to the detriment of many developing nations [UN, 2002a].

Unfortunately, the current model of globalization is widening inequalities between and within countries. The benefits of globalization are not reaching enough people. Meeting the target of sustainable development calls for a radical change of thinking. It means starting new companies, creating decent jobs, and investing in health, education, and food safety. The goal is more satisfying levels of human development for all, including the most vulnerable, and accelerating the pace of economic transformation, growth, and sustainable development.

Intensive growth of employment is needed to meet the common goal of the international community to reduce global poverty. Governments, the private sector, international financial institutions and development agencies, and civil society representatives all seem to agree that current inequality trends must be reversed and global governance structures reviewed. It is no longer feasible to conduct "business as usual" in international economic policy.

Several Nobel laureates have recognized the importance of good governance and the need for timely reform. Incomplete information, inadequate institutions, and local capacity limitations can distort the income distribution and deepen inequality. This calls for a new role for governments to complement market activities that ensure poverty reduction and improvements in the living standards of the most needy. There is a need to reorient current austerity policies from just reducing government debt, toward social and environmental accountability. The management of economic policy in individual countries needs to include the identification and consideration of "soft" issues like local values and cultural heritage. Yet such processes of cultural change call for innovative approaches, which makes the challenge of coping with globalization even more complex.

Thus the time for consensus-building and new thinking toward sustainable, gender-sensitive, people-centered development has arrived. Existing social and economic divides leverage major threats against global prosperity, security, and stability. Widely spread terrorist attacks have demonstrated that globalization is not only about economic integration. It confirmed ILO's credo that "universal and lasting peace can be established only if it is based upon social justice" and that "poverty anywhere" accompanied by inequality and marginalization "constitute a danger to prosperity everywhere" and are among the causes of today's ills: terrorism, crime, and corruption.

Such inequalities compel enhanced collaboration among global development partners and stakeholders. There is a need to identify pathways to a sustainable future through an inclusive globalization of the world economy. We should steer the liberalization of markets toward putting a "human face" on the globalization process, thus introducing a social conscience into the global economy so that markets work for all.

Despite general awareness of these mounting problems, the relationship between globalization and labor remains largely unexplored. Analytical research is thus thrust to center stage to help assess the social impact of globalization and trade liberalization.

A number of studies have analyzed the effects of globalization on the well-being of people, and the benefits of trade liberalization for the poor. The findings of several of these studies have been challenged and on both methodological and empirical grounds. One inquiry concluded that "the proposition that trade liberalization by itself leads to higher growth remains unproven" and that "trade liberalization has resulted in both an increase and a decline in the growth rate depending on country circumstances." The single way of legitimizing globalization worldwide is to ensure a sustainable livelihood through full employment.

Some researchers have pointed out the need to improve risk management capacity at both global and national levels, including development of an "early warning system" where problems might be identified and communicated early, so that appropriate mitigating measures can be activated. Protecting the most vulnerable population groups minimizes social costs. Measures to alleviate the social costs of globalization would include improving the functioning of labor and credit markets, a social safety net, and active labor market policies to assist displaced workers.

Lessons of the past decades call for careful considerations in policy formulation. Policies should serve the needs of the majority of people — but not sacrifice the destinies of the remaining minority by experimenting with new, unproven policies. Wise development policy implements positive measures that have worked in other countries. The Political Declaration of the World Summit of Sustainable Development [UN, 2002b] in Johannesburg recognized that:

- Sustainable development requires a long-term perspective and broad-based participation in policy formulation, decision making and implementation at all levels and a stable partnerships with the private sector, labor, civil society and all major groups.
- Successful private corporations have a responsibility to contribute to the evolution of equitable, sustainable communities; the private sector should operate within a transparent, stable regulatory environment.
- Dialogue and cooperation among all the world's peoples and civilizations is of prime importance.

The Summit declared that the achievement of the goals of sustainable development entails a democratic system of global governance with enhanced and accountable international and multilateral institutions.

11.4 The Oxford Martin Commission

The report, *Now for the Long Term,* published by the Oxford Martin Commission for Future Generations [OMCFG, 2013], calls for urgent action and a radical shakeup in politics and business to deliver progress on climate change, poverty, governance, and disease. Composed of prominent global leaders and chaired by Pascal Lamy, former WTO director-general, the Commission argues that the ability to address today's global challenges is undermined by the absence of a collective societal vision and urges leaders to promote shared global values to protect the prospects for future generations. Searching for new ways to manage our collective interests, the Oxford Martin commission claims that failure to address the long-term issues exposes current generations to unacceptable instability and risk, and threatens our ability to build a sustainable, inclusive, and resilient future for all. Based on past successes and failures, it proposes three actions to overcome deep political and cultural divides in the world:

- *Create a coalition to counteract climate change,* to accelerate action with measurable targets for energy-efficient buildings, faster market penetration of efficient vehicles, and tracking harmful emissions.

- *Establish a voluntary taxation and regulatory exchange* to address tax abuse/avoidance, harmonize company taxation arrangements, promote information sharing, and enhance transparency and governance.
- *Introduce "CyberEx," a new early warning platform,* to promote better understanding of common cyber threats, identify preventive measures, and minimize future attacks for the shared benefit of government, corporate, and individual interests.

The report asserts that achieving sustainable globalization is an imperative rather than an option and that sustainable development can only be reached through the active participation of all stakeholders — not only government agencies but also legislators, businesses, trade unions, academia, and religious and non-governmental organizations. It points to the great challenge of combining the centralized management of governments with the decentralized decision making of market participants.

11.5 Globalization and Poverty

The impact of globalization on sustainable development and poverty reduction has been the subject of extensive debate over the past decades. Despite remarkable progress in the fight against poverty in some parts of the world, efforts often ignore the underlying causes of poverty and inequality, considering them only byproducts of growth. The relationship between globalization and growth is theoretically ambiguous. Even the simpler question of how trade affects economic growth is still under debate, perhaps because growth itself is less well understood than the economics of static markets [Deardorff & Stern, 2001]. While trade affects the income opportunities and levels of the poor (both positively and negatively), the linkages between trade and poverty are not as direct and immediate as with other national policies. Trade reforms will create some losers who suffer temporary adverse shocks (some even in the long run), and exacerbate poverty with spells of unemployment. Yet, appropriate policy responses can help alleviate hardship and facilitate adjustment, rather than abandoning reform [Ben-David, *et al.*, 1999].

Studies of poverty and relative deprivation are usually founded on a comparison of income against basic material needs for food, shelter and clothing. From an early point they have also encompassed a wider appreciation of many cumulative effects on the life of poor people, perhaps best summed up as the loss of dignity or the humiliation that poverty engenders. Dignity is, of course, much less susceptible to quantification as it requires a sense of self-respect and respect from others, as well as material well-being. Yet surveys indicate that the most injurious and debilitating characteristic of poverty is loss of dignity, because it weakens relationships within families and communities and persons in authority, and thus reduces the capacity to escape from a cycle of deprivation that can endure for generations [ILO, 2001a].

The efforts of the international community in the fight against poverty have been remarkable, culminating in the Rio +20 conference. A consensus was reached to pursue poverty reduction and sustainable development through the means of employment-intensive growth. Further results reached in 2013 are significant, with a global accord signed during the WTO ministerial meeting at Doha, with the Monterrey conference, with the Johannesburg summit. On all these occasions it was argued that to meet sustainable development goals, current trends of production, consumption, and distribution need to be halted.

11.6 Partnerships for Sustainable Globalization

The global economy demands adjustments that increase competitiveness and advance technological change to enhance productivity. Consultative and participatory approaches are needed to develop and implement effective socioeconomic policies at the national and global levels. The poverty effects of trade liberalization are transmitted via four broad groups of institutions (whether net suppliers or end users of the goods or services in question): enterprises, distribution channels, the government, and households. Policies promoting decent employment opportunities, complemented by social protection and well-functioning labor markets institutions, are crucial.

Many people are endowed with specific capital, *i.e.*, skills or equipment needed by industry. As industries and markets change, people gain or lose along with their employers — and can find the basis for their livelihood destroyed. Public policy can only partially acknowledge and mitigate such costs that can continue for months (or even years), as unemployed people search to relocate, retrain, reinvest, and otherwise readjust. Those later in life may never recover. Economists therefore usually favor only a gradual movement toward free trade, so that adjustment costs can be accommodated within the routine ups and downs of market dynamics [Deardorff & Stern, 2001].

Sustainable development requires mechanisms that permit the government and the private sector to develop "shared" vision, planning, and decision making. Economic planning and policymaking need to become more prudent and transparent, respecting the interests of future generations. This calls for a new type of partnership that redefines the roles and responsibilities of public and private sector organizations. Employers' and workers' organizations may find that they should review their roles and responsibilities and take a more central role in national policy and program cycles. Consultations at all levels will contribute to consensus-building, accountability, and transparency. Civil society representatives and other national and international partners, together with central and regional government, should be actively involved in addressing specific issues of local development. Such joint efforts will strengthen the three pillars of sustainable development:

- pursuing economic, social, and environmental objectives,
- linking sector strategies to macroeconomic concerns,
- ensuring policy coherence.

A better understanding of the causal mechanisms of globalization and consultation with social partners might contribute to the development of an early warning system and increase social risk management. In turn, this might enable countries to offset the transitional social costs of globalization and alleviate attendant increases in poverty. A broad participation of social partners is needed to bring key information into the policy implementation process. When implementing trade-related reforms, policymakers need to be aware of potential shocks — who would win and who would lose. All stakeholders need to adapt to the new situation. This can be done through a socially and environmentally responsible restructuring of the economy, modernizing the institutions and the industrial base, and building a national capacity to foster innovation. Flexibility should be increased by developing negotiating and administrative skills for crisis management [Essama-Nssah, 2000].

Table 11.1 The roles of social partners for sustainable development.

Government	Employers' Organizations	Trade Unions
• Social protection • Employment strategies	• Define new business and restructuring plans • Labor force analysis identifying skill mix and new skill requirements	• Agreements
SOCIAL DIALOGUE TO SHARE THE BURDEN		

In response to the challenges of globalization, the private sector is more widely addressing its role in sustainable development as companies realize that it is in their commercial interest that the community be vibrant and prosperous. There is increasing evidence of private sector willingness to invest in social projects, as part of building success in their core business. Also, businesses are backing traditional philanthropic initiatives [World Bank Group, 1998].

Socially and environmentally responsible initiatives toward sustainable growth are essential and should be widely promoted. Table 11.1 below outlines the main roles for each of the social partners.

11.7 Social Assessment

In today's global world, national economies are integrated through production, distribution, and consumption chains — and a downturn in any country easily spills over to others. Recent financial crises demonstrate the need to enhance social protection systems. Policies should concentrate on social security, as well as employment security. Mechanisms of social assessment (SA) are needed both for domestic policy interventions and to counteract external financial and economic shocks.

Article 22 of the Universal Declaration of Human Rights [UN, 1948] states that "everyone, as a member of society, has the right of social security." Article 9 of the International Covenant of Economic, Social and Cultural Rights [UN, 1966] refers to the "right of everyone to social security, including social insurance."

The report of the secretary-general to the special session of the General Assembly on *Assessing the Social Impact of Economic Measures Taken in Response to Financial Crises in Developing Countries* [UN, 2000a] recognized that in countries undergoing structural adjustments and economic reforms, there is a need for regular and frequent monitoring and evaluation of the social impact of such changes and reforms. Affected groups of the population need to be better targeted so that emergency programs can be better designed. The report stresses that social assessment (SA) is particularly important for countries where representative democracy is weak. SA can serve to demonstrate the positive economic impact of social policies and programs (such as social protection, the identification of labor standards, investments in health, education, and basic social services) on the productivity of the workforce. In this way it can contribute to increased output and improved competitiveness and profitability of enterprises.

Typical indicators of social impact measure employment, and absolute and relative income; levels of education, health, housing, and other social services; as well as social integration. The report stresses the importance of the timing and sequencing of policy measures so that their impact becomes positive, improving work conditions. This all depends on the effectiveness of investments in infrastructure and the development of social and human resources. Social assessment (SA) can assist to:

- forecast and evaluate the impact of policies, programs, and projects;
- identify factors that improve the response of the poor to incentives for raising their productivity and income;
- analyze the poverty-reduction and employment content of public investments;
- design social protection systems for the poor;
- strengthen the ownership of programs by participatory processes that involve their beneficiaries and other relevant actors.

Forecasting the social impact of policies and programs and evaluating them *ex post* has been a common practice for some time. The critical importance of SA was earlier underscored at the World Summit for Social Development convened by the UN Economic and Social Council

(ECOSOC) in Copenhagen [UN, 1995]. The program of action stated that an integrated socioeconomic approach to development requires, *inter alia:*

- *analyzing and reviewing* macroeconomic, microeconomic, and sectoral policies and their impact on poverty, employment, social integration, and social development;
- *assessing* the extent, distribution, and characteristics of poverty, unemployment, social tension, and social exclusion;
- *developing quantitative and qualitative indicators* of social development, poverty, employment, social integration, *etc.*

SA is usually considered to be an essential component of policy formulation and a tool to understand how the social welfare of different groups will be affected by development initiatives. Yet, some main questions of SA [World Bank, 1998] often remained unanswered:

- What will be the impact of globalization on various stakeholders, particularly on women and vulnerable groups?
- Are there plans to mitigate adverse impacts?
- What social risks might affect project or program success?
- What institutional arrangements are needed for participation and project delivery?
- Are there adequate plans to build the capacity required at the appropriate level?
- How can existing tools and techniques be used to study the social impact of proposed reforms?
- Have alternative policy options been considered?
- How can policies be appropriately sequenced?

These questions all aim at a better understanding of the channels through which globalization and trade-related policies impact the income distribution, employment, and poverty.

Part III

Remembering Times Past and Honoring Four Great Scholars

by Sten Thore

Part III

Overview

During the early work on this book, the thought occurred to me how privileged I have been in my long life to meet, work with, and be inspired by some great scholars — and that I should try to relate to the reader some small daily episodes from my contacts with them. These rambling notes, then, are not biographic in any sense and certainly not providing a balanced presentation of their academic careers and published work. Instead, they provide a glimpse for posterity of how one eager student (with enthusiasm, awe, and sometimes even despair) responded to his good luck of meeting some of the towering personalities of his profession.

The notes span a long time interval, from my first meeting with Tinbergen in 1954, via my year with Abe Charnes at Northwestern University 1963–1964, eventually rejoining him at The University of Texas in Austin in 1978 — where one year earlier George Kozmetsky, the great benefactor, had launched the Institute for Constructive Capitalism (later morphing into the IC^2 Institute). With The University of Texas at Austin celebrating its centennial in 1981, he named Bill Cooper, Ilya Prigogine, and fourteen others as his "Centennial" fellows. I was a member of this illustrious academy of scholars during the years 1981–1996.

The four scholars portrayed here form, as it were, the four pillars that support the analysis in Part I of the present volume. Tinbergen is the hero of the entire book. Abe Charnes and Bill Cooper created the envelopment techniques (and Bill actively participated in the planning and writing of this book). Prigogine's analysis of far-from-equilibrium conditions in physics or economics models finally lets us look forward to a more realistic understanding of the economic world.

During my retirement years in the Algarve, Portugal, I have been fortunate to be able to maintain contacts with former PhD students from many parts of the world, including the Instituto Superior Técnico in Lisbon where for two years I held a Luso-American chair in the commercialization of high technology. Many of the memories recounted below were told over a cup of coffee on the *esplanada* (terrace) outside our house overlooking the sun-drenched Atlantic Ocean. Ruzanna Tarverdyan, then still working for the International Labour Office in Geneva, has come here several times, charming, enthusiastic, and artistic. My old friend David Gibson, Associate Director of the IC^2 Institute, has dropped by several times in connection with his regular visits as he works with universities across Portugal. Thanks David, for suggesting that I pen down these notes!

Chapter 12

Jan Tinbergen
(1903–1994)

The picture of Tinbergen that I have chosen as a frontispiece to this essay is the way I remember him when I saw him for the first time at the meeting of the Econometric Society in Uppsala, Sweden, in August 1954. He was then 51 years old — dynamic, slim, tall, with a bounce in his step, and with his characteristic crewcut hairdo. He was one of the leading economists of his generation, and I had read a good deal of his work. As a young graduate student in economics, I owned a copy of Tinbergen's famous study *Statistical Testing of Business Cycles,* two volumes [1939] commissioned by the League of Nations. The "Lundequistska" book shop in Uppsala was a treasure trove and I bought all important works in economics that I could put my hands on. Having an undergraduate background in mathematics and statistics, I was attracted to Tinbergen's approach to economics. In his inaugural address as professor at Erasmus University in Rotterdam, Tinbergen had declared that he would pursue "statistics and mathematics in the service of business cycle research."

In the thirties, the very idea that one should try to collect statistics to verify (or reject) economic theory was looked upon with suspicion. Reviewing Tinbergen's work in the *Economic Journal* in 1939, J. M. Keynes derided his pioneering econometric work as "statistical alchemy . . . giving quantitative precision to what, in qualitative terms, we know already as the result of a complete theoretical analysis."

And yet, despite the incomprehension and ridicule, a new science was born: econometrics. The two leaders of the new discipline were Ragnar Frisch and Jan Tinbergen, working independently but pursuing a very similar progression of thought. Those early days, econometrics was still conceived by its founders as a branch of economics. In his textbook *Econometrics* (my own early copy bought at the Lundequistska book shop is in French and titled, *Econométrie* [1941]) Tinbergen surveyed central fields of economics like consumer demand, production, labor markets, and financial markets supporting the theory by data and statistical estimations. Later, unfortunately, under the hands of Klein and others, econometrics was to be converted into a discipline of methods only, being pursued by narrow specialists.

The meetings of the Econometric Society served as one of the most important fora for economists of all stripes to meet and exchange ideas. The 1954 meeting at Uppsala was organized by Herman Wold, head of the Statistical Institute at Uppsala and one of the luminaries of the new science of econometrics. The University of Uppsala, founded in 1477, was those days one of the foremost centers of learning in the world. Any academic subject was taught by the Herr Professor, with his students reverently absorbing his every word. When I was only 22 years old, Herman Wold let me join his graduate research seminar.

With his monumental study *Demand Analysis* [1952], Wold had codified one of the central fields of econometric research. Earlier, with his dissertation in 1938, he more or less single-handedly had created the mathematical discipline of stochastic processes (a forerunner to control theory and cybernetics). Now his formidable energy was directed to the preparations for the meeting of the econometric society.

To set the tone for the upcoming conference, Herman Wold wanted to present a body of new research work developed by him, with his research seminar. And so during the academic year leading up to the conference, we set to work, meeting every week at the Statistical Institute, a mixed group of some very green students (where I belonged) and established researchers in the departments of statistics and economics. The goal was to develop new micro theory and new market theory under uncertainty and to illustrate the novel concepts by numerical experiments. The computer had not yet emerged as a tool in practical research work, but we could draw on the efforts of a small army of calculating clerks from Estonia, supported by the Swedish government.

In particular, Wold wanted to investigate the properties of systems of economic time series. Building directly on Tinbergen's work, he illustrated the causal structure of such systems with the help of the "Tinbergen diagram" [Tinbergen, 1940]. For our numerical work, Wold decided on a causal chain for a single market, consisting of a demand relation, a supply relation and a price strategy.

When the conference opened, each participant was handed a thick mimeographed volume containing the reports of our seminar. Several of these were later published by the new publishing house of North Holland, and duly refereed in *Econometrica* Our work on "an ignorant monopolist" [Thore, 1964; Billström & Thore, 1964] not knowing the location of the demand curve facing him was well received and opened up a research field that would later be harvested by others.

The conference turned out to be a great and resounding success. Important European economists showed up, including Erich Schneider from Kiel, Jan Tinbergen from Amsterdam, and Richard Stone from Cambridge — seated in a group in the first few rows of the huge auditorium. Wold was supposed to sit in his chair at the podium, but my memory shows him running up to the blackboard all the time — intervening, directing, commenting, and filling the board with his usual clutter. This was his show. The attendees craned their necks to take it all in. (The presentations were all in *plenum*; the concept of parallel sessions not yet being invented).

My next memory of Jan Tinbergen is from the spring of 1956, when he taught a class in economic policy at the *Institut Universitaire d'Études Europeennes* (IUSE) at Turin, Italy. The Institute is generously endowed by the Fiat Foundation, headquartered in Turin, and my own role at IUSE was that of a research scholar during the academic year 1955–1956. A surprising list of eminent guest scholars had been engaged, one week at a time, giving classes to the master students of European Studies. In particular, I remember an impressive series of lectures by Oscar Lange and the classes led by Tinbergen (and by Herman Wold, of course). His was the brain behind it all, as he and the amiable secretary Gustavo Malan had put together the roster of speakers. In addition to the Institute's teaching program, a panel that included F. Brambilla, E. Schneider, J. Tinbergen, and H. Wold had been assembled to advise the Institute on its research activities. As the first resident research scholar of the Institute, I was free to attend the classes that appealed to me, but would otherwise pursue the Institute research theme [Thore, 1956].

My main impression from listening to Tinbergen at Turin was his strong social commitment to the conduct of economic policy in the Netherlands, to the common social and cultural European heritage, and to the bettering of economic and social conditions in the third world. Naturally, he would respond to a call from a university institute of European Studies. There was no common market yet; its precursor, the European Coal and Steel Community, had been set up only in 1950. Perhaps it was this social commitment that made it easy for Tinbergen to postulate the existence of an idealized mathematical function of economic and social welfare.

I should mention a few words about the violent infighting that broke out inside the nascent discipline of econometrics, when Tinbergen's work was praised by one side and an alternative doctrine arose under the leadership of authors such as Klein and Haavelmo. Tinbergen's large models of the 1930s were all causally recursive systems, as illustrated in the typical *Tinbergen arrow diagram*, see Figure 12.1. The diagram illustrates the causal structure of the interaction between variables over time.

Tinbergen's diagram is a case of *causal chains*: each variable is determined causally by the history of the entire system (at times $t-2$ and $t-1$) and by the current performance (time t) of the *preceding* variables in the chain.

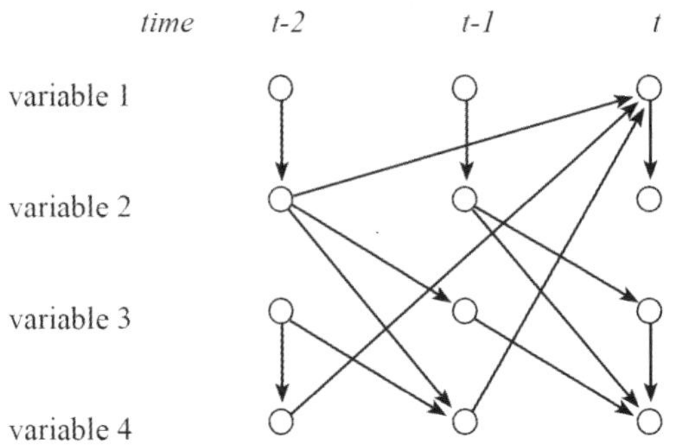

Figure 12.1 Tinbergen arrow diagram.

The alternative to the causal chain is an *interdependent* system that may include definitional relations and equilibrium conditions. For instance, the simple equation *demand* = *supply* cannot be represented as a causal chain, because it simultaneously determines two variables.

While Tinbergen in all his writings and applied econometric work had used causal chains empirically, my mentor Herman Wold during the 1960s emerged as the high priest of causal chains, exploring and codifying their mathematical properties. A typical work of his is the 1964 volume *Econometric Model Building: Essays on the Causal Chain Approach*. To Wold, the causal chain was the formal expression of causality itself. Faced with a market condition *demand* = *supply*, Wold immediately would ask "Why is demand equal to supply? How did it come about?" and his answer invariably would be in terms of a causal chain (such as the market price responding with some time lag to small differences between demand and supply).

To me, those were the glorious days of econometrics. But the fun was to be spoiled. *A Textbook of Econometrics* by Lawrence Klein [1953] and the school of interdependent systems no doubt represented massive mathematical advance, but at a terrible cost: the discipline of econometrics became the battleground of ever more sophisticated mathematicians and lost touch with the common economist. The journal *Econometrica,* which had been one of the flagship journals of the economic profession at large, eventually was to become just one among many journals specializing in the statistical estimation of economic relationships.

In 1963 I saw the writing on the wall and I decided that my love relationship with econometrics was over. I left econometrics for good, and turned my attention to operations research instead. While the econometric profession at large would churn out ever larger econometric models of the US and other economies, to this day I still believe that this work is misdirected. The Tinbergen arrow diagram somehow got lost along the way.

During the 1950s and 1960s, Tinbergen's international fame was growing and his work on economic planning won general acclaim (see Chapter 1 in this book). It was only natural that he (together with Ragnar Frisch) would be selected in December 1969 as the first recipient of the newly created Prize in Economic Science in memory of Alfred Nobel, instituted by Sveriges Riksbank (the central bank of Sweden) to celebrate its 300th anniversary.

Tinbergen's Nobel lecture, *The Use of Models: Experience and Prospects* [1969], must have surprised the listeners, as they heard him stress the limited reach of economic knowledge. Rather disarmingly, he confessed that his decade-long statistical studies of the fluctuations in investment activity during the business cycle never led to any confident conclusions and that, as head of the Netherlands central planning bureau, he found it safer to "ask industrialists for their investment programs" rather than to rely on econometric explanations. He had also found government expenditure difficult to forecast. (Both variables are determined by a small number of decision makers.) Random fluctuations are important.

To Tinbergen, social policy was a major determinant of the development of the economic system. Discussing the need to expand the economic analysis to include educational variables, Tinbergen pointed out that the budget for education in the Netherlands at this time was among the largest of the various ministries. *Educational variables* to be included in the analysis could be gross enrollment data in schools or educational facilities or — even better — the number of students specified by type of education.

Another set of social variables would characterize the *income distribution*. He was concerned about the negative effects of too uneven distributions but hoped that "Models ... may soon be used to study in a more precise way ... the possibilities to change income distribution and, for example, to find out what degree of inequality is inevitable." Surprisingly enough, he does not refer to the Gini index.

A third set of social variables mentioned would be the sets and costs of *economic and social institutions*. What Tinbergen seemed to have in mind here was not only central and local government agencies but the organization of economic and social life in general, such as it might differ under capitalism or state socialism. As an example he mentions the costs of tax collection. Had he lived today and seen the mushrooming modern welfare state in all Western countries, he would no doubt have added to his list the cost of operating welfare systems, administrative costs, and perhaps even costs in terms of lost incentives.

What about the overarching preference or utility function of his earlier works? It was still very much in his thoughts. "It is better first to specify the social welfare function as precisely as possible," he said, "and then... use it for finding the socioeconomic optimum." As he concluded his speech, he expressed the hope that one day comparative studies of the socioeconomic optimum would lead to "a discussion of a more scientific character... about the relative merits of various existing socioeconomic orders, especially those of Eastern and Western Europe." He ended by suggesting that "more fundamental research in economics deserves relatively more attention and resources than the more superficial versions of economic research directed at forecasting and analyzing very short-term fluctuations . . . ."

Chapter 13

Abe Charnes
(1917–1992)

A letter from the Technological Institute, Northwestern University arrived on Herman Wold's desk in Uppsala in May of 1963 — a letter that was to change the lives of my family and me forever. A. Charnes, a prolific contributor to the rapidly expanding new science of operations research, had written to Wold that he had a position available for a visiting research scientist in the upcoming academic year. He asked whether Wold could recommend some young PhD among his students who would be willing to travel to the States for a year to work with him.

In retrospect, it is easy to understand Charnes's intentions. He and Bill Cooper were busy at the time developing the methods of chance-constrained programming (originally designed to deal with a problem of scheduling the production of heating oil at the Esso Standard Oil Company) [Charnes, Cooper & Symonds, 1958]. Wold was one of the leading authorities in the world on stochastic processes.

As all Wold's graduate students, I knew all the ins and outs of Wold's doctoral dissertation of 1938. His famous "decomposition theorem" had in one stroke made Wold one of the portal figures of stochastic processes, together with Kolmogorov. The timing of the letter was fortuitous — with my doctoral work on household savings, I had ended up right in the firing line between the two ruling but fiercely antagonistic schools of econometrics: causal chains (the "baby" of my mentor Wold) and interdependent systems (represented by Haavelmo, faculty opponent at the public hearing of my dissertation). Being essentially a peaceful person, I had become thoroughly disenchanted with the future of econometrics and had decided to leave this field of research entirely. I was on the lookout for new green pastures. The offer to move into operations research under the guidance of one of its founding scholars was a heaven-sent opportunity.

Three months later, in the sweltering August heat, our small family arrived at O'Hare airport, Chicago: my wife Margrethe and I, our three-year-old daughter, our newborn son, and our nanny. Charnes had sent his research assistant Ken Kortanek to meet us (who would later set his mark on semi-infinite programming). He picked us up in a gigantic blue Cabriolet and drove us to our lodgings on Michigan Avenue, a few blocks south of Northwestern University.

My travel luggage included the two volumes of *Management Models and Industrial Applications of Linear Programming* [1961], a magistral work that summed up the essentials of a flood of some forty papers on the subject that Charnes & Cooper had published, jointly or separately, during the preceding decade. I was reading it with increasing enthusiasm. Up to now, linear programming had seemed to me essentially an abstract mathematical procedure — but here was a wealth of practical real-life applications.

I was soon to discover the downside of the practical appeal of Charnes's work. It was virtually impossible to meet with him at his office. At an early point I and my family had been invited to his home, meeting with his charming wife Kay and their children, but at the office — no. His secretary told me: "Dr. Charnes is very, very busy. He has scheduled meetings or other events every single day for the next two months." Perhaps she could fit me in some time in December!

Charnes was a magnetic teacher. His graduate seminar was jammed with people, many of them coming straight from the department of mathematics. Two students would be assigned to write an abstract of each class, type it, and distribute it in mimeographed form for the next class meeting. The task was sought after, but not easy, because the material that Charnes would cover would sometimes be made up on the spot, only to appear in a new journal article some months later, perhaps even featuring the student as a coauthor. We were in awe. We were in the presence of a genius.

The set date in December finally arrived. I had carefully prepared myself. As always, Charnes wanted to be presented with a practical real-life problem. I presented him with a case of calculating the needs of a bank to hold liquid reserves in the face of fluctuating levels of demand deposits. I wrote two lines of math on the black board featuring a chance-constrained lower limit on the level of liquid reserves — a constraint that would be permitted to be violated sometimes but not too often. Charnes did not say anything, just regarded me in silence. More silence. Then, feverishly, he started filling the entire black board with new math. I got lost almost immediately, I did not dare to ask him, and I just tried to visually memorize a few formulas without understanding them.

At that very moment, the phone rang. The local police office was calling. My wife Margrethe who had been speeding to the hospital with our sick baby boy had been stopped and brought to the police station. I was needed immediately and in person to post bail! Aghast, I left the office in a great hurry.

The following months I worked hard to reconstruct what Charnes had shown me on the black board before the phone rang, and five months later I presented him with a draft joint paper. He read it, changed a couple of words in the introduction, and I submitted it to *The Journal of Finance* where it was promptly accepted for publication [Charnes & Thore, 1966]. I had worked hard for one full academic year. He had worked hard for one hour. And yet, the paper is truly a joint product, shared equally — a fairly pedestrian approach from my side, ennobled by Charnes's inspired mathematical insight.[13]

At the time, I never quite understood how the most famous research team in operations research in the world — Abe Charnes, Bill Cooper, and their numerous collaborators and PhD students — actually operated. During some of their most productive years (1957 to 1968) they lived 500 miles

[13]For the reader who would like to see in some detail how Abe Charnes' genius worked, I might here indicate the key step of deduction that he came up with during that aborted meeting. In the published paper, the chance-constrained formulation (16) essentially reproduces the math that Abe was considering on the black board. Converting, he was led to the convex programming problem (19). How could it be solved? In an extraordinary *tour de force*, Abe found a two-step maneuver that reduced the entire programming problem at hand to an unconstrained maximization problem.

apart — with Charnes at Northwestern University on the shores of Lake Michigan, and Cooper never leaving their common alma mater Carnegie Institute of Technology (rechristened Carnegie Mellon in 1965) in the steel town of Pittsburgh. Communication was not made easier by the fact that Charnes preferred to travel by train in the 1960s. (He claimed that he would get a lot of work done on the train, but the truth was that he was afraid of airplane accidents, at the time not uncommon).

They had originally met over lunch at Carnegie Institute of Technology in 1948 when Charnes began his postdoctoral career as an assistant professor of mathematics. Their collaboration began when Charnes joined a team including B. Mellon of Gulf Oil Company to work on processes associated with the blending of aviation gasolines, and led to the seminal papers [Charnes, 1952; Charnes, Cooper & Mellon, 1952] which in one stroke converted the early developments of linear programming by J. von Neumann into a practical and easy-to-use tool.

The work that Charnes and Cooper did for Gulf Oil was followed up by a series of other practical applications. These included assignments for General Electric (leading to the development of goal programming) and for the Standard Oil Company of New Jersey (chance-constrained programming). The key to the extraordinary fecundity of their research was no doubt their strong bonds of friendship, a strong sense of joint purpose, and their accelerating insight into the potential of the new operations research techniques that they invented. Some sciences are more or less sterile, having been harvested over and over again. Operations research under their hands became a new exploding science.

The importance of their work was quickly recognized by their peers, as manifested by the launching of The Institute of Management Science (TIMS) with Cooper as the first (founding) president. Charnes became its vice president, then president and the editor of *Management Science*, the society's journal.

More than 10 years were to pass before I saw Abe Charnes again. We would exchange Christmas cards, and I would send him copies of some of my publications (several of which dealt with the management of bank portfolios under uncertainty). His old friend George Kozmetsky, now dean at the Graduate school of Business at The University of Texas at Austin, offered him a prestigious chair at the business school, where he would also be directing a new Center for Cybernetic Studies. He transferred from Northwestern University to The University of Texas at Austin in the fall of 1968.

A couple of days before Easter 1975, I was taking a hot bath in our home in Bergen, Norway when the telephone rang. I recognized the soft voice immediately. Charnes, calling from Texas, asked if he could send first class return tickets to my wife and me: Bergen-to-Mexico City. There would be a meeting organized by the Mexican Banking Association and Charnes was putting together a program on operations research in banking.

Charnes loved Mexico, only an hour by air from his home in Austin, Texas. There he and his wife would thoroughly relax. Our two families took some time off from the conference proceedings to take a full day's tour to see the Teotihuacan pyramids some 25 miles north of Mexico City. The next day our wives went shopping; just walking along the aisles of the crammed bazaar in the center of Mexico City is an unforgettable experience. Explosions of color!

13.1 Early Developments of Linear Programming

One afternoon, over a glass of wine, I asked Charnes to tell me about the early days of linear programming. There was a special reason why I raised this issue, which I could not mention to him at the time. In the spring of 1972 I had been asked by the secretary to the Nobel Committee in Stockholm to prepare a report detailing the early developments of linear programming in economics. Such reports are routinely being compiled and kept up to date by the Committee to serve as background material for the selection of possible future Nobel prizes in economics. A couple of months later I had fallen ill and I had written to the Nobel Committee asking to be relieved from the assignment. (It was later transferred to some other Scandinavian professor of economics but I do not know whom.)

Charnes impressed upon me that John von Neumann was the true "father" of linear programming. Around the year 1947 he presented in his lectures the main features, including the simplex method; he also indicated the nature of the dual theorem. His work was continued by his students including G. Dantzig. Much of this work was published in the *Cowles Commission Monograph no. 13*, 1951. It should be noted that at this early date, no practical application of linear programming had ever been reported in the literature. There was no clear understanding of the interpretation of the dual problem. Only in the summer of 1951, at a meeting of the American Mathematical Society, Charnes and Greenberg presented a practical example where a straightforward interpretation could be accorded to both the direct and the dual variables.

Early attempts at practical application of linear programming had invariably been stranded because the simplex calculations ran into indeterminacy and degeneracy. At the time nobody knew how to deal with this. The problem of degeneracy was finally solved by Charnes in his paper *Optimality and Degeneracy in Linear Programming* [1952]. His solution introduced so-called non-Archimedean field extensions into the mathematical programming literature — a mathematical strategem to which he would repeatedly return, in his future research.

When Charnes submitted his paper to *Econometrica* the editor W. B. Simpson sent it on to George Dantzig for review. This was not a good choice. It was difficult for Dantzig to write the referee report in an impartial manner since he was known to have strong negative feelings about Charnes. Upon the advice of L. Hurwicz, Simpson therefore passed the refereeing task on to N. Georgescu-Roegen, and the paper was immediately accepted for publication.

Dantzig responded by submitting a "Note on Charnes's paper on optimality and degeneracy in linear programming" to the journal. Simpson sent it on to Charnes so that he could answer in the same issue of the journal — a common practice. Charnes did indeed write an answer "Rejoinder to G. B. Dantzig: A comparison of perturbation methods" pointing out mathematical errors in Dantzig's opus. Dantzig then withdrew his Note; it was never published, nor was the Charnes Rejoinder ever published. (For further details, see the account in *Management Models and Industrial Applications*, vol. 1, pp. 428–429).

Thus started a lifelong shadow boxing match between Charnes and Dantzig, a kind of scholarly one-upmanship that took both tragic and sometimes comic forms. I will return to that in a moment.

With the degeneracy problem satisfactorily dealt with, it was finally possible to turn to a real-life application of linear programming: the blending of aviation gasoline. It was a classic joint effort, Charnes having developed the math, Cooper doing the calculations on an old-fashioned hand-operated calculator, and Mellon supplying the specific industry knowledge. This pathbreaking work appeared in the April 1952 issue of *Econometrica* [Charnes, Cooper & Mellon].

So, who got the Nobel prize for the development of linear programming in economics, handed out in 1975? Two names always stood at the top of the list: L. Kantorovich and Tj. Koopmans. The Nobel committee decided to limit the coverage of the prize to economics proper, not entering into the matter of mathematical priorities. Kantorovich got his prize for his work on industrial scheduling in Leningrad before the war, and Koopmans for the development of the transportation model in international trade, and for activity analysis.

In September 1977 a large symposium was organized by Charnes's many students all over the world to honor him on his 60th birthday. Our symposium committee was headed by Ken Kortanek, A. Fiacco, and Darwin Klingman; the proceedings were held at The University of Texas at Austin and later published in the volume with Kortanek and Fiacco as editors [1980]. Charnes had the ability to attract outstanding students that remained warmly attached to him over the years and it was a wonderful experience for us to meet again, in the lecture halls and in the beautiful home of Kay and Abe Charnes, located not very far from the campus. On the last evening, they hosted an elegant dinner as a band of Mexican *mariachis* concerted on their instruments.

While visiting in Austin, we all had a chance to admire the gleaming new facilities of the business school, now rapidly climbing to national prominence under the leadership of Dean Kozmetsky. And there was a secret, Charnes confided to me. An offshoot of the business school, a think tank dedicated to the study of capitalism, was about to be launched, funded by the vast wealth of the Kozmetsky family. Would I be interested?

And so it came about — a year later, in midsummer of 1978 — that my wife and I with our two children who were still in school, settled down in an attractive residential area in Austin, at first on a three year assignment. I became a research fellow of the new Institute for Constructive Capitalism, a position that later, in connection with the centennial celebrations of the establishment of The University of Texas at Austin in 1883, was converted into a "Centennial" fellowship named after Gregory A. Kozmetsky, the son of Dean Kozmetsky.

13.2 The Value-transfer Economy

As I started working at the Institute for Creative Capitalism, a new mathematical economic model had recently been discovered by Charnes and Cooper: the "resource value-transfer" economy. On the surface, it seemed to deliver precisely what an institute for creative capitalism presumably would be all about. The model reflects a view of the economy which is very different from orthodox economic equilibrium theory, but which corresponded to the way in which many people then perceived economic reality — that resource prices and the horizontal income distribution are the results of a political struggle, rather than being determined in competitive markets.

This political struggle occurs on two levels: first, there is a struggle between the resource-owners for sharing the total resource-earnings accruing in the economy. The resource-owners bargain for higher prices (wages, the price of oil, coal, rare metals). Second, there is a struggle among various consumer groups for sharing national income. In many countries the horizontal income distribution is determined by the relative bargaining power of labor unions, farmers, *etc.*

In 1974 Charnes and Cooper published a mathematical model to capture the characteristics of such an economy, which they called a "resource value-transfer economy." They assumed that, as a result of bargaining and restrictive practices, resource-owners receive a fixed and given sum of money from the sale of each resource. They further assumed that the horizontal distribution of income resulted in a fixed and given sum of money becoming available for expenditure by each consumer group. In other words, there were fixed and given shares of the "cake" both in the earning and spending of national income. They discovered a sophisticated optimization principle that solves such an economy.

I was slightly taken aback when I received a reprint of their publication and saw that the paper was published in a venerable Italian journal that I did not even know existed: the *Rendiconti Accademia Nazionale de Lincei,* the proceedings of the academy of "lynxes" (smart observers) founded by Galileo Galilei. This was part of the never-ending game of hide and seek with George Dantzig: burying their paper in an obscure journal, Dantzig would presumably not discover their work immediately, thus giving Charnes and Cooper time to develop their model further without interference from others. But alas, Dantzig had eyes of a "lynx" too, and within 18 months his own work on an institutionalized "divvy" economy appeared in print in the *Journal of Economic Theory*.

What happened then, to the resource value-transfer model? Very little, I am afraid. With the perspective of 35 years of hindsight, one must say that it turned out to be a dead end. I am not aware of any further publication that brought the model significantly forward, neither theoretically nor empirically. This is unfortunate, because as I write these lines the thought strikes me that, as the orthodox model in economics has come crushing down these few last years, and a new worldwide battle among nations for the control of oil and rare minerals is under way, the fight over the divvying-up of the cake is more intense than ever.

Instead, other priorities quickly presented themselves for both Charnes himself and for the new Institute for Constructive Capitalism. A new and tremendously powerful computational tool invented by Charnes and Cooper appeared on the scene in 1978, termed by them "data envelopment analysis." Originally conceived of as a method of ranking the achievements of preschool education, it now started its triumphal march, growing into a major tool of empirical work in economics in our own day. I shall relate the explosion of scholarly work in this area in the essay on W.W. Cooper.

The Institute for Constructive Capitalism under the direction of its creator George Kozmetsky in the early 1980s moved with full force into the area of commercialization of new technology. That too is a huge success story, but it falls outside the scope of my present concern.

13.3 Chance-constrained Programming

As I settled down to my daily tasks at the Institute for Constructive Capitalism, my collaboration with Charnes did not come out as successfully as I had hoped. I did some work with him and Ken Kortanek on the resource value-transfer economy, but the results were not spectacular and without publication results. Seeing him regularly at his office, he would seat me at a small rickety table in front of him. Bringing up various points of mathematical analysis, he would search the vast shelves with mathematical treatises behind him, pull out one thick volume after another and thrust them on the table. Opening the books, he would criticize the author's text and immediately turn to some alternative development by another author. These were all household names in mathematical analysis, but they did not find favor for Charnes's critical eyes. A basic sin that authors of mathematical texts often commit is to introduce assumptions up front that are excessively stringent. Routinely, they would assume continuity or convexity, even though much weaker assumptions might suffice for the argument to follow. Charnes hated such inexactitude.

It was a privilege to witness close-hand how one of the sharpest mathematical minds of the century worked. First there would be a lengthy session of beating about the bush, as it were — a monologue of small talk about similar problems that he had dealt with in the past, and episodes from the writing of earlier papers. Most sentences he spoke were never completed, just odd glimpses into his train of thoughts, but since I was pretty familiar with most of his work I usually managed to follow him. After these introductory rituals, he would mobilize the sum total of his intellectual energy in one blow, attempting to crack some problem head on. Each time I saw it I was equally impressed. I cannot solve mathematical problems that way — head-on by sheer mental concentration; I need time.

The basic truth was that I fell short of the mathematical gifts that greater collaboration would have demanded. I felt more comfortable returning instead to some of the well-established Charnes-Cooper programming techniques, such as chance-constrained programming. I was more convinced than ever that Charnes and Cooper had developed many specialized programming tools of operations research that had a great future in economics proper. As I settled down at my job at the Institute for Constructive Capitalism, this became my credo and the guiding light for my work.

Although the work of Charnes always presupposed numerical calculations, he himself did little numerical work. This aspect was often delegated to coauthors. He himself was therefore not really involved in the dramatic revolution in data processing and new simplified data codes that arrived in the 1980s. Yet, it is important to touch on this issue here because this revolution transformed some of the highly sophisticated programming techniques that Charnes and Cooper would routinely use (*i.e.*, chance-constrained programming, integer programming, programming with zero-one variables, and nonlinear programming) into simple numerical tools readily available to a vast audience.

The revolution occurred on two levels: the development of new simplified computer languages and the arrival of the personal computer. When I arrived at The University of Texas at Austin, I had used the software package Mathematical Programming System (MPS) for many years and was thoroughly familiar with it, both for linear and nonlinear programming. It was the workhorse of management science those days, and it did what it was supposed to do. But it required considerable processing capabilities on a large university computer. I quickly became a fixed presence in the computing rooms of The University of Texas at Austin's Computing Center and in the Business School Computing Center. At that time, you submitted the program via a computer terminal (featuring a monitor and a keyboard), and went back to the Computing Center some six hours later to retrieve a printout of the results. To preclude renewed runs asking for more details about the solution, a single standard printout often featured hundreds of pages.

David Kendrick of the Department of Economics had, for a couple of years, been involved in an ambitious project at the World Bank to develop a new programming language for the solution of large and complex mathematical programming models. This new software tool was called General Algebraic Modelling System (GAMS). When I arrived at The University of Texas at Austin in 1978, Kendrick gracefully shared with me a preliminary version of the program package, so that I was able to use it for several years before it was introduced to the market. (Kendrick was the sole star in a rather miserable department mainly devoted to pursuing Marxist "heterodox" theory. Things went so bad in the 1980s that there was talk of closing down the department entirely.)

For me, the availability of GAMS turned out to be a huge blessing, enabling me to solve numerically a variety of models of chance-constrained programming. I applied this programming method to spatial equilibrium [Thore, 1986] and to activity analysis [Thore, 1987]. When I later prepared a comparison of the performance of Western free markets to state capitalism in the Soviet Union and in Eastern Europe, my mathematical tool was, again, chance-constrained programming.

One of the most pressing challenges of contemporary economic research, as I saw it, was to reveal the self-deception in economic science of the achievements of the Soviet Union and Eastern Europe, and the denial and cover-up of their dismal economic performance. The original name of our research institute, the Institute for Constructive Capitalism, had filled me with delight and hopes, and had been a major factor when I accepted the invitation to join the institute in 1978. To me, with my European background, it was important. I grieved when the name of our institute in 1981 was changed to "IC^2 Institute," preserving the same acronym which was now to stand for *Innovation, Creativity, and Capital*. It was done to placate Europeans, like Henri Theil. In retrospect, perhaps it was necessary. My own teacher from England, Frank Hahn, did no longer want to shake my hand. I had badly betrayed the great don of leftist Cambridge, by working for an "institute of capitalism!"

In the 1970s, the academic professions at many European universities were under assault by strident leftist students. I had received my share of this at the Norwegian Business School at Bergen. Serving for a while as the dean of the economic subjects, during faculty meetings I was pushed from one losing battle to another as ten representatives of the Marxist student union outvoted all sensible decisions — students who once conducted a strike in the effort to block my access to my office. But in Texas, this was all very far away. Most Americans feel that capitalism is as American as apple pie. When I came to Texas, the dominant political party was the Democratic Party — and most Texans were old-fashioned, conservative Southern Democrats (long before the Bush years!).

I never had any political discussions with my colleagues at the Institute and I do not know the political views of Abe Charnes. I think the truth was that he saw everything through the eyes of a mathematician. He was proud of his contacts with the Nobel laureate Kantorovich, who sent a paper to the 1977 Austin symposium honoring Charnes's 60th birthday. Abe wanted to reach out to scholars all over the world, beyond the confines of "operations research" or "management science" as understood in the West. So, when moving from Northwestern University to The University of Texas at Austin, Abe named his research center in the business school "The Center for Cybernetic Studies." To him "cybernetic" was a term of more global outreach.

Benefiting from my work on chance-constrained programming, I was brought to the idea that key differences between Western capitalism and Soviet planning could be expressed in terms of chance-constraints. Under both political systems, output of produced goods is uncertain and may fail to cover demand. In the capitalist economy, total output is uncertain because of technological uncertainty surrounding manufacturing, distribution, and marketing. Capitalism therefore needs to accumulate buffers of inventories to meet demand. Under state socialism, output is uncertain for very different reasons: there is bureaucratic uncertainty in the planning process that leads to supply bottlenecks, late delivery of raw materials and spare parts, and changes in production plans in the middle of the planning period. The result is chronic shortages of consumer goods, indicating that the central planning agency does not even attempt to meet demand. [Land, Lovell & Thore, 1992].

Pursuing these ideas [Land, Lovell & Thore, 1993; 1994], we later developed chance-constrained DEA and applied this new programming tool to compare the economic performance of a group of Western European market economies with that of state socialism (see Chapter 3). Finally, a viable tool to numerically determine the economic short-comings of state socialism. I tried to convey my enthusiasm to Abe, but I am not sure that he understood my feelings. By then the Soviet Union had disappeared from the map and most centrally planned economies with it.

13.4 Game Theory

In addition to his pathbreaking contributions to mathematical programming, Charnes was a pioneer in the theory of games. As early as 1928 von Neumann had proved the minimax theorem for all matrix games ("a saddle-point exists, defining an optimal strategy and the value of the game"), but it was only with the book *Theory of Games and Economic Behavior* by von Neumann and Morgenstern [1947] that modern research in the area got under way. In a classic paper, Charnes [1953] showed how the new theory of linear programming could be brought to bear on the game concepts developed by von Neumann and Morgenstern.

As always, the guiding star for Charnes was his desire to aid and serve practical applications. Discussing a game played by players subject to linear constraints, he demonstrated how it could be transcribed into an equivalent linear programming problem. Together with his work on resolving degeneracy in linear programming, this opened the door for actual large-scale numerical solution of real-life games. Thus, in effect, Charnes turned game theory into a tool for both qualitative characterizations and practical numerical solution. As an example I might mention the characterizations and computations of the optimal landing fees at Birmingham airport in England (each aircraft movement being a player in a more than 13,000 person game) carried out by his PhD student Stephen Littlechild [Littlechild & Thompson, 1977].

An important lesson to be drawn from Charnes's 1953 work is this: In many ways the saddle-point problem provides a more general formulation than its two uni-extremal equivalents, one max problem and one min problem. Each of these two employs additional variables stemming from the constraints and the objective function of the other. Neither problem requires any information on the other problem's optimal solution. In this sense, the max problem and the min problem are completely separable and each problem has its own interpretation. In my conversations with Charnes in the 1980s, we repeatedly returned to these observations. During those years, I was doing the groundwork on my monograph *Economic Logistics* (eventually published in 1991), in which I surveyed an array of operations research models dealing with transportation, production, and storage — most of them formulated as constrained maximization problems (maximizing "quasi-welfare" being a function of quantities demanded by consumers). For each of them there exists an alternative minimization formulation (minimizing "indirect quasi-welfare" being expressed as a function of prices). So, here too, a fundamental saddle-point principle is at work.

Abe had put in my hands a 1982 work titled, *Game Theory* by G. Owen, and I immersed myself in the treatment of two-person infinite games. In an "infinite" game each player may select from a continuum of choices over some given closed interval. For any logistics model, there then exists a saddle-point problem with a "quantum player" controlling all production and distribution, and a "price player" setting all prices. The saddle-point can be solved by a max problem in quantum variables or a min problem in price variables; the two problems are completely separable and each one has its own interpretation. Thus the insights of Abe Charnes from 1953 ultimately led to an overarching saddle-point formulation of any programming problem of economic logistics.

In the late 1980s a most unfortunate event occurred, a tragedy that befell Abe Charnes and Bill Cooper alike. Two good friends who had shared so much of their academic lives had a serious falling out and they stopped working together. Worse than that: they did not even talk to each other. They never made up. There was no reconciliation.

I never knew what happened or when. First, people around them assumed that it was just a matter of some passing hot temper. Eventually the awful truth sank in. Everybody was baffled: of course they had strong personalities and they were both uncompromising in their scientific rectitude and honesty. But they had been friends for so many years and they were both charming and open-minded persons. The two families knew each intimately, and their wives Kay Charnes and Ruth Cooper were longstanding, good friends. My wife Margrethe has reminded me of the following episode: When she, together with Ronya and George Kozmetsky, and a few close friends, arranged a festive dinner for Ruth on her 75th birthday in 1990, the Charnes couple was not present.

This rift between the two friends did not seem to put a damper on their separate innovative powers or routines of hard work. Each of them continued to inspire his own team of students and collaborators. For several years Abe Charnes continued to bring a number of outstanding Chinese PhD students to Texas, publishing with them in his usual ferocious tempo.

When I last visited Charnes at his office, he was ill. Abe Charnes died in February 1993. A beautiful celebration of his life was held at the CBA Hall of Honors at The University of Texas at Austin.

Author's Note:

In this essay on Abe Charnes and the following one on Bill Cooper I am describing their joint work as I myself encountered it over a time span of more than 30 years. I am telling this story the way I experienced things, in a very personal and subjective way. It is certainly not in any way a balanced and objective biography. My account of Charnes covers the following operations research techniques:

- early developments of linear programming,
- the resource-value transfer economy,
- chance-constrained programming,
- game theory.

In the essay on Bill Cooper I have found it natural to discuss:

- goal programming,
- data envelopment analysis.

This division of material only reflects my own preoccupations as I was working in the shadow of these two great scholars. All their work published under their two names was truly joint work. Together they garnered many awards, including the John von Neumann Theory Prize in 1982, as seen below.

Chapter 14

W. W. Cooper
(1914–2012)

When I first met Bill Cooper, he was one of the luminaries of Carnegie Mellon University: founding member and first president of The Institute for Management Science (TIMS), associate editor for *Operations Research*, and departmental editor of *Management Science*. The modern reader may not be aware of the unique position of Carnegie Mellon University in the academic world of the 1960s and 1970s. Over time, information theory — the IT revolution — has spread over the entire academic spectrum, but in those days Carnegie Mellon ruled the IT kingdom. The university had brought together a unique set of superstars, including polyhistor Herbert Simon, who held a chair in computer science and psychology. Seen today as the father of artificial intelligence, Herb's efforts matured into the construction of "Big Blue," the IBM chess-playing machine that beat Kasparov in 1994.

I just could not believe my luck in installing myself and my family as a young visiting professor at the Graduate School of Industrial Administration (the business school at Carnegie Mellon) in the fall of 1969. These were hallowed grounds. The brainpower of the faculty was matched by awesome digital resources in hardware. I remember my stupefaction when my wife and I were invited to dinner at the home of Gerald Thompson, one of the professors in the GSIA, and he took me down to the basement to show his "home computer." A home computer? Even the concept was new to me, a computer was something that you needed a huge university facility with scores of employees to run. Gerry explained to me that his was the first satellite computer that Carnegie Mellon had built, connected to the mainframe via a dial-up mechanism.

On a small scale, I was to benefit from the huge computing resources at the university (as was my research assistant Finn Kydland whom I had brought along for the fall of 1969, and who later made a glorious career at Carnegie Mellon, capped by a Nobel prize in 2004).

I met Bill Cooper for the first time in September 1969. It was not quite what you would call an orderly introduction. The occasion was the dean's annual party for faculty and wives. Dean Richard Cyert (later chancellor of the university) lived in a posh area of town and as my wife and I drove up to the house, the driveway and surrounding streets were crammed with parked Chevrolets and Lincolns. Those were the days of the large American car with hundreds of horsepower under the hood. I myself owned a glorious pastel blue Buick Electra. Inside we were greeted by the hosts, a huge dinner buffet, and two servants (dressed in livery) carving and serving slices from two gigantic roasts of beef.

But the house was surprisingly small and there was no empty sitting space to be seen. Balancing our full plates with some generous helpings of brown sauce, we piloted our way to the adjoining room, following the maelstrom of guests, but no luck. Behind us people were pushing, so we stumbled down a narrow staircase and entered the childrens' rooms downstairs. The first one, full again — the second, ah — some available sitting room on a bouncy double bed (already occupied by several couples eagerly enjoying their dinner). As I tasted my first mouthful of the roast beef, I realized that an energetic guest on the other side of the bed was lecturing everybody who cared to hear, about the need to develop new mathematical techniques to measure social processes. Thus I met the legendary Bill Cooper.

At this time, Bill was already a dean himself, head of the innovative School of Urban and Public Affairs. The school was his own brainchild and the first of its kind in the United States. The idea is easy to explain: during the last decade Carnegie Mellon had strengthened its position as the leading academic center promoting mathematical and computer-based techniques for the study and management of business firms, and now Bill wanted to expand these activities to the field of social policy.

The idea to use mathematics and computers as a tool to solve management problems goes back to World War II, when mathematicians would calculate optimal bombing runs over enemy country, or the deployment of submarines to protect convoys. The new mathematics developed for this purpose was called "operations research." After the war, the idea was born to adapt the same techniques to some kind of "scientific" conduct of regular business operations — "management science." Two intellectual giants stood out in these efforts, young researchers at the Graduate School of Industrial Administration, Carnegie Mellon University: A. Charnes and W. W. Cooper. In hundreds of pathbreaking papers, they would establish management science as a reputable and impressive new field of scholarly research.

In these efforts, Charnes and Cooper struck up a lasting friendship with George Kozmetsky, a young researcher at Harvard. Kozmetsky decided to test the theory that this new mathematics could be used to make money. He founded Teledyne (with Henry Singleton), which would become one of the largest industrial combines in the nation. The three friends (with others) started The Institute of Management Science, a society having the objective of "identifying, extending, and unifying scientific knowledge that contributed to the understanding and practice of management." Cooper was its first president. Kozmetsky guaranteed financial standing for the society's new journal, *Management Science*.

But Bill Cooper's ambition went beyond making money out of operations research. Not that money didn't mean anything to him. He had always managed without a surplus of money. As an undergraduate student at the University of Chicago in the mid-1930s, Cooper supported himself as a professional boxer at nights. (Bill's legacy from those days was that he had a wonderful physique. He was the kind of person you would not want to meet in a dark alley at night in the seedier districts of Chicago.) "I learned from that to be prepared and take advantage of all opportunities," he said to a reporter in 2002. "If a guy drops his guard, you move in. If you wait until a punch is thrown, it's too late." That wisdom, he allowed, has served him in academia as well as in the ring.

The great overriding inspiration driving Cooper was instead to find out if the new mathematical methods of operations research could successfully be applied to *public* management science. That's where he wanted to "move in." He saw his opportunity to do just that with the joint development of the Charnes-Cooper technique of "goal programming."

14.1 Goal Programming

The initial developments of goal programming were presented in Charnes, Cooper, and Ferguson [1955], and involved setting goals for executive compensation. Typical applications to public or social management have dealt with resource allocation in a marine environmental protection program, and budgetary decisions in a consumer protection regulatory agency. (For reference to these works and many others, see the survey article Charnes and Cooper [1977].)

In 1968, Bill Cooper and Otto Davis had prepared a proposal to the Richard King Mellon Foundation to create a School of Urban and Public Affairs (SUPA). The proposal found favor with the Mellon family who donated 10 million dollars for the purpose. Cooper became the first dean.[14] Directing the educational program and the research carried out at the new school, Cooper became one of the early pioneers of the branch of economics that today is known as "environmental economics."

It is easy to explain how goal programming can account for environmental and social considerations. Suppose that a policymaker feels that the exploitation of some resource X is excessive and detrimental in the long run, such as the deforestation of wildlife tracts and tropical rain forests, eventually leading to erosion of soil and climate change. The employment of other resources may be observed as lacking, such as the use of unskilled labor, workers with handicaps, *etc.* In short, assume that it is possible to encapsulate the various considerations regarding the use of the resource into a single numerical goal g and write

$$X = g + g^{+} - g^{-}$$

[14]In 1992 the school was renamed as the H. John Heinz III School of Public Policy and Management in honor of Senator H. John Heinz III.

Deviations from the goal are permitted, both in the positive direction (an over-fulfillment or excess is here denoted by g^+) and in the negative direction (an under-fulfillment or deficit being denoted by g^-). Deviations from the goal are associated with penalties. For instance, in the case of supply of ground water there will be some large penalty to be paid for over-withdrawal from the aquifer. No penalty will be levied for withdrawals of ground water that fall short of the goal figure. Let the unit penalties be M and N respectively, and total penalties are then

$$Mg^+ + Ng^-$$

The larger the penalty that is associated with deviation from a goal, the more likely it is that the goal will be satisfied. Whether penalties are charged in cash or are suffered as a psychological inconvenience, in the goal programming formulation they are, in all circumstances, counted as costs of doing business — like costs for raw materials, power, water, *etc.*

A key question in all goal programming is this: Who will enforce the optimal solution? Clearly, some mechanism of enforcement is needed, otherwise the solution will revert to the free market solution. Few producers will voluntarily adjust their use of inputs unless they are induced to do so by being forced to pay goal penalties, or by being paid goal subsidies, directly or indirectly. There are several answers to this question. One possibility is social and attitudinal change: some producers may become aware of the urgency of environmental factors; they will then act as if bonuses and penalties are assessed for goal deviations. But no bonuses would actually be paid and no penalties collected in dollars and cents. Another possibility is that local or central government actually pays the bonuses and collects the penalties in cash. Examples of the latter are provided by the US steel industry, which since the mid-1960s has had to comply with environmental guidelines, and pay cash fines for excessive pollution of air and/or water.

A third possibility is that local or central government computes the dual variable (shadow price) of the goal constraint, as shown above, and introduces a system of unit *subsidies* or *excise taxes* connected with the use of resources. The possibility of such subsidies and excise taxes was discussed in 1915 by A. C. Pigou in his book *The Economics of Welfare.* The use of Pigou taxes have become widespread in the modern economy, for instance as excise taxes on cigarettes, liquor, and gasoline.

Speaking in terms of modern welfare analysis, the purpose of the Pigou tax is to *internalize* the negative external economies associated with the use of the good in question. But a Pigou tax is not the only way this can be done. Sometimes it is possible to define property rights to the environmental factors which are being damaged, and to let the owner of these property rights charge a market price for the use of his property. For instance, the owner of a large wilderness tract may charge cash for hunting permits, or the owner of a river may charge a fee for permitting an upstream factory to release toxic waste into his waters.

The beauty of Charnes-Cooper goal programming is that it provides the analyst with a computing tool that not only calculates the optimal possibilities of satisfying as closely as possible the environmental targets, but also in one stroke via the corresponding dual program supplies the optimal Pigou taxes (and/or subsidies).

Cooper had become something of a national celebrity and other universities eyed his success at Carnegie Mellon with jealousy. Finally, Harvard University made him an offer that he "just could not refuse." He spent the five years at Harvard (1975–1980), but he never felt at home there — he never could stomach the intellectual snobbishness of the place. He longed to return to his beloved ranch outside Pittsburgh, which had been such an important part of his life. There was also the matter of the successful Pittsburgh law practice of his wife Ruth.

At this point in the story, the three friends Charnes, Cooper, and Kozmetsky closed ranks. Kozmetsky, who still owned a major part of the industrial giant Teledyne, had left running the company to his partner Singleton so that he could return to academia as dean of the business school at The University of Texas at Austin. Having demonstrated to himself and the world that "scientific management" could be harnessed to build an industrial empire, he now set himself the task of building a world-leading business research environment. He had already signed up Abe Charnes as a faculty member. Bill was still at Harvard. Kozmetsky realized the unique opportunity at hand — he could bring Charnes and Cooper together again on one single campus. Here was the most famous research team within the field of operations research who, except for two short years, had lived their careers separated from each other.

In 1977, Kozmetsky established the Institute for Constructive Capitalism[15] as a research unit within the business school to promote research in technology commercialization. Bill agreed to join Kozmetsky in Austin as a professor in the business school and as a fellow at the IC^2 Institute. The three friends were together again. The moment was precipitous. Abe and Bill were at the zenith of their creative powers, and a well-funded research organization was waiting to develop their work.

From this point on, I can report on events as a direct observer. I had joined the Institute for Constructive Capitalism in 1978, only a couple of months after it started operations. During the first few years, the research staff of the institute was quite limited but — with the construction of a new futuristic building a mile from campus — the organization became more structured and a team of "centennial" scholars under the direction of Kozmetsky was assembled. Bill Cooper was appointed to a centennial fellowship named after Kozmetsky's only daughter, Nadia. The team included a Nobel prize winner (Ilya Prigogine) and a former national security adviser (Walt Rostow).

In my essay on Abe Charnes, I have already mentioned my initial work at the institute on various models of transportation, production, and warehousing, exploring the saddle-point nature of the models and eventually bringing together my publications on the subject in a large graduate textbook. It was going to be one of the first volumes in a series on management and management science to be published by the Institute. Bill was serving as the editor of the book series and, to my good fortune, it fell upon him to critique my work.

This was the first time I had the privilege of working with Bill. He was a kind, caring person and a hard worker, digging down to the roots of any matter at hand. In my draft manuscript I had sketched a chapter on saddle-point theory, summing up the Kuhn-Tucker saddle-point theorem. Bill returned my original pages with both margins filled with comments and a number of new handwritten pages. He suggested that I also cover the matter of saddle-points in two-person games, and briefly drafted the

[15]The Institute for Constructive Capitalism founded by George Kozmetsky is now known as the IC^2 Institute; the acronym IC^2 stands for Innovation, Creativity, and Capital.

necessary math. Gratefully I realized that the end product would be a chapter jointly authored by the two of us, which he accepted.

But there were more chapters (*many* more chapters), and this amounted to a huge burden of reading. Bill took the entire manuscript with him for his annual holiday on the island paradise of St. Croix where he and his wife Ruth owned a beach apartment. I fear he spent little time enjoying the ocean, for he spent most of his morning hours scrutinizing my text and filling every page with comments.

Bill was more than a towering mathematician. He wrote fluent, beautiful, and precise English. His personal style was easy to recognize — when publishing with Abe Charnes he was always responsible for the verbal form of the final product. Bill wanted me to also write good English, and thus I received a most valuable lesson as he taught me to enjoy the writing process, rather than fear it.

Half a year later, with the manuscript getting close to its final form, I asked Bill: "The title of my manuscript (*The Optimization of Spatial and Sectoral Resource, Production, and Distribution Systems*) is really very long and tedious. Could I possibly compress the title to *Economic Logistics*? I know that there is no such recognized term — logistics is a word used in operations research, not economics — but I strongly feel that the material should be considered as belonging to economics proper."

Bill's answer still rings in my ear. "If you feel that way, then go ahead. Don't be afraid. It is our duty to show the way forward."

14.2 Data Envelopment Analysis

One of Bill's students at Carnegie Mellon was E. Rhodes, who for his dissertation research was evaluating the program Follow-Through — an educational program for disadvantaged children undertaken in US public schools with federal government support. The program recorded the performance of schools in terms of outputs such as student scores in reading and math, and included an index to measure a child's self-esteem. There were also statistics on numbers of teachers, a counseling index, and more. What kind of social or educational theory could be used to analyze such a bewildering array of data? Yet for a long time Bill had talked of tackling precisely such a complex problem. As it turned out, this research was to open the door to a new world of understanding of economic theory and policymaking.

The Charnes, Cooper, Rhodes paper on project Follow-Through was published in 1978. A year later Abe still talked about it continuously, and the breakthrough it represented: data envelopment analysis (DEA) had been born. I attended Abe's presentation of the joint paper the Institute of Management Sciences in Hawaii in 1980. It was a sensation.

The novel idea of DEA is to discard the standard assumption of optimality that pervades most of economic theory. Some school districts are manifestly more efficient than others in implementing the Follow-Through program. So, instead of forcing assumptions on the analysis which are not warranted, let us accept that most of the schools are not located on an optimality "frontier" (or "envelope"). Only a few of the schools make up the frontier. The others are falling behind. Those that fall behind are ranked. That is, the calculations yield a diagnostic for each school: its deficit performance is measured.

The truth is, it took several years for us to all realize that this new plaything of Abe and Bill really constituted a scientific revolution. Perhaps they themselves divined as much, naming it "data envelopment analysis," thus presenting the technique as a new method for processing general data — but such wide adoption was yet several years away.

As always, the PhD students of Abe and Bill were the first researchers to get into the act. R. D. Banker had been Bill's student at Harvard; his research prompted the development of a slightly different DEA model, permitting variables rates of return of the output variables (rather than the constant returns to scale that were subsumed in the Follow Through program study). The BCC-model (Banker, Charnes and Cooper) of DEA was published in 1984, to be distinguished from the CCR-model of Charnes, Cooper, and Rhodes [1978].

The calculations involved in data envelopment analysis can present numerical subtleties and — in those early days — a solution was dependent on access to rather sophisticated software. At the business school of The University of Texas at Austin, Abe directed the "Center for Cybernetic Studies" and at this time, many DEA calculations were carried out using the software package that his students had collectively assembled. Things became easier later, and in the mid-1980s, I myself wrote a program in the general algebraic modelling code GAMS. Today, specialized commercial program packages are readily available (*i.e.*, the Banxia software that was used for the calculations in Part I of this book).

With these three building blocks in place (the CCR-model, the BCC-model and numerical codes), the stage was set for data envelopment analysis to conquer the world. A major milestone was the conference on New Uses of DEA in Management and Public Policy held at the IC^2 Institute in September 1989. The resulting publication *Data envelopment analysis, Theory, Methodology and Applications,* by Charnes, Cooper, Lewin and Seiford bears the dedication, "... to George Kozmetsky for his early championing of DEA and for his lifelong commitment to nurturing creativity." The publication of the book was delayed for a couple of years and appeared in 1994. By this time, the book recorded 472 published articles and dissertations related to DEA. Unfortunately, Abe Charnes never saw the book; he died in 1992.

In evaluating the social and economic performance of nations, goal programming can be a useful complement to the standard DEA model. Rather than striving to achieve full effectiveness along the DEA frontier, an international organization such as the Organisation for African Unity (OAU) may declare certain targets for its member states. Deviations from these goals on either side are possible but may not be desired. For instance, there may be laid down goals of social and educational policy that reflect a more moderate ambition than the achievements in other parts of the world. While these goals should still pose a challenge, they should be attainable in light of the performance of other countries to which the country currently investigated may reasonably be compared.

Like all novel statistical techniques, DEA has sometimes been misunderstood. A common fallacy is to believe that it somehow represents an alternative to linear regression. It does not. Linear regression enables the researcher to search through a catalog of possible explanatory factors and to determine the factors that deliver the best goodness of fit. It provides a tool for testing the presence of possible causal factors. DEA does not test the chosen list of input and output variables at all. The causality is subsumed and is never tested.

Even after Abe's death, Bill remained in the forefront of DEA research, popularizing envelopment analysis to ever new fields of application and coauthoring several influential textbooks [Cooper, *et al.,* 2004; Cooper, *et al.*, 2006]. In 2003 George Kozmetsky also died. But while his old-time friends were no longer with him, Bill's life did not change much. He still went to his office at the business school every day, sometimes meeting with a group of smart PhD students.

It remains for me to account for Bill's involvement in joint work with Ruzanna Tarverdyan and me on problems related to the activities of the International Labour Organization. To Bill, this work reminded him of ideas about Quality of Life pursued by Nestor Terleckyj at the National Planning Association in the early 1970s [Charnes, Cooper & Kozmetsky, 1973; Terleckyj, 1975]. To Terleckyj, Quality of Life was a multidimensional concept and it should be possible to measure it numerically, using both national account statistics and data from interviews and special studies [Cooper & Ijiri, 1983].

The other intellectual root of our joint work [Cooper, Thore & Tarverdyan, 2011] is the original DEA paper [Charnes, Cooper & Rhodes, 1978] that featured a fractional programming model for determination of the efficiency rating of a decision making unit. Compressed to the bare essentials, the 2011 model can be presented as follows.

Let Y_j be a vector of indicators of the Quality of Life of individual j and $V(Y_j)$ his utility function. Let X_j be a vector of factors generating Quality of Life and $U(X_j)$ his cost function. The Quality of Life rating of individual j is then defined as the ratio $V(Y_j)/U(X_j)$. Maximize this rating for individual $j = 0$, subject to the conditions that the rating can never exceed 1, neither for the individual $j = 0$ himself, nor for any other individual j considered:

$$\begin{aligned} &\max\ V(Y_0)/U(X_0) \\ &\text{subject to } V(Y_j)/U(X_j) \leq 1, \quad \text{all } j \end{aligned}$$

The beauty of this formulation is that it rediscovers the fractional programming problem as originally presented [Charnes, Cooper & Rhodes, 1978]. In our correspondence, Bill several times expressed his satisfaction with this aspect of our work. It should be remembered that the fractional programming approach was the standard formulation of the envelopment procedure during the first few years of DEA and was routinely referred to as the "primal" program. But eventually it seemed that the interpretation in terms of a fractional program was less important. With the 1984 publication [Charnes, Cooper & Banker] the "dual" program involving an equiproportional shrinking of the inputs entered the scene as the obvious entry point to understanding the envelopment procedure. Finally, Abe and Bill both decided to switch the names, referring from then on to the fractional programming version as the "dual" one. (Note the sentence "Here the names Primal and Dual are interchanged from those of earlier published papers," in Charnes, Cooper, Lewin & Seiford [1994, p. 26.])

Considering the 33 years spanning the time from Bill's first work on the fractional program of DEA to his last, I consider myself lucky and fortunate of being a member of the research team that uncovered the earlier unknown potential of the fractional formulation. One of the very last projects that occupied Bill's mind was the prolific ideas of our coauthor Ruzanna Tarverdyan, dreaming of creating a foundation in Geneva dedicated to the pursuit of international assessments of national economic and social policy, based on envelopment calculations.

Chapter 15

Ilya Prigogine
(1917–2003)

As Ilya Prigogine stepped up to receive his 1977 Nobel prize in chemistry from the hands of Carl Gustaf, King of Sweden, two university presidents watched him with intense pride: the heads of the Free University of Brussels and of The University of Texas at Austin. Brussels had been his *alma mater* and his home town (his family settled there after fleeing from the Russian Revolution that occurred only a couple of months after he was born.) He had been appointed Professor at the university in 1950; nine years later he was appointed Director of the International Solvay Institute.

To Lorene Rogers, the president of The University of Texas at Austin, the ceremony in Stockholm was a moment of great achievement. Prigogine's contacts with The University of Texas at Austin went back a long time, and had eventually led to an appointment as a regental professor of physics and chemical engineering. He was one of the bright stars of an otherwise sleepy Southern university and Rogers had eagerly accepted the invitation to travel to Stockholm. To mark the day and honoring Prigogine, she ordered the landmark university tower in Austin to be lit up in the university's color: burnt orange. This was traditionally done to celebrate the Texas Longhorns football team winning a game. This time it signified something else: as an academic institution, the university had finally come of age.

When I arrived at The University of Texas at Austin one year later, the academic community was still abuzz. Rogers had from the start been a controversial person, the very first woman to be appointed to the post of president of a Southern university. There was some nasty gossip in the staid glossy magazine *Texas Monthly* about her travel to Stockholm and a shopping spree there, to the point that even Prigogine himself found it necessary to send a letter to the editor pointing out that:

> At the time I received the Nobel prize, I was, as I am still, professor at both the University of Brussels and The University of Texas at Austin. Therefore, the Nobel Foundation invited presidents of both universities to the ceremony. Both attended. This is a routine procedure, and it would have been strange indeed to refuse the invitation . . . . I have heard that my Nobel prize is a Russian Nobel prize because I was born in Moscow, that it is a Belgian Nobel prize because I am a citizen of Belgium, and that it is a Texas Nobel prize because an important part of the work was done in Austin. I leave this choice to anyone interested.
>
> *Texas Monthly*, November 1982

In the fall of 1983 The University of Texas at Austin celebrated the Centennial of its foundation. To mark the occasion, the university had conducted a spectacular funding drive, matching every dollar raised with a dollar from university funds. One man who eagerly responded to this opportunity was George Kozmetsky — co-creator of the vast industrial conglomerate Teledyne, Inc. and head of the business school of The University of Texas at Austin, at the time listed as one of the nation's 400 wealthiest individuals. Through his investment vehicle the RGK Foundation, he had established 16 new endowed faculty positions.

Six years earlier Kozmetsky had started the Institute for Constructive Capitalism (the IC^2 Institute) as an arm of the business school. Morphing into the Institute for Innovation, Creativity, and Capital, the IC^2 is now organized as an independent research unit of the university. The new research positions were all recognized as "Centennial Fellowships." Prigogine was named as the RGK Foundation Centennial Fellow.

I have a vivid memory of the day when I met Prigogine for the first time. We had all assembled on the second floor in the newly completed IC^2 building, seated around the enormous glass table in the boardroom. "We" were all the freshly baked centennial fellows, each one of us holding a fellowship honoring Kozmetsky's business associates, friends or family.

I had been part of the research staff at the Institute since its inception. My new colleagues were world class researchers, handpicked by Kozmetsky from across the entire university, representing departments as diverse as Medical Chemistry, Economics, Management Science, Marketing, Government, Biotechnology, and Robotics. And there was Ilya Prigogine, Director of the Center for Studies in Statistical Mechanics. Watching them all, I felt immensely proud — and humble. This was indeed a Learned Academy.

Prigogine had the air of old European nobility (he was indeed to have the title of viscount bestowed upon him by the King of Belgium a couple of years later), dressed immaculately, and spoke in a soft and friendly tone, singing on the vowels with his characteristic French accent. Each Centennial Fellow was asked to present himself to the others by summing up his current research with a few words. Prigogine spoke of "dissipative structures" in thermodynamics. It was the first time I had even heard of the concept. Reading up on the matter later, I learned that the term was actually coined by Prigogine himself, to describe thermodynamic systems under far-from-equilibrium conditions.

A leading theme of George Kozmetsky's was the need to establish an academic environment that would promote creativity and the spawning of new ideas. With magnetic power he would talk to us in his weekly seminar about the starting-up and management of new companies, about the new "technopolis" in Silicon Valley, and about his dreams of creating something similar at The University of Texas at Austin. In this quest he wanted his Centennial Fellows to be his standard-bearers.

Academic lecturing is good, but so are social contacts. The Kozmetskys spent considerable efforts (and money) on launching memorable social events that brought us all together. During the first years, while George Kozmetsky was still head of the business school, he would invite the entire school to an annual black tie dinner party at the posh and venerable Driskill hotel. After dinner, there would be dancing in the huge ballroom lit up by crystal chandeliers hanging down from the domed ceiling richly decorated with scenes from Texas history. My son recounts with some relish the following story: As he arrived with our car late that night to pick us up at the Driskill hotel, Prigogine spotted him entering and told him: "Your mum is a terrific dancer." The Nobel laureate must have had some difficulty following her in the Charleston!

Other opportunities for the Centennial Fellows to become more acquainted included the annual excursion to the Kozmetsky ranch west of Austin, in the "hill country." Even by Texas standards it was a respectable "spread" that included an entire river; to go there you had better bring your pickup truck because the river was fairly deep and you had to splash right through it! The excursion was for the people working at the RGK Foundation and the IC^2 Institute. Kozmetsky junior (Greg) would organize the annual baseball game pitting the RGK against IC^2 . Every able-bodied person had to participate. The barbeque itself was served up by the nearby Cow Town, on a steam-driven rebuilt agricultural tractor from the 1930s. As night fell, we would all sit on the low wall of the circular pit, lazily looking at the flames of the huge log fire. Prigogine would talk about dissipative structures.

I shall try below to recount some of Prigogine's views on irreversible processes, dissipative systems, chaos, and bifurcations. He loved to talk about these matters, and his Nobel prize gave him a platform for expressing his views in interviews on radio and television programs. He had thought hard and long on many of the most difficult problems in physics and cosmology, and he wanted to share his thinking and his results with a broad audience. The interested reader can find a number of video clips of his lectures and interviews on "YouTube."

Prigogine belongs to that rare brand of physicists and thinkers who have helped define not only what we see in the world around us, but also what we are, and our role in the universe. The first steps along this road were taken by the Greek philosopher Epicurus (341–270 BC). As a follower of Democritus, he believed that everything that has ever existed and that will ever exist is made out of indestructible building blocks, irreducibly small in size and unimaginably vast in number: atoms.

In his book *The End of Certainty* [1996], Prigogine discusses the fundamental dilemma raised by Epicurus: What can be the meaning of human freedom in a deterministic world of atoms? Epicurus used atomistic theory to develop a philosophical system seeking ethical ends. If the simplest fact of existence is rational and if there exists a natural explanation for everything, then man would be liberated from superstition, even the wrath of the gods, and could instead pursue a life of seeking pleasure in simple things. Epicurus lived a frugal life in a secluded garden in Athens.

But the great physicists of times who followed him would be haunted by doubts. With natural sciences revealing the great laws of the universe, what role is there left for the human mind? Prigogine cites Einstein:

> . . . a Being endowed with higher insight and more perfect intelligence, watching man and his doings, [would] smile about this illusion of his that he was acting according to his own free will.

If you believe that the world is just one big automaton following mathematical laws, then what room is left for human reasoning, hopes, and dreams? Like Einstein, a generation of modern physicists have been filled with pessimism and *Weltschmerz*. Particularly, there is the Second Law of Thermodynamics which traditionally is understood to place mankind in crushing dilemma, formulated by Rudolf Clausius in the mid-19th century. He developed a theory for the working of the steam engine, stating that "heat cannot by itself pass from a colder to a hotter body" and stressed the concept of entropy (dissipation of available energy). Whenever work is done, an amount of usable energy is irrevocably lost. All matter and energy in the universe will eventually degrade into a state of inert uniformity or heat death.

And so, the world clock ticks slowly and inexorably toward the final extinction of the universe and of time itself. For some, such as Stephen W. Hawking, in his *Brief History of Time*, we are close to the end. Prigogine asks "How can we conceive of creativity or ethics in a deterministic world?" [*ibid.,* p. 6].

More than a decade has passed since Prigogine died peacefully in Brussels. Already it is becoming clear that posterity will look upon Prigogine as the greatest physicist since Newton. Not only did he make some of the most fundamental discoveries of his age in chemistry, thermodynamics, and physics — but, more importantly, he has given back to modern man a belief in himself and in the future. Following in Prigogine's footsteps, scientists continue to discover new patterns on all levels of existence, from the biology of molecules to the cosmology of the universe. Prigogine transformed physics, giving it a new cultural relevance. In the arts, medicine, business, social science, and technology, professionals have acknowledged their debts to his fundamental and resounding insights. As Prigogine himself put it:

> Mankind is at a turning point, the beginning of a new rationality.... We are observing the birth of a science that views us and our creativity as part of a fundamental trend present at all levels of nature. [*ibid.*]

How did it all happen? As a young student at the Université Libre in Brussels, Prigogine hit upon the key question that was going to pursue him relentlessly during his entire scientific career: What is time? Time was not mentioned in his physics classes. Physics did not deal with time. Newton's system of planetary motion is reversible in time, it works just as well backwards as forwards. The movements of a pendulum can be repeated exactly backwards in time. Obtaining his PhD in chemistry and named a professor in 1947, he would remember one of the most famous scientists of the day attending one of his lectures, addressing him, "I am surprised that you give more attention to irreversible phenomena, which are essentially transitory, than to the final result of their evolution, equilibrium." Prigogine was so stunned that he was unable to respond.

15.1 The Chemical Clock

To introduce his theories, Prigogine liked to bring up the subject of the "chemical clock." It is an oscillating chemical reaction discovered by German chemists in the early nineteenth century. As two clear liquids are filled into a glass, the resulting mixture suddenly turns red; a while later it turns blue, then turns red again, continuing to blink at regular intervals. As a chemical experiment it can be carried out in any school laboratory.

Because of the chaotic motion of the molecules in the vessels, one would expect them to mix and the color of liquid to appear as "violet." But that is not what happens. Instead, there seems to be some inherent capability of the chemicals for reorganizing themselves at regular intervals into two alternative states.

Prigogine did not invent this experiment, but he saw deeper into the nature of such "dissipative" (energy-releasing) processes than anybody else. His theories obtained a dramatic empirical proof in 1958 with the publication of the details of a chemical clock now referred to as the Belousov-Zhabotinsky reaction. The reaction occurs at states far from equilibrium and it is self-organizing. The concentrations of various chemicals oscillate with clock-like precision.

The chemical clock demonstrates all the characteristics of a dissipative structure. *First, the system is far from equilibrium but there is order*. In this case, the order takes the form of a bifurcation, splitting into two alternative states. In other situations, the process can generate regular time patterns, or dissolve into any number of regular sub-processes. The order is unstable at all times — it hangs in a thread at "the edge of chaos."

To analyze the chemical clock mathematically, Prigogine formulated differential equations for chemical kinetics, and in particular for competing biopolymers. Applying the same mathematics to the growth and interaction of biological populations and social systems, he found surprising examples of order in far-from-equilibrium ecosystems, like termites building their nests. After an initial random search, the insects proceed to construct successions of regular pillars and walls — chaos producing order.

With the book *Self-Organization in Nonequilibrium Systems* [1977], Prigogine and his pupil G. Nicolis placed themselves among the pioneers of modern chaos theory. The same mathematics can be used to illustrate the chaotic supergrowth of high tech companies like Google or Apple, or the supergrowth of countries like China and India. These chaotic growth paths are in wild disequilibrium. But they define platforms of new order.

Second, the chemical clock is irreversible in time. It is not possible to unscramble the two ingredient liquids back into their original form. There is an "arrow of time" pointing away from the past and toward the future. To a physicist brought up into a Newtonian world of mechanistic and time-invariant laws, this is a most disturbing fact. You cannot "undiscover" the inventions of the Apple iPhone, iPod, or iPad. The company can go under, but the technology will remain. And you cannot run the huge economic boom in China backwards in time. The growth rate may slow down but the new Chinese middle class will have their ambitions and dreams raised forever. The arrow of time points forward.

Actually, history itself is irreversible in time, starting with the moment of the big bang and reaching up to our own times. The reversible and timeless Newtonian system should not be discarded but it needs to be amended to account for the presence of irreversible processes.

Third, the chemical clock illustrates the possibility of evolution. Evolution occurred on our planet even before the advent of life: the slow cooling of the planet, and the formation of geological strata, rivers, and seas. The historic formation of the Nile with its tributaries and the climatic conditions created a "time clock" of alternating seasons of flooding in upper Egypt, generating an order of regular growing and harvesting seasons downstream, thus putting in place the conditions for one of the first civilizations on our planet.

15.2 Evolution and Creativity

The subject of evolution of plants and animals brings us to Darwinian evolution. In many ways Prigogine emulates what Darwin did in biology, formulating an evolutionary approach to physics. Extending the mathematics of chemical thermodynamics, Prigogine discusses the concept of a "niche" — a population of molecules or biological individuals that stays unabsorbed and maintained inside a larger medium: a pocket of gas or a liquid, or a biological species.

As new species evolve, they occupy new niches of subsistence and survival. Here is an example from my own observation post in southern Portugal where I live in retirement. Sometimes I spot storks along the rivers. Why has the stork developed that long funny beak? To catch frogs and small fish deeper down in the muddy freshwaters than other birds manage to reach, I guess. Why does the stork build its nests on the top of erect poles, often more than seven meters above the ground? A smart way of protecting the eggs and the young from intruding guests, presumably. The stork has found a safe niche that serves it well.

Imagine a magic Carl von Linneus living a couple of million years ago, strolling the earth, notebook in hand, identifying, registering, and cataloging all the plants and animals there. He would describe an orderly system of course, with classes, families, and species, all with alluring Latin names. There would be order — but, as we know, it would not be in equilibrium. Actually, it would be very, very far from equilibrium. Every plant and animal would be on a path of evolution — some of them establishing more solid niches, and others desperately adapting and modifying their features in order to hang on to life. Presumably, there would even be a precursor to the stork, living in a precursor niche. The niches themselves evolve. Nicolis and Prigogine write:

> The increasing effectiveness of the exploitation of each resource provides a basis for understanding the notion of "survival of the fittest" familiar from Darwin's

> theory. In particular, our arguments show that a definition of the "fittest" can only be obtained through a suitable analysis of the evolution equations describing the ecosystem [*ibid*, p. 458].

Deterministic processes can be seen only in isolated, artificial systems. The natural world, on the other hand, is a world of irreversible processes, of self-organization. Prigogine perceives nature on Earth in exactly the opposite way it was viewed in classical physics. He no longer conceives of nature as a passive object. It is an active object in our lives. What we see here on Earth is just the opposite of entropy. Instead of going to heat death, we see successive diversification. We see evolution. Prigogine views energy dissipation as the driving force of evolution. He notes that, despite the increase in organization and complexity of living systems, there has been an acceleration of biological evolution in the course of time. Each new step increasing the functional organization has in itself the germs for further evolution.

Prigogine offers a guardedly optimistic alternative to the pessimistic view of mankind's future — entropy and all-reigning disorder spreading throughout the universe. In an interview with *OMNI* magazine in 1983, he said:

> The classical view divided the universe between spiritual self and the physical, external world. Yet inside us we see time, activity; we experience change. This internal experience is in complete contrast with the view of the world as a timeless automaton. As we begin to discover the roots of time outside us, this duality tends to disappear. We see a convergence between the world outside and the world inside us. With the paradigm of self-organization we see a transition from disorder to order. In the field of psychological activity this is perhaps the main experience we have — every artistic or scientific creation implies a transition from disorder to order.

Prigogine discusses the "narrow path" in the last chapter of *The End of Certainty* [1997]:

> We have tried to follow ... a narrow path between two conceptions that both lead to alienation: a world ruled by deterministic laws, which leaves no place for novelty, and a world ruled by a dice-playing God, where everything is absurd, acausal, and incomprehensible....We have attempted to make this book a journey along the narrow path, and thereby illustrate the role of human creativity in science (pp.187–88).

It was my good fortune to be delegated the editorial task of processing the paper "Instability, Complexity, and Bounded Rationality in Economic Change" that Prigogine wrote together with his two pupils P. Chen and K. Wen as his contribution to a volume of essays honoring George Kozmetsky [Cooper, *et al.*, 1997]. To my knowledge this is the only paper where Prigogine put together in one place his thoughts on economics. Ping Chen would bring new versions of the paper to me, and I had long discussions with him, he himself having authored a piece on the growth of the Chinese economy as an evolutionary and self-organizing process [Chen, 1993].

According to the authors, there existed two different views on how the earlier stagnant Chinese economy could be brought to development. One was a big bang theory arguing that "you cannot leap over a chasm in two steps." Shock therapy would knock the former economic system out of the orbit provided by central planning. Market forces would steer the entire economic system into a new, stable regime. But social change is a complex, path-dependent, and unpredictable process. Great uncertainty attaches to the bifurcation and transition stage.

The alternative was a decentralized, bottom-up approach to reform insisting that "you can only walk across a river by feeling first for the stones." There would be experimentally based changes of economic and social institutions at the grassroots level. Self-organization under nonequilibrium constraints would adapt the economic system to the prevailing environment, making it robust against perturbations. Nonequilibrium promotes growth and development.

Perhaps Prigogine and his coworkers were able to do something that economists of the twenty-first century have not yet been able to do: to find a fitting label for the explosive growth of the Chinese economy. It is not capitalism. It is not central planning. It is a self-organizing disequilibrium process.

References

Abad, C., Thore, S. & Laffarga, J. (2004). Fundamental analysis of stocks by two-stage DEA, *Manage. Decis. Econs.*, 25:231–41.

Afsa, C., Blanchet, D., Marcus, V., Mira d'Ercole, M., Pionnier, P. A., Ranuzzi, G., Rioux, L. & Schreyer, P. (2008). Survey of existing approaches to measuring socioeconomic progress. Working Paper. Commission on the Measurement of Economic Performance and Social Progress, Paris.

Arrow, K. J. (1958). Tinbergen on economic policy, *J. Am. Statist. Assoc.*, 53:89–97.

Arthur, W. B. (1989). Competing technologies, increasing returns, and lock-in by historical events, *Econ. J.*, 99:116–31.

Balassa, B. (1989). *Comparative Advantage, Trade Policy and Economic Development.* (Harvester Wheatsheaf: New York).

Balassa, B. (1989). *New Directions in the World Economy.* (Macmillan: New York).

Bana e Costa, C. & Thore, S. (2002). The many dimensions of an R&D project: Multi-criteria analysis, ed., Thore, S., *Technology Commercialization: DEA and Related Analytical Methods for Evaluating the Use and Implementation of Technical Innovation,* (Kluwer: Boston), pp. 23–44.

Bana e Costa, C., de Corte, J. M. & Vansnick, J-C. (2012). MACBETH, *Int. J. Inf. Tech. Decis.*, 11:359–87.

Bandura, R. & Saisana, M. (2012). *An Inventory of 300 Composite Indicators.* European Commission, JRC-IPSC, Italy (No EUR 25560 EN).

Banker, R. D., Charnes, A. & Cooper, W. W. (1984). Some models for estimating technical and scale inefficiencies in data envelopment analysis, *Mgmt. Sci.*, 30:1078–92.

Bass, F. M. (1969). A new product growth model for consumer durables, *Mgmt. Sci.*, 15:215–27.

Ben-David, D., Nordstrom, H. & Winters, A. (2001). *Trade, Income, Disparities and Poverty, Special Studies 5*. (World Trade Organization: Geneva).

Billström, F. & Thore, S. (1964). Simulation experiments with dynamic price strategies in monopoly theory, ed., Wold, H., *Econometric Model Building* (North-Holland: Amsterdam), pp. 283–96.

Bouyssou, D. (1999). Using DEA as a tool for MCDM: Some remarks, *J. Oper. Red. Soc.*, 60:974–978.

Charnes, A. (1952). Optimality and degeneracy in linear programming, *Econometrica*:160–170.

Charnes, A. (1953). Constrained games and linear programming, *P. Natl. Acad. Sci. USA*, 39:639–41.

Charnes, A. & Cooper, W. W. (1961). *Management Models and Industrial Applications of Linear Programming*, 2 vols. (Wiley: New York).

Charnes, A. & Cooper, W. W. (1962). Programming with Linear Fractional Functionals, *Nav. Res. Logist. Q.*, 9:181–96.

Charnes, A. & Cooper, W. W. (1974). An extremal principle for accounting balance of a resource value-transfer economy, *Rend. Accad. Naz. Lincei.*, 4:556–61.

Charnes, A. & Cooper, W. W. (1977). Goal programming and multiple objective optimizations, *Eur. J. Oper. Res.*, 1:39–54.

Charnes, A. & Thore, S. (1966). Planning for liquidity in financial institutions: The chance-constrained method, *J. Financ.*, 21:649–74.

Charnes, A., Cooper, W. W. & Rhodes, E. (1978). Measuring the efficiency of decision making units, *Eur. J. Oper. Res.*, 2:429–44.

Charnes, A., Cooper, W. W. & Ferguson, R. O. (1955). Optimal estimation of executive compensation by linear programming, *Mgmt. Sci.,* 1:138–51.

Charnes, A., Cooper, W. W. & Kozmetsky, G. (1973). Measuring, monitoring and modeling quality of life, *Mgmt. Sci.*, 19:1172–88.

Charnes, A., Cooper, W. W. & Mellon, B. (1952). Blending aviation gasolines: A study in programming interdependent activities, *Econometrica*, 20:135–59.

Charnes, A., Cooper, W. W. & Symonds, G. H. (1958). Cost horizons and certainty equivalents: An approach to stochastic programming of heating oil, *Mgmt. Sci.*, 4: 235–63.

Charnes, A., Cooper, W. W., Golany, B., Seiford, L. & Stutz, J. (1983). Pareto-optimality, efficiency analysis and empirical production functions, *Research Report CCS 479*, Center for Cybernetic Studies, The University of Texas at Austin.

Charnes, A., Cooper, W. W., Lewin, A. Y. & Seiford, L. M. (1994). *Data Envelopment Analysis: Theory, Methodology, and Application*. (Kluwer: Boston).

Chen, P. (1993). China's challenge to economic orthodoxy: Asian reform as an evolutionary, self-organizing process, *China Econ. Rev.*, 4:137–42.

Cherchye, L. & Moesen, W. (2004). *Institutional Infrastructure and Economic Performance: Levels versus catching up and frontier*. (Catholic Univ: Leuven).

Cobb, C., Halstead, T. & Rowe, J. (1995). *The Genuine Progress Indicator: Summary of Data and Methodology. Redefining Progress*. (OECD: Washington).

Cooper, W. W. & Ijiri, Y., eds. (1983). *Kohler's Dictionary for Accountants*, 6th ed. (Prentice-Hall: New York).

Cooper, W. W., Seiford, L. M. & Tone, K. (2006). *Introduction to Data Envelopment Analysis and its Uses: With DEA Solver Software and References*. (Springer: New York).

Cooper, W. W., Seiford, L. M. & Zhu, J. (2004). *Handbook on Data Envelopment Analysis*. (Kluwer: Boston).

Cooper, W. W., Thore, S., Gibson, D. & F. Phillips F., eds., (2007). *IMPACT: How IC^2 Research Affects Public Policy and Business Markets — A volume honoring George Kozmetsky's receipt of the National Medal of Technology* (Greenwood: Westport).

Cooper, W. W., Thore, S. & Tarverdyan, R. (2011). A utility function approach for evaluating country performances with DEA — the twin goals of Decent Work and A Fair Globalization ed., L. Hockley, *Global Operations Management*. (Nova Sci: New York) pp. 49–72.

Daly, H. & Cobb, J. (1989). *For the Common Good. Redirecting the Economy Toward Community, the Environment and a Sustainable Future*. (Beacon: Boston).

Deardorff, A. & Stern, R. (2001). *What You Should Know About Globalization and the World Trade Organization*. (Univ. Michigan: Ann Arbor).

Essama-Nssah, B. (2000). *New Dimensions of Poverty-Focused Evaluation within a Comprehensive Development Framework* (World Bank: Washington).

Esty, D. C., Levy, M., Salteli, A., & Dahl, A. (2005). *2005 Environmental Sustainability Index*. (Yale University with Columbia University, the World Economic Forum, and the Joint Research Centre of the European Commission).

European Commission (2009). *A Roadmap for Action: GDP and Beyond — Measuring Progress in a Changing World. COM (2009)* 433 of 2.8.2009.

European Commission (2012). *European Competitiveness Report 2012: Reaping the Benefits of Globalization*. ec.europa.eu/enterprise.

Fiacco, A. V. & Kortanek K. O., eds. (1977). *Extremal Methods and Systems Analysis: An International Symposium on the Occasion of Professor Abraham Charnes 's Sixtieth Birthday* (Springer Verlag: New York).

Fuchs, H. W., Farrish, R. O. P. & Bohall, R. W. (1974). A model of the US apple industry: A quadratic interregional intertemporal activity analysis formulation, *American J. of Agricultural Economics*, 56:739–50.

Golany, B. & Thore, S. (1997a). The competitiveness of nations, eds. Cooper, W. W., Thore, S., Gibson, D. & F. Phillips F., *IMPACT: How IC^2 Research Affects Public Policy and Business Markets — A volume honoring George Kozmetsky's receipt of the National Medal of Technology* (Greenwood: Westport), pp. 189–208.

Golany, B. and Thore, S. (1997b). The economic and social performance of nations: Efficiency and returns to scale, *Socio. Econ. Plan. Sci.*, 31:191–204.

Golany, B. and Thore, S. (1997c). Restricted best practice selection in DEA: An overview with a case study evaluating the socioeconomic performance of nations, *Ann. Oper. Res.*, 73:117–40.

Goreux, L. M. (1981). *Independence in Planning: Multi-level Programming Studies of the Ivory Coast*. (World Bank: Washington).

Goreux, L. M. & Manne, A. S., eds. (1973). *Multi-Level Planning: Case Studies in Mexico*. (North-Holland: Amsterdam).

Hawking, S. (1988). *A Brief History of Time: From the Big Bang to Black Holes* (Bantam Books: New York).

Hueting, R. (1974). *New Scarcity and Economic Growth*, Dutch ed., Agon (Elsevier: Amsterdam). (1980) English ed. (North-Holland: Amsterdam).

ILO (1999). *Decent Work*. Report of the Director-General. (International Labour Organization: Geneva).

ILO (2001a). *Poverty Reduction and Decent Work in a Globalizing World*. (International Labour Organization : Geneva).

ILO (2001b). *Reducing the Decent Work Deficit: A Global Challenge*. Report of the Director-general. (International Labour Organization: Geneva).

ILO (2003). *Working out of Poverty*. Report of the Director-general. (International Labour Organization: Geneva).

ILO (2004). *Constitution of the International Labour Organization. Declaration concerning the Aims and Purposes of the ILO*. http://www.ilo.org/public/English/about/iloconst.htm, Geneva 2004.

ILO (2005). *Decent Work and the Millennium Development Goals*. Information folder. (International Labour Organization: Geneva).

ILO (2008). *ILO Declaration on Social Justice for A Fair Globalization*, 10 June. (International Labour Organization: Geneva).

Klein, L. R. (1953). *A Textbook of Econometrics*. (Row, Peterson & Co: White Plains).

Krugman, P. (1994). Competitiveness: A dangerous obsession, *Foreign Affairs* 7:28–44.

Kuznets, S. (1971). *Modern Economic Growth: Findings and Reflections,* Nobel prize lecture, Nobelprize.org. Nobel Media AB 2013.

Land, K. C., Lovell, C. A. K. & Thore, S. (1992). Productive efficiency under capitalism and state socialism: The chance-constrained programming approach, *Public Finance* 47:109–21. Supplement: *Public Finance in a World of Transition* ed. by P. Pestieau.

Land, K. C., Lovell, C. A. K. & Thore, S. (1993). Chance-constrained data envelopment analysis, *Manage. Decis. Econ.*, 14:541–54.

Land, K. C., Lovell, C. A. K. & Thore, S. (1994). Productive efficiency under capitalism and state socialism: An empirical inquiry using chance constrained data envelopment analysis. *Technol. Forecast. Soc.*, 46:139–52.

Lawn, Philip A. & Sanders, R. D. (1999). Has Australia surpassed its optimal macroeconomic scale? Finding out with the aid of "benefit" and "cost" accounts and a sustainable net benefit index. *Ecol. Econ.*, 28:2:213–29.

Leontief, W., Carter, A. P. & Petri, P. (1977). *The Future of the World Economy — A United Nations Study*. (Oxford Univ: New York).

Levi-Faur, D., ed. (2012). *The Oxford Handbook of Governance*. (Oxford University: Cambridge.)

Littlechild, S. C. & Thompson, G. F. (1977). Aircraft landing fees: A game theory approach, *Bell J. Econ.*, 8:186–204.

Loh, J., Green, R. E., Ricketts, T., Lamoreux, J., Jenkins, M., Kapos, V. & Randers, J. (2005). The Living Planet Index: Using species population time series to track trends in biodiversity. *Phil. Trans. R. Soc. B.* 360:289–95.

Marks, N. (2010). *Happy Planet Index*. www.happyplanetindex.org.

Meadows, D. H., Meadows, D. L., Randers, J. & Behrens, W. W. III (1972). *The Limits to Growth*. (New American Library: New York).

Nicolis, G. & Prigogine, I. (1977). *Self-Organization in Nonequilibrium Systems: From Dissipative Structures to Order through Fluctuations* (Wiley-International: New York).

Nordhaus, W. & Tobin, J. (1972). *Is growth obsolete?* (Columbia University: New York).

OECD/EC JRC (2008). *Handbook on Constructing Composite Indicators, Methodology, and User Guide.* (OECD Publishing, Paris).

OMCFG (2013). *Now for the Long Term*. (Oxford: Cambridge).

OMNI Magazine (1983). *Ilya Prigogine: Wizard of Time*, interview by R.B. Tucker, May 1983 at www.edu365.cat.

Osberg, L., and Sharpe, L. (2002). An Index of Economic Well-being for Selected OECD Countries, *Rev. Income Wealth*, 48: 291–316.

Owen, G. (1982). *Game Theory*, 2nd ed. (Academic: New York). Now in 4th ed. (2013).

Pearce, D. W. (1980). *The MIT Dictionary of Modern Economics* (MIT: Cambridge).

Pearce, D. W., & Atkinson, G. (1993). Capital theory and the measurement of sustainable development: An indicator of weak sustainability, *Ecol. Econ.*, 8: 103–8.

Porter, M. (1980). *Competitive Strategy*. (Free Press: New York).

Porter, M. (1985). *Competitive Advantage*. (Free Press: New York).

Porter, M. (1990). The competitive advantage of nations, *Harvard Business Review*, March, April.

Porter, M. (1990). *The Competitive Advantage of Nations*. (Free Press: New York).

Prigogine, I. (1997). *The End of Certainty: Time, Chaos, and the New Laws of Nature* (Free Press: New York).

Prigogine, I. & Stengers, I. (1984). *Order out of Chaos* (Bantam: New York).

Rees, W. E. (1992). Ecological footprints and appropriated carrying capacity: What urban economics leaves out. *Environ. Urban.*, 4:121–30.

Samuelson, P. A. (1952). Spatial price equilibrium and linear programming, *Am. Econ. Rev.*, 42:283–303.

Seiford, L. M. & Thrall, R. M. (1990). Recent Developments in DEA: The Mathematical Programming Approach to Frontier Analysis, *J. Econometrics*, 4:7–38.

Serra N., & Stiglitz, J. E., eds. (2008). *The Washington Consensus Reconsidered: Towards a New Global Governance*. (Oxford Univ: New York).

Stiglitz, J. E., Sen, A., & Fitoussi, J.-P. (2009). *Report by the Commissionon the Measurement of Economic Performance and Social Progress*. CMEPSP.

Takayama, T. & Judge, G. G. (1971). *Spatial and Temporal Price and Allocation Models*. (North-Holland, Amsterdam).

Terleckyj, N. (1975). *Improvements in the Quality of Life 1974–1983: Estimates of Possibilities in the United States* (National Planning Association: Washington).

Thore, S. (1956). *A Critique of the Theory of the Consumption Function* (Institution University d'Études Européennes: Turin). With a foreword by H. Wold.

Thore, S. (1964). Price strategies of an "ignorant" monopolist, ed., Wold, H., *Econometric Model Building* (North-Holland: Amsterdam), pp. 283–96.

Thore, S. (1986). Generalized network spatial equilibrium: The deterministic and the chance-constrained case, *Pap. Reg. Sci. Assoc.*, 59:93–102.

Thore, S. (1987). Chance-constrained activity analysis, *Eur. J. Oper. Res.*, 30: 267–9.

Thore, S. (1991). *Economic Logistics: The Optimization of Spatial and Sectoral Resource, Production, and Distribution Systems*. With a chapter on "Some elements of saddle-point theory" coauthored by W. W. Cooper and S. Thore. (Quorum: Westport).

Thore, S. (1995). *The Diversity, Complexity, and Evolution of High Tech Capitalism*. (Kluwer: Boston).

Thore, S. (1996). Economies of scale in the US computer industry: An empirical investigation using data envelopment analysis, *J Evol. Econ.*, 6:199–216.

Thore, S. (1999). Enterprise in the information age, eds. Halal, W. E. & Taylor, K. B., *Twenty-First Century Economics* (St. Martin's: New York).

Thore, S. (2003). Global optimization of economic and social policy, ed., Wang, J., *Encyclopedia of Business Analytics and Optimization*, in press 2014.

Thore, S. and Tarverdyan, R. (2008). Using data envelopment analysis to screen the possibility of A Fair Globalization, *Portuguese Journal of Management Studies*, 13:129–51.

Thore, S. and Tarverdyan, R. (2009). Using data envelopment analysis to quantify ILO objectives and identify policies conducive to Decent Work in a globalized world, *Socio. Econ. Plan. Sci.*, 43:151–164.

Thore, S., ed. (2002). *Technology Commercialization: DEA and Related Analytical Methods for Evaluating the Use and Implementation of Technical Innovation.* (Kluwer: Boston), 2nd ed., Springer 2012.

Tinbergen, J. (1939). *Statistical Testing of Business Cycle Theories,* 2 vols. (League of Nations: Geneva).

Tinbergen, J. (1941). *Econométrie,* (Noorduijn: Gorinchem).

Tinbergen, J. (1952). *On the Theory of Economic Policy* (North-Holland: Amsterdam).

Tinbergen, J. (1956). *Economic Policy: Principles and Design* (North-Holland: Amsterdam). http://repub.eur.nl/resource/ pub_16740/index.html.

Tinbergen, J. (1969). The use of models: Experience and prospects, ed., Lindbeck, A., *Lectures to the Memory of Alfred Nobel, December 12, 1969, in Nobel Lectures, Economics 1969–1980*. (World Sci.: Singapore, 1992).

UFC (2004). *The Barcelona Agenda.* (Universal Forum of Cultures: Barcelona).

UN (1948). *Universal Declaration of Human Rights*, of the General Assembly. (United Nations: New York).

UN (1966). *International Covenant of Economic, Social, and Cultural Rights*, of the General Assembly. (United Nations: New York).

UN (1995). *Report of the World Summit for Social Development.* (United Nations: Copenhagen.)

UN (2000a). *Assessing the Social Impact of Economic Measures Taken in Response to Financial Crises in Developing Countries*, Report of the Secretary General to the Special Session of the General Assembly. (United Nations: Geneva).

UN (2000b). *United Nations Millennium Declaration.* (United Nations: New York).

UN (2001a). *Enhancing Social Protection and Reducing Vulnerability in a Globalizing World*, Report of the Secretary General, Economic and Social Council. (United Nations: Geneva).

UN (2001b). *Road Map Toward the Implementation of the United Nations Millennium Declaration.* (United Nations: New York).

UN (2002a). *Deepening Democracy in a Fragmented World.* (United Nations: Geneva).

UN (2002b). *Political Declaration.* World Summit on Sustainable Development, Johannesburg. (United Nations: Geneva).

UN (2004). UN Department of Economics and Social Affairs, Division for Sustainable Development, *Monterrey Consensus of the International Conference on Financing for Development*, March 22, 2002. (United Nations: New York).

UN (2005). *2005 World Summit Outcome*, Resolution adopted by the General Assembly. (United Nations: New York).

UN (2006). UN Economic and Social Council, *Creating an Environment at the National and International Level Conducive to Generating Full and Productive Employment and Decent Workfor All.* Report of the Secretary General. (United Nations: Geneva).

UN (2012a). *Millennium Development Goals Indicators.* (United Nations: Geneva).

UN (2012b) *The Future We Want, of the Rio +20 Conference.* (United Nations: Geneva).

UN (2013). *A New Global Partnership: Eradicate Poverty and Transform Economies Through Sustainable Development,* Report of the High Level Panel of Eminent Persons On The Post-2015 Development Agenda. (United Nations: Geneva).

UNWCED (1987). *Our Common Future* a.k.a the Brundtland Report, by UN World Commission on Environment and Development. (Oxford University: Cambridge).

USCC (2006). *The Competitiveness Index: Where the US Stands*, www.compete.org. US Council of Competitiveness.

USCC (2013). *Making Impact*, Annual report 2012–2013. US Council of Competitiveness.

van de Kerk, G. & Manuel, A. R. (2008) A comprehensive index for a sustainable society: The SSI — the Sustainable Society Index, *Ecological Economics*, 66(2–3):228–42.

von Neumann, J. & Morgenstern, O. (1947). *Theory of Games and Economic Behavior* (Princeton University: Princeton, NJ). Now available in a 60th Anniversary Commemorative Edition (2007).

Wackernagel, M. (1994). *Ecological Footprint and Appropriated Carrying Capacity: A Tool for Planning Toward Sustainability* (PhD thesis). Vancouver, Canada: School of Community and Regional Planning. The University of British Columbia.

Waldrop, M. M. (1992). *Complexity: The Emerging Science at the Edge of Order and Chaos* (Simon & Schuster: New York).

WCSDG (2004a). *A Fair Globalization: Creating Opportunities for All.* (World Commission.)

WCSDG (2004b). *The Social Dimension of Globalization.* (World Commission).

WEF (2014). *The Global Competitiveness Report 2014–2015*, Geneva 2014.

Williamson, J. (2008). A short history of the Washington consensus, eds., Serra, N. & Stiglitz, J. E., *The Washington Consensus Reconsidered: Towards a New Global Governance.* (Oxford University: New York).

Williamson, J., ed. (1990). *Latin American Adjustment: How Much has Happened?* (IIE: Washington).

Williamson, J. & Wold, H. (1964). *Econometric Model Building. Essays on the Causal Chain Approach* (North-Holland: Amsterdam).

Wold, H. & Jureen, L. (1952). *Demand Analysis. A Study in Econometrics* (Almquist & Wiksell: Uppsala).

World Bank (1998). *The Social Development Family in the Environmentally and Socially Sustainable Network.* (World Bank: Washington).

World Bank & IMF (2004). *Policies and Actions for Achieving the MDGs and Related Outcomes*, Global monitoring report. (World Bank: Washington).

World Bank & IMF (2006). *A Common Vision for the World Bank Group.* (World Bank and IMF: Washington).

World Bank & IMF (2006). *Millennium Development Goals: Strengthening Mutual Accountability, Aid, Trade, and Governance*, Global monitoring report. (World Bank: Washington).

World Bank Group (1998). *Partnerships for Development: Proposed Action for the World Bank.* (World Bank Group: Washington).

Yorke, J. & Li, T.-Y. (1975). Period three implies chaos, *Am. Math. Mon.*, 82:985–92.

Index